# Relationship Marketing in Franchising and Retailing

This book offers an accessible and comprehensive introduction to relationship marketing in franchising and retailing, especially in areas such as business and marketing management as well as strategic marketing.

The topics this book covers include (but is not limited to): (1) relationships in the context of e-commerce within the franchising sector; (2) franchisees with multiple stakeholder roles: perceptions and conflict in franchise networks; (3) Why franchisors recruit franchisees from the ranks of their employees; (4) franchisee advisory councils and justice; and (5) determinants of overall franchisee satisfaction.

This book is ideal for students, practitioners and professionals interested in Relationship Marketing, Customer Services, and Marketing Communications. The chapters in this book were originally published as a special issue of *Journal of Strategic Marketing*.

**Park Thaichon** is Associate Professor of Marketing at the School of Business, University of Southern Queensland, Australia. His research, teaching, and consulting focus are on digital marketing, technology, relationship marketing, and consumer behaviour.

**Lorelle Frazer** is Dean of the School of Business and Creative Industries at the University of the Sunshine Coast in Australia. Her research focuses on franchising relationships, and she has been honoured by the Franchise Council of Australia for her 'significant contributions to the education of the Australian franchise community'.

**Scott Weaven** is Professor and Head of the Department of Marketing at Griffith University, Australia. His recent research has focused on examining digital, relational and hybridized methods of international market entry, e-commerce and encroachment issues in franchise systems, hybrid sales structures, online relationship marketing and consumer sentiment analysis and market segmentation in a variety of business contexts.

# Relationship Marketing in Franchising and Retailing

*Edited by*
**Park Thaichon, Lorelle Frazer and Scott Weaven**

Routledge
Taylor & Francis Group

LONDON AND NEW YORK

First published 2023
by Routledge
4 Park Square, Milton Park, Abingdon, Oxon OX14 4RN

and by Routledge
605 Third Avenue, New York, NY 10158

*Routledge is an imprint of the Taylor & Francis Group, an informa business*

Introduction © 2023 Park Thaichon, Lorelle Frazer and Scott Weaven
Chapters 1, 2, 5 and 6 © 2023 Taylor & Francis
Chapter 3 © 2020 Aveed Raha and Ilir Hajdini. Originally published as Open Access.
Chapter 4 © 2020 Peter Balsarini, Claire Lambert and Marie M. Ryan. Originally published as Open Access.

*British Library Cataloguing in Publication Data*
A catalogue record for this book is available from the British Library

ISBN13: 978-1-032-42798-0 (hbk)
ISBN13: 978-1-032-42799-7 (pbk)
ISBN13: 978-1-003-36435-1 (ebk)

DOI: 10.4324/9781003364351

Typeset in Myriad Pro
by Newgen Publishing UK

**Publisher's Note**
The publisher accepts responsibility for any inconsistencies that may have arisen during the conversion of this book from journal articles to book chapters, namely the inclusion of journal terminology.

**Disclaimer**
Every effort has been made to contact copyright holders for their permission to reprint material in this book. The publishers would be grateful to hear from any copyright holder who is not here acknowledged and will undertake to rectify any errors or omissions in future editions of this book.

# Contents

# Citation Information

The following chapters were originally published in the *Journal of Strategic Marketing*, volume 30, issue 2 (2022). When citing this material, please use the original page numbering for each article, as follows:

**Chapter 6**

*Determinants of overall franchisee satisfaction: application of the performance feedback theory*
Michal Jirásek, Susanne Maria Gaffke and Josef Windsperger
*Journal of Strategic Marketing*, volume 30, issue 2 (2022), pp. 221–238

For any permission-related enquiries please visit:
www.tandfonline.com/page/help/permissions

# Notes on Contributors

**Peter Balsarini**, School of Business and Law, Edith Cowan University, Perth, Australia.

**Isaac Cheah**, School of Marketing, Curtin University, Perth, Australia.

**Lorelle Frazer**, School of Business and Creative Industries, University of the Sunshine Coast, Australia.

**Susanne Maria Gaffke**, Department of Business Decisions and Analytics, University of Vienna, Vienna, Austria.

**Anthony Grace**, USC Business School, University of the Sunshine Coast, Sunshine Coast, Australia.

**Ilir Hajdini**, Department of Business Analytics and Decision, University of Vienna, Vienna, Austria.

**Michal Jirásek**, Department of Corporate Economy, Masaryk University, Brno, Czech Republic.

**Zhanna Kremez**, Griffith Business School, Griffith University, Brisbane, Australia.

**Claire Lambert**, School of Business and Law, Edith Cowan University, Perth, Australia.

**Johan Liang**, School of Marketing, Curtin University, Perth, Australia.

**Munyaradzi Nyadzayo**, UOWD Faculty of Business, University of Wollongong in Dubai, Dubai, United Arab. Emirates

**Helen Perkins**, Department of Marketing, Griffith Business School, Griffith University, Brisbane, Australia.

**Ian Phau**, School of Marketing, Curtin University, Perth, Australia.

**Sara Quach**, Department of Marketing, Griffith Business School, Southport, Australia.

**Aveed Raha**, Department of Business Analytics and Decision, University of Vienna, Vienna, Austria.

**Marie M. Ryan**, School of Business and Law, Edith Cowan University, Perth, Australia.

**Wei Shao**, Department of Marketing, Griffith Business School, Griffith University, Brisbane, Australia.

**Anwar Sadat Shimul**, School of Marketing, Curtin University, Perth, Australia.

**Park Thaichon**, School of Business, University of Southern Queensland, Australia.

**Scott Weaven**, Department of Marketing, Griffith University, Australia.

**Josef Windsperger**, Department of Business Decisions and Analytics, University of Vienna, Vienna, Austria.

# Introduction: Relationship marketing in franchising and retailing

Park Thaichon, Lorelle Frazer and Scott Weaven

## Overview

This book *"Relationship marketing in franchising and retailing"* presents a series of chapters covering topics to gain a better understanding of relationship marketing in franchising and retailing. The book is including research topics relating to business management, marketing management, and strategic marketing associated with relationship marketing in franchising and retailing. The topics that book includes but are not limited to: (1) relationships in the context of e-commerce within the franchising sector; (2) franchisees with multiple stakeholder roles: perceptions and conflict in franchise networks; (3) Why franchisors recruit franchisees from the ranks of their employees; (4) franchisee advisory councils and justice; and (5) determinants of overall franchisee satisfaction.

Franchising has been considered an appealing means of expanding a business and certainly offers many benefits to small businesses. Research in franchising and retailing is becoming more advanced (Rosado-Serrano, Dikova, & Paul, 2018). This book addresses one of the major issues in franchising research, which is the lack of understanding of relationship marketing in franchising and retailing (Roberts et al., 2022). However, there has been limited research by leading journal outlets on relationship marketing in franchising (Roberts et al., 2022; Thaichon et al., 2020). Besides, there have been restricted researchers on the topic (Quach et al., 2019, 2020; Kremez et al., 2019a, b) This has been the case since the special issue by the *Journal of Retailing* in 2011 and by *Journal of Business Venturing* in 1999.

In fact, relationship marketing involves the development of strong relationships between exchange partners that enhance satisfaction, trust, value, and commitment, and ultimately improve profitability (Bolton, Lemon, & Verhoef, 2004; Chiu, Hsieh, Li & Lee, 2005; Liang & Wang, 2006; Morgan & Hunt, 1994; Weaven, Baker, & Dant, 2017). It highlights the significance of the continuous interaction between involved parties in developing a long-term relationship (Palmatier, Dant, Grewal, & Evans, 2006; Weaven, Grace, Frazer, & Giddings, 2014). As the success of a franchise in retail is dependent on the relationship between the franchisor and franchisees, and between the sellers (franchisors/franchisees) and the customers, it is imperative to advance our knowledge of relationship marketing in franchising in retailing (Beitelspacher, Baker, Rapp, & Grewal, 2018).

We would like to express our sincere gratitude to all authors who submitted their work originally to the special issue "Relationship marketing in franchising and retailing" of the *Journal of Strategic Marketing* and to all reviewers who provided their service to ensure the quality of the special issue. We have only a few manuscripts following a rigorous review process to include in the special issue. The end result represents a deep thought-provoking edition for the journal.

## References

Beitelspacher, L. S., Baker, T. L., Rapp, A., & Grewal, D. (2018). Understanding the long-term implications of retailer returns in business-to-business relationships. *Journal of the Academy of Marketing Science*, *46*(2), 252–272. 10.1007/s11747-017-0553-6

Bolton, R. N., Lemon, K. N., & Verhoef, P. C. (2004). The theoretical underpinnings of customer asset management: A framework and propositions for future research. *Journal of the Academy of Marketing Science*, *32*(3), 271–292. 10.1177/0092070304263341

Dant, R. P., & Kaufmann, P. J. (1999). Introduction: Special issue on franchising. *Journal of Business Venturing*, *14*(4), 321–322. 10.1016/S0883-9026(98)00022-6

Kremez, Z., Frazer, L., & Thaichon, P. (2019a). The effects of e-commerce on franchising: Practical implications and models. *Australasian Marketing Journal*, *27*(3), 158–168.

Kremez, Z., Frazer, L., Weaven, S., & Quach, S. (2019b). Ecommerce structures for retail and service franchises: Ecommerce implementation in mature franchise systems. *Asia Pacific Journal of Marketing and Logistics*, *33*(6), 1292–1308.

Liang, C. J., & Wang, W. H. (2006). The behavioural sequence of the financial services industry in Taiwan: Service quality, relationship quality and behavioural loyalty. *The Service Industries Journal*, *26*(2), 119–145. 10.1080/02642060500369131

Morgan, R. M., & Hunt, S. D. (1994). The commitment-trust theory of relationship marketing. *Journal of Marketing*, *58*(3), 20–38. 10.2307/1252308

Palmatier, R. W., Dant, R. P., Grewal, D., & Evans, K. R. (2006). Factors influencing the effectiveness of relationship marketing: A meta-analysis. *Journal of Marketing*, *70*(4), 136–153. 10.1509/jmkg.70.4.136

Quach, S., Weaven, S. K., Thaichon, P., Baker, B., & Edwards, C. J. (2020). Gratitude in franchisor–franchisee relationships: Does personality matter? *European Journal of Marketing* *54*(1), 109–144.

Quach, S., Weaven, S., Thaichon, P., Grace, D., & Frazer, L. (2019). A model of entrepreneurship education in franchising–application of outside-in marketing with a behavioural focus. *Journal of Business & Industrial Marketing*, *35*(1), 116–133.

Roberts, R. E., Frazer, L., & Thaichon, P. (2022). A Western franchise in Shanghai, China: a late entrant's success. *Journal of Strategic Marketing*, *30*(6), 606–626.

Rosado-Serrano, A., Dikova, D., & Paul, J. (2018). International franchising: A literature review and research agenda. *Journal of Business Research*, *85*, 238–257. 10.1016/j.jbusres.2017.12.049

Thaichon, P., Weaven, S., Quach, S., Baker, B., & Frazer, L. (2020). What to expect after the honeymoon: evolutionary psychology of part-time franchising. *Journal of Strategic Marketing*, *28*(8), 702–726.

Weaven, S. K., Grace, D., Frazer, L., & Giddings, J. (2014). The effect of pre-entry information on relational outcomes in franchising: Model conceptualisation and gender comparison. *European Journal of Marketing*, *48*(1–2), 193–217. 10.1108/EJM-06-2011-0301

Weaven, S., Baker, B. L., & Dant, R. P. (2017). The influence of gratitude on franchisor–franchisee relationships. *Journal of Small Business Management*, *55*(S1), 275–298. 10.1111/jsbm.2017.55.issue-S1

# Consumer attitude and intention toward ridesharing

Isaac Cheah, Anwar Sadat Shimul, Johan Liang and Ian Phau

**ABSTRACT**

This paper aims to examine the factors affecting consumer's intention to participate in the sharing economy in particular toward ridesharing services. Data were collected from UberX users in Australia (n = 278) and New Zealand (n = 295) using online survey and analysed through Structural Equation Modelling in AMOS 25. The research model is tested and compared across three studies. The results show that perceived usefulness and word-of-mouth significantly influence the consumers' attitude toward ridesharing. The results across two samples show that the positive relationship between perceived usefulness as well as word of mouth and attitude toward service innovation is moderated by the consumers' attitude toward the advertising. In addition, currently the ridesharing application ridesharing requires more effort from the users, especially those who have a lower self-efficacy or are risk adverse towards using this type of service innovation. This paper suggests ridesharing services utilise the power of the word of mouth and peer recommendations in the brand's promotional strategies. Furthermore, personalised e-guides and instructions can form part of the service user interface which would help curb the negative perception around app usage and complexity, and thus increase consumer confidence.

## 1. Introduction

With on-demand start-ups from Uber to Handy disrupting their industries, Uber and its imitators are modern-day franchises without many of the upsides of joining a franchise network where independent contractors are quasi-franchisees. Like franchises, the on-demand platforms offer small-business owners affiliation with a big brand and use that brand to aggregate consumer demand and drive leads. In the U.S., Uber alone has more than 160,000 active independent operators (Benoit, Baker, Bolton, Gruber, & Kandampully, 2017; Davidson, Habibi, & Laroche, 2018), whom it recruited with the promise of being their own boss. However, high franchise fees and steep commissions have impeded the uptake of these on-demand platforms. In many ways, the platforms' trendy business models offer a lower value proposition than a franchise, at a much higher cost to the business owner (Standing & Mattsson, 2018). Therefore, it is important that these on-demand platforms mitigate these negative perceptions by maintaining a strong relationship with their franchisees through support mechanisms and initiatives, while at the same time seeking to develop a better understanding of their key stakeholders' demands as a means to improve service quality.

The rapid growth of the sharing economy, exemplified by ridesharing platforms Uber and Lyft, as well as home-sharing platforms Airbnb and Couchsurfing, is changing the patterns of ownership and consumption of goods and services. 'Collaborative consumption' or 'sharing economy' (Benoit et al., 2017; Davidson et al., 2018) are used as synonyms to describe the economic activities of firms that connect other interdependent economic as actors as 'sellers' and 'buyers' in service contexts such as transportation (e.g. Uber.com), accommodation (e.g. Airbnb.com), or financial services (e.g. Lendingclub.com). In a sharing economy, consumers exchange services in a peer-to-peer fashion, through matching markets facilitated by social networks and online applications (Breidbach & Brodie, 2017). Businesses such as Uber or Airbnb help individuals to gain economic benefits from underutilized resources such as cars or spare rooms. By becoming 'peer-to-peer services for hire' (Cusumano, 2015, p. 34), these firms differ from early sharing platforms like Napster, which focused on the exchange of resource ownership only, but did not include monetary rewards. In contrast, platform businesses like Uber or Airbnb facilitate resource access, and promise monetary rewards for those willing to engage in their context (Breidbach & Brodie, 2017). In the transportation sector, fast-expanding Uber has taken a dramatic amount of business from taxi companies in cities where it operates around the world. In 2015, for example, the company was signing up over 1100 new ridesharing partners every month in Australia (Allen, 2015). A 2014 survey report of consumers by PricewaterhouseCoopers (PWC, 2015) found that the majority agreed that the sharing economy made life more convenient and efficient (83%), was better for the environment (76%), built a stronger community (78%) and provided more fun than engaging with more traditional companies (63%) (PWC, 2015). In addition, the adoption of collaborative consumption services has also been shown to be driven by familiarity, service quality, trust, and utility (Möhlmann, 2015). It has also been proposed that consumers are attracted by the social benefits the sharing economy might provide. Guests of Airbnb, for example, experience community-focused and social atmosphere at their host's house, and even gain local connections with the host's help (Kim, Yoon, & Zo, 2015).

A literature review showed that studies on the sharing economy can be divided into two categories, organizational-level studies and individual-level studies, with the former being predominant (e.g. Breidbach & Brodie, 2017; Lee, Chan, Balaji, & Chong, 2018). The majority of organizational-level studies have been conceptual and qualitative in nature and focused on proposing business models of the sharing economy and discussing their applications to different industrial sectors (e.g. Benoit et al., 2017; Binninger, Ourahmoune, & Robert, 2015; Choi, Cho, Lee, Hong, & Woo, 2014). However, individual-level studies on the sharing economy have not received commensurate scholarly attention, with a few notable exceptions empirically examining the motivating factors of users' intention to participate in the sharing economy (e.g. Hamari, Sjöklint, & Ukkonen, 2015; Möhlmann, 2015; Rayle, Dai, Chan, Cervero, & Shaheen, 2016). Furthermore, few studies have investigated how consumers are motivated to accept and adopt ridesharing application (RA). While the research on the sharing economy has started to emerge (e.g. Puschmann & Alt, 2016; PWC, 2015), and a scientific understanding of the phenomenon is still evolving (Lee et al., 2018) there still remains a dearth of understanding as to why people participate in collaborative consumption (Hamari et al., 2015), particularly in geographically dispersed markets such as Australia and New Zealand.

This study bridges these research gaps by systematically examining the effects of perceived benefits (e.g. perceived usefulness and perceived ease of use) and social commerce (e.g. word of mouth communication) on user's attitude and their intention to participate in the sharing economy. Furthermore, this study draws on a number of theoretical model and framework including the extended valence framework (Kim, Ferrin, & Rao, 2009), consumer innovation adoption models (Lee, 2012; Saaksjarvi, 2003), the theory of planned behaviour (Ajzen, 1991; Hsu & Chiu, 2004; Pavlou, Liang, & Xue, 2006) and the technology acceptance model (TAM) (Wang, Lin, & Luarn, 2006) to systematically examine the inhibiting, motivating, and technological factors affecting users' intention to participate in the sharing economy. The study also aims to examine large-scale collaborative consumption data across UberX users from Australia and New Zealand – two countries that share similar cultural values and norms. This study therefore sets forth to empirically investigate factors that affect consumer adoption of ridesharing applications and provides significant theoretical underpinnings that contributes to the emerging literature on the sharing economy through the lens of technology acceptance. The following sections of this paper consist of literature review and hypothesis development, methodology, result, discussion, implications, and future research directions.

## 2. Literature review and hypotheses development

### 2.1. Research on the sharing economy

The sharing economy services are no longer a niche market but an emerging and profitable one that attracts millions of users and huge investments from businesses (Möhlmann, 2015). These services have permeated every aspect of our personal lives, from transportation and accommodation to entertainment (Horpedahl, 2015). In the context of shared mobility, P2P car rental is a popular collaborative consumption practice: platform providers (e.g. Drivy and GetAround) have developed online marketplaces that allow car owners (peer service providers) to rent out their private vehicle to other drivers (consumers) for a limited period of time (e.g. Münzel, Boon, Frenken, & Vaskelainen, 2018). The collaborative consumption practice chosen for this study is ridesharing (i.e. carpooling). Ridesharing has been defined as adding additional passengers to a pre-existing trip (Benoit et al., 2017; Davidson et al., 2018). Uber is essentially a ridesharing application (RA) or a mobile application provided by a transportation network company to order a car ride online. From a consumer perspective, RAs are attractive because they offer lower prices, better accessibility, great flexibility, ease of use, and 'a user-focused mission' including transparency and interactive communication (Dredge & Gyimóthy 2015; Wallsten, 2015).

A review of literature showed that previous studies can be loosely classified into two types: organizational-level studies and individual-level studies. Organizational-level studies focuses on proposed business models of the sharing economy and discussed their applications to different industrial sectors (e.g. Binninger et al., 2015; Choi et al., 2014) or motivations and barriers for adopting the sharing economy business model in addition to its potential effects on traditional business (e.g. Denning, 2014; Nica & Potcovaru, 2015). However, it is noted that individual-level studies on the sharing economy remain scant (Lee et al., 2018). Among the few existing studies, the majority have explored the motivating factors of participating in the sharing economy. Extrinsic and intrinsic benefits were found to positively influence user participation in the sharing economy (e.g. Hamari et al., 2015).

## 2.2.  Theory of Planned Behaviour (TPB) and Technology Acceptance Model (TAM) in

One of the most widely used conceptual frameworks for theorizing why users accept or reject a certain information technology (IT) is the technology acceptance model (TAM) (Wang et al., 2006). TAM includes a concise structure with perceived usefulness (PU) and perceived ease of use (PEOU) (Davis, 1989), which is popular for its under-standability and simplicity (King & He, 2006). Consumer perceived ease of use (PEOU) had been seen as an important factor to influence consumer's adoption of innova-tion. Davis (1989) defines PEOU as the degree to which a person believes that using a particular system or innovation would be free of effort. This construct reflects users' subjective assessments of a system or innovation, which may be representative of objective reality. Innovation acceptance will suffer if users do not see a system or innovation as easy to use (e.g. Davis et al., 1989). A large number of studies have embraced TAM as a fundamental theoretical framework, and some have extended TAM by adding specific variables to different subjects such as perceived playfulness to World Wide Web (Moon & Kim, 2001), social factors to online gaming (Hsu & Lu, 2004), perceived enjoyment to hedonic information systems (Van der Heijden, 2004) and perceived risk and trust to online payment (Yang, Liu, Li & Yu, 2015). Similarly, derived from the same theory of reasoned action (TRA) with TAM, the theory of planned behavior (TPB) (Ajzen, 1991) explains behavior intention by paying more attention to attitude, subject norm and perceived behavior control in an organization setting. In addition, by introducing social (such as word of mouth communications) and individual cognitive variables (e.g. PEOU), the extended or decomposed TPB models explain much more of users' intention than TPB and TAM do (Hsu & Chiu, 2004; Pavlou et al., 2006). Therefore, individual factors are crucial in enhancing the explanatory power of an acceptance model, especially in the market setting of personal information technology such as RA. For the purpose of this study and from the consumer's view, the higher perceived ease of use and perceived usefulness will cause a more positive attitude toward service innovation, thus increasing consumer adoption:

$H_1$. Consumer PU of service innovation is positively related to consumer attitude toward service innovation.

$H_2$. Consumer PEOU of service innovation is positively related to consumer attitude toward service innovation.

## 2.3. Communal sharing and consumer word of mouth

Ridesharing practices among family and friends are also used to illustrate 'online-facilitated offline sharing' (Belk, 2014a, p. 15) or 'Internet-facilitated sharing' (Belk, 2014b, p. 1596), as well as commons-based peer production (Benkler & Nissenbaum, 2006). Benkler (2004) also argued that 'sharing nicely' is a pro-social practice, but one that relies on the economic system to collaborate and produce wealth within communities. This kind of social relationship has been labeled 'communal sharing' because it involves kindness, altruism, love, cooperation, collectivism, and shared identity (Fiske, 1992). In a communal style, participants ideologically associate collaborative consumption with a social exchange opportunity (e.g. keeping company). As such, the communal style is more likely performed by the participants who have had previous experience in creating pro-social relationships through collaborative consumption and who are concerned with belonging to a community (i.e. in particular, the original ridesharing community). As a collaborative consumption practice, RAs such as Uber noted significant business growth from word-of-mouth (WOM) by customers, in particular, 34% of new customers used Uber based on peer recommendations (Rayle et al., 2016). For instance, Uber's referral program is also a communal sharing opportunity using WOM as a facilitator where the RA offers a free ride to both a referrer and a new rider upon a successful referral. The program provides frequent riders the incentive to introduce new customers to the service and because of this, they were quick to tell everyone they knew about the company-referring friend-after-friend which only helped to fuel Uber's revenue base.

As a form of social commerce, word-of-mouth (WOM) represents one of the most influential sources of information transfer by consumers (Keiningham, Rust, Lariviere, Aksoy, & Williams, 2018). WOM both in an online and offline context, affects our behavior as consumers by creating awareness, changing, or confirming our opinions, creating interest in purchasing products and brands (Pitt, Eriksson, Plangger, & Dabirian, 2019; Risselada, Verhoef, & Bijmolt, 2014; Zuo, Zhu, Chen, & He, 2019) in addition to accelerating new purchases and adoption (Kumar, Bezawada, Rishika, Janakiraman, & Kannan, 2016; Libai, Muller, & Peres, 2013) and encouraging repeat purchase (Iyengar, Van den Bulte, & Lee, 2015). WOM, if positive, is highly effective for several reasons. First, it is customised, as the informer portrays the information in a relevant way to the recipient (Godes & Mayzlin, 2004; Trusov, Bucklin, & Pauwels, 2009). Second, as a more unbiased and largely credible source of information, WOM recommendations saves the recipient time and money in identifying appropriate information (Hogan, Lemon, & Libai, 2004). Third, at least if offered through informal sources, it is independent, as the informer has no vested interest in the sale of the service, which adds to its credibility (e.g. Hewett, Rand, Rust, & van Heerde, 2016). Given its non-commercial nature, WOM communication is viewed with less scepticism than firm-initiated promotional efforts (Godes & Mayzlin, 2004). Therefore, as part of social exchange opportunity, consumer's WOM is predicted to relate positively to consumer attitude toward service innovation:

$H_3$. Consumer's WOM is positively related to consumer attitude toward service innovation.

## 2.4. Behavioural intention

Mathur (1999) showed that adoption of an innovation involved both cognitive (awareness and interest) and behavioral (trial and adoption) steps. According to Reasoned Action Theory, behavior is determined by intentions, which are in turn determined by attitudes and subjective norms (Fishbein & Ajzen, 1980). The relationship between attitude and behavioral intentions has been widely examined and supported. Meta-analysis, combining samples of over 10,000 participants, supports the strong attitude-intention-behavior linkage (Kim & Hunter, 1993). RAs such as Uber is perceived as a service innovation and transport option that serves previously unmet demand for fast, flexible, and convenient mobility in urban areas (e.g. Rayle et al., 2016). Within the context of Uber and Airbnb, Yang, Song, Chen, & Xia (2017) find that consumers' perceived confidence and social benefits result in commitment and positive behavioural intention toward the sharing-economy services. Based on the theoretical expectations and empirical findings, it is expected that consumer attitude toward service innovation will positively influence consumer's intention to use service innovation:

$H_4$. Consumer attitude toward service innovation is positively related to consumer's intention to use service innovation.

## 2.5. Consumer attitude toward the advertisement

Advertising can act as a powerful representational tool, and having marginalized groups represented in mainstream advertising can have a profound effect amongst minority consumers seeking acceptance and validation. Attitude towards the Advertisement is defined as 'a learned predisposition to respond in a favourable or unfavourable toward advertising in general' (MacKenzie & Lutz, 1989, p. 53). Mitchell and Olson (1981) and Shimp (1981) have introduced and suggested the important role that attitudes towards the advertisement construct plays in understanding advertising effectiveness.

Haley & Baldinger (1991) suggested that positive affect (e.g. one's propensity to experience positive emotions and interact with others) towards an advertisement may be one of the best indicator to determine advertising effectiveness. This notion is supported by a number of empirical studies which have found positive affect to be a useful measure of advertising effectiveness relating to brand attitudes and perceptions (Biehal, Stephens, & Curio, 1992; Shimp, 1981), affective responses (Batra & Ray, 1986; Gelb & Pickett, 1983; Kim, Baek, & Choi, 2012). In addition, empirical work by Mitchell and Olson (1981) found evidence of the mediating role of the attitude towards the advertisement construct when results their experiment concluded that they were able to better predict brand attitude and behavioural intention if attitude towards the ad was taken in consideration, together with beliefs about certain product attributes. Similarly, using a classical conditioning perspective, Shimp (1981) suggested as consumers are exposed to products in the advertisement which are portrayed in a manner in which the consumer perceives it as appealing or attractive (e.g. with use of pleasant stimuli such as music or a likeable character), these positive perceptions become conditioned over time and are eventually transferred to the brand that represents the product/advertisement.

In short, a positive affective response through a process of conditioning will not be just for the ad, but also to the branded product that is the subject of the ad (Gelb & Pickett, 1983;

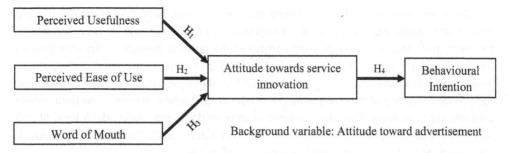

**Figure 1.** Conceptual model.

Shimp, 1981). Building on the existing literature, the study investigates consumer attitude toward the advertisement as a moderator on the relationships hypothesised ($H_1$ to $H_4$) in the conceptual model. Therefore, it is hypothesized that:

$H_5$: Consumers' attitude toward the advertisement will moderate the relationships hypothesised in $H_1$ to $H_4$.

Based on the above discussion, Figure 1 shows the antecedents and consequence of consumer attitude toward service innovation as a conceptual model.

## 3. Study 1

### 3.1. Method

Study 1 tests hypothesis 1–5 based on Australian samples. The survey instrument consists of seven sections and was developed using established scales. First section included a real-life printed advertisement of UberX as the survey stimulus followed by the screening questions to examine the brand familiarity (Becker-Olsen & Hill, 2006) and usage of UberX service. Second section measured perceived usefulness of UberX service (Barabino, Deiana, & Tilocca, 2012; Swan & Bowers, 1998). Third section measured perceived ease of use (PEOU) of UberX service (Kraft, Rise, Sutton, & Røysamb, 2005). Fourth section measured word of mouth of Uber service innovation (Widianti et al., 2015). Fifth section measured respondents' attitudes towards service innovation of UberX service (Lee, 2012). The next section measured respondents' behavioural intention (Bansal, Irving, & Taylor, 2004). Then, the respondents' attitude toward an Uber advertisement was measured (Lee, 2012). The respondents' demographics were asked in the final section. All items are measured on a 5-point Likert scale with 1 representing 'strongly disagree' and 5 representing 'strongly agree'.

Due to the Internet-savvy target audience of UberX users, an online survey with assistance from a market research company was employed for data collection (e.g. Lee et al., 2018). The market research company sent the survey link to a pool of consumers with random sampling. In addition to recording their past usage of UberX services, respondents were screened and limited to those who scored 3 and above on the 5-point Likert scale for brand familiarity (Becker-Olsen & Hill, 2006). A higher level of brand familiarity score has been considered in this research with the notion that the consumers who are not familiar with UberX may lack the understanding of the ridesharing services and thus may provide inappropriate responses to the survey questions. Moreover, past studies suggest that compared to familiar brands, unfamiliar brands have lower advertisement effectiveness and faster wear out (Campbell & Keller, 2003). Therefore, it was imperative to control the brand familiarity as this research examines the moderating influence of the consumers' attitude toward advertisement. The data collection took approximately 4 weeks, covering both weekdays and weekends. A total of 295 valid and useable responses were considered completed, valid and useable for study 1. A brief overview of the sample profile is presented in Table 1.

An Exploratory Factor Analysis (EFA) was conducted to ensure the unidimensionality of each variable. Each scale has a satisfactory Cronbach alpha score (more than 0.70) to prove the data has a strong reliability (Nunnaly, 1978). Structural Equation Modelling (SEM) was used to test the conceptual model and hypothesised relationship. Data were analysed using IBM SPSS Statistics 25 and AMOS 25. Several assumptions for the SEM were checked. For example, the Variance Inflation Factor (VIF) were below 3.0 (Hair, Black, Babin, Anderson, & Tatham, 2010) that assured the absence of multicollinearity. Furthermore, Common Method

**Table 1.** Profile of respondents.

| Characteristics | Categories | Australia (n = 295) Percent | New Zealand (n = 278) Percent |
|---|---|---|---|
| Usage status | User | 49.0 | 49.0 |
| | Non-user | 51.0 | 51.0 |
| Gender | Male | 52.5 | 53.6 |
| | Female | 47.5 | 46.4 |
| Age | 18–24 | 21.7 | 20.5 |
| | 25–34 | 27.1 | 32.7 |
| | 35–44 | 13.2 | 23.7 |
| | 45–54 | 11.2 | 14.0 |
| | 55–64 | 15.6 | 7.2 |
| | 65 and above | 11.2 | 1.8 |
| Education | Secondary/High School | 21.0 | 8.6 |
| | Diploma/Certificate | 29.2 | 27.0 |
| | Undergraduate Degree | 35.3 | 43.2 |
| | Postgraduate Degree | 14.2 | 21.2 |
| Income (AUD/NZD) | 20,000 and under | 11.5 | 10.4 |
| | 20,001–45,000 | 22.4 | 13.7 |
| | 45,001–60,000 | 15.3 | 20.1 |
| | 60,001–75,000 | 10.8 | 16.2 |
| | 75,001–90,000 | 11.5 | 8.6 |
| | 90,000–110,000 | 10.2 | 7.6 |
| | 110,001–150,000 | 9.5 | 14.7 |
| | 150,000 and above | 6.4 | 3.6 |
| | Not sure/Prefer not to say | 2.4 | 1.4 |
| Occupation | Student | 14.6 | 13.7 |
| | Professional | 19.3 | 27.0 |
| | Business | 7.8 | 10.1 |
| | Education | 4.7 | 5.0 |
| | Medical | 2.4 | 1.5 |
| | Information Technology | 6.1 | 5.4 |
| | Design | 0.3 | 0.7 |
| | Executive | 2.7 | 18.6 |
| | Home Maker | 9.5 | 8.3 |
| | Skilled Worker | 7.1 | 4.0 |
| | Self- employed | 3.7 | 1.4 |
| | Retired | 7.5 | 2.9 |
| | Others | 14.2 | 1.4 |

Bias (CMB) was examined with Harman's (1967) one-factor test whereby an exploratory factor analysis was run on all the items of the six variables of this research. The unrotated principal components factor analysis indicated a multiple factor solution and a first-factor variance provide a value of less than 0.50 and so CMB is not a legitimate threat to the validity of the research (e.g. MacKenzie & Podsakoff, 2012).

The two-step procedure (Anderson & Gerbing, 1988) was followed for testing the conceptual model and hypotheses. In this purpose, the factor structure was assessed through measurement model, which were respecified based on item reliability, factor loadings, standardized residuals, and modification indices. The internal consistency, convergent validity, and the discriminant validity were examined under the measurement model. The internal consistency of the constructs were assessed with the composite reliability (CR) of a value greater than 0.70 (Hair et al., 2010). An Average Variance Extracted (AVE) value greater than 0.50 was considered for the convergent validity (Malhotra, 2010). Furthermore, discriminant validities of the constructs were achieved once the square root of the AVE values are higher than the pair-wise inter-construct correlations.

Next, the model fit was assessed and postulated relationships were tested through a structural model. The adequacy of model fit was examined through the following five goodness-of-fit indices (Barrett, 2007; Hu & Bentler, 1999): $\chi^2$/df, Standardized Root-Mean-Square Residual (SRMR), Root-Mean-Square Error of Approximation (RMSEA), Comparative Fit Index (CFI) and Tucker–Lewis index (TLI). As suggested by Kline (2011), Tucker–Lewis index (TLI) and the comparative fit index (CFI) were assessed on the threshold values of 0.90, whereas the maximum acceptable value for the root-mean-square error of approximation (RMSEA) was 0.08. In addition, the ideal $\chi^2$/df value was assessed as less than 3 (Kline, 2011) and the benchmark for Standardised Root Mean Residual (SRMR) was less than 0.08 (Hu & Bentler, 1999).

### 3.2. Results

Then, the reliability and validity of the constructs were tested by running the confirmatory factor analysis, optimizing the measurement model, and purifying the scale items. Two items from perceived usefulness were removed due to high modification indices. The measurement model resulted good fit with $\chi^2$ = 384.00, df = 141, $\chi^2$/df = 2.73; RMSEA = 0.07, SRMR = 0.04, CFI = 0.95, and TLI = 0.94. The model further provided satisfactory composite reliabilities, convergent, and discriminant validities for the constructs (Table 2). A summary of the factor loading, AVE and composite reliabilities for the construct measure is presented in Table 3.

**Table 2.** Validity measure for study 1 and 2.

| | Study 1 | | | | | Study 2 | | | | |
|---|---|---|---|---|---|---|---|---|---|---|
| | 1 | 2 | 3 | 4 | 5 | 1 | 2 | 3 | 4 | 5 |
| 1.Purchase intention | **0.88** | | | | | **0.91** | | | | |
| 2.Perceived usefulness | 0.51 | **0.80** | | | | 0.40 | **0.77** | | | |
| 3.Perceived ease of use | 0.57 | 0.48 | **0.79** | | | 0.36 | 0.67 | **0.79** | | |
| 4.Word of mouth | 0.74 | 0.47 | 0.68 | **0.92** | | 0.46 | 0.54 | 0.81 | **0.92** | |
| 5.Attitude toward service innovation | 0.84 | 0.58 | 0.54 | 0.80 | **0.85** | 0.43 | 0.56 | 0.74 | 0.84 | **0.87** |

Figures in the diagonal (values given in bold) are the square root of the Average Variance Extracted (AVE); those below the diagonal are the correlations between the constructs.

**Table 3.** Scale items for construct measure.

| Latent variables with indicators | Australia | | | New Zealand | | |
|---|---|---|---|---|---|---|
| | Factor loading | AVE | CR | Factor loading | AVE | CR |
| Perceived usefulness | | 0.78 | 0.87 | | 0.59 | 0.85 |
| Convenience of the service (mobile app is easy to use). | 0.80 | | | X | | |
| Punctuality of the service (service is delivered on time). | 0.83 | | | 0.75 | | |
| Affordability of the service (service is reasonably priced). | 0.80 | | | X | | |
| Availability of the service (service covers most major cities and inner suburbs). | 0.74 | | | 0.78 | | |
| Security of the service (service is safe). | X | | | 0.82 | | |
| Driver's knowledge of travel routes (service is efficient). | X | | | 0.72 | | |
| Perceived ease of use | | 0.63 | 0.87 | | 0.63 | 0.87 |
| I can easily make a booking for an UberX service. | 0.73 | | | 0.73 | | |
| I have the resources available to book an UberX service. | 0.70 | | | 0.70 | | |
| I expect that I will be able to book for an UberX service conveniently and without any hassles. | 0.87 | | | 0.87 | | |
| If I wanted to, I would not have any problems with booking an UberX service. | 0.85 | | | 0.86 | | |
| Word of mouth | | 0.84 | 0.94 | | 0.84 | 0.94 |
| I would speak positive things to others about UberX services in general. | 0.88 | | | 0.88 | | |
| I would recommend UberX services to people who need my advice about a ride-sharing service. | 0.93 | | | 0.93 | | |
| I would recommend UberX services to my friends and relatives. | 0.94 | | | 0.94 | | |
| Attitude toward service innovation | | 0.73 | 0.91 | | 0.75 | 0.90 |
| I think UberX is a good mobile ride-sharing app. | 0.81 | | | X | | |
| The UberX service makes me feel good. | 0.85 | | | 0.84 | | |
| The UberX service is my first preference. | 0.84 | | | 0.85 | | |
| I like the UberX service. | 0.90 | | | 0.91 | | |
| Purchase intention | | 0.78 | 0.94 | | 0.83 | 0.94 |
| I would intend to purchase or use an UberX service. | 0.90 | | | 0.90 | | |
| I would consider to purchase or use an UberX service. | 0.80 | | | X | | |
| I would expect to purchase or use an UberX service. | 0.91 | | | 0.91 | | |
| I would plan to purchase or use an UberX service. | 0.92 | | | 0.92 | | |

AVE = Average Variance Extracted, CR: Composite Reliability, X = Item deleted in the process of CFA.
Background variable: Attitude toward advertisement.

The structural model also achieved good fit with $\chi^2 = 395.86$, df = 144, $\chi^2/df = 2.75$; RMSEA = 0.07, SRMR = 0.05, CFI = 0.95, and TLI = 0.94 (Table 4). The results show that perceived usefulness and word of mouth have a significant positive impact on ATSI. Thus, $H_1$ and $H_3$ are supported. Furthermore, $H_4$ is supported as consumers' ATSI has a significant positive impact on purchase intention. However, against the expectation ($H_2$), perceived ease of use did not result in positive ATSI (Table 5).

The sample was divided into two sub-samples with a median score of 4.25 for the attitude toward the advertisement (AtAd). A model level comparison did not show any significant difference between the two sub-samples ($\Delta\chi^2 = 3.948$, $\Delta df = 4$, p = 0.413).

**Table 4.** Structural model results.

| Sample | $\chi^2$ | df | $\chi^2/df$ | CFI | SRMR | RMSEA |
|---|---|---|---|---|---|---|
| Australia (n = 295) | 395.86 | 144.00 | 2.75 | 0.95 | 0.05 | 0.07 |
| Australia user (n = 145) | 347.78 | 144.00 | 2.42 | 0.90 | 0.07 | 0.08 |
| Australia non-user (n = 150) | 268.95 | 144.00 | 1.87 | 0.95 | 0.06 | 0.07 |
| New Zealand (n = 278) | 346.30 | 112.00 | 3.09 | 0.94 | 0.06 | 0.08 |
| New Zealand user (n = 135) | 129.84 | 112.00 | 1.16 | 0.99 | 0.06 | 0.03 |
| New Zealand non-user (n = 143) | 176.35 | 112.00 | 1.58 | 0.96 | 0.07 | 0.06 |

**Table 5.** Summary of the hypothesis testing.

| | | Relationship | | | $\beta$ | t-test | P-value |
|---|---|---|---|---|---|---|---|
| Study 1 | Australia (n = 295) | | | | | | |
| | $H_1$ | Perceived usefulness | → | ATSI | 0.26 | 5.341 | *** |
| | $H_2$ | Perceived ease of use | → | ATSI | -0.05 | -0.847 | 0.397 |
| | $H_3$ | Word-of-mouth | → | ATSI | 0.72 | 11.402 | *** |
| | $H_4$ | ATSI | → | Purchase intention | 0.85 | 17.718 | *** |
| | Australia UberX user (n = 145) | | | | | | |
| | $H_1$ | Perceived usefulness | → | ATSI | 0.49 | 4.362 | *** |
| | $H_2$ | Perceived ease of use | → | ATSI | -0.26 | -1.623 | 0.105 |
| | $H_3$ | Word-of-mouth | → | ATSI | 0.69 | 5.206 | *** |
| | $H_4$ | ATSI | → | Purchase intention | 0.78 | 9.334 | *** |
| | Australia UberX non-user (n = 150) | | | | | | |
| | $H_1$ | Perceived usefulness | → | ATSI | 0.26 | 3.612 | *** |
| | $H_2$ | Perceived ease of use | → | ATSI | -0.03 | -0.371 | 0.711 |
| | $H_3$ | Word-of-mouth | → | ATSI | 0.67 | 8.813 | *** |
| | $H_4$ | ATSI | → | Purchase intention | 0.84 | 13.016 | *** |
| Study 2 | New Zealand (n = 278) | | | | | | |
| | $H_1$ | Perceived usefulness | → | ATSI | 0.21 | 4.329 | *** |
| | $H_2$ | Perceived ease of use | → | ATSI | -0.04 | -0.598 | 0.55 |
| | $H_3$ | Word-of-mouth | → | ATSI | 0.77 | 11.407 | *** |
| | $H_4$ | ATSI | → | Purchase intention | 0.86 | 15.726 | *** |
| | New Zealand UberX user (n = 135) | | | | | | |
| | $H_1$ | Perceived usefulness | → | ATSI | 0.07 | 0.933 | 0.351 |
| | $H_2$ | Perceived ease of use | → | ATSI | 0.08 | 1.054 | 0.292 |
| | $H_3$ | Word-of-mouth | → | ATSI | 0.8 | 7.298 | *** |
| | $H_4$ | ATSI | → | Purchase intention | 0.75 | 7.19 | *** |
| | New Zealand UberX non-user (n = 143) | | | | | | |
| | $H_1$ | Perceived usefulness | → | ATSI | 0.14 | 1.852 | 0.064 |
| | $H_2$ | Perceived ease of use | → | ATSI | -0.13 | -1.186 | 0.236 |
| | $H_3$ | Word-of-mouth | → | ATSI | 0.8 | 6.046 | *** |
| | $H_4$ | ATSI | → | Purchase intention | 0.8 | 7.86 | *** |

Next, a path level comparison was conducted which showed that relationship postulated in $H_1$ (Perceived usefulness → ATSI) was stronger for the sub-sample with low AtAd. The strength of the relationship was invariant for $H_2$, $H_3$, and $H_4$ across two subsamples.

The conceptual model was also compared across the UberX user and non-user in Australia. The measurement model provided validities for both subsamples (Table 6). The model did not significantly differ across the two groups (p = 0.265). Path level comparison showed that the positive relationship between perceived usefulness and ATSI ($H_1$) was stronger among users than the non-users. Otherwise, the rest of the findings for $H_2$, $H_3$, and $H_4$ were invariant between the UberX users and non-users in Australia.

Next, the moderating influence of AtAd was examined for the UberX users in Australia. The conceptual model was significantly different between high and low AtAd subsamples ($\Delta\chi^2$ = 8.52, $\Delta df$ = 4, p = 0.074). The path level comparison showed that the positive relationship between word of mouth and ATSI was only significant for the high AtAd sub-sample.

Finally, conceptual model was not significantly different while compared between the high and low AtAd sub-samples within UberX non-users in Australia ($\Delta\chi^2$ = 2.19, $\Delta df$ = 4, p = 0.701). However, the positive relationship between perceived usefulness and ATSI ($H_1$) was only significant for the low AtAd sub-sample. The significant influences of AtAd on the hypothesised relationships are presented in Table 7.

**Table 6.** Validity measures for user and non-user subsamples.

| | CR | AVE | 1 | 2 | 3 | 4 | 5 |
|---|---|---|---|---|---|---|---|
| Australian user sample | | | | | | | |
| 1.Purchase intention | 0.90 | 0.70 | **0.84** | | | | |
| 2.Perceived usefulness | 0.86 | 0.60 | 0.62*** | **0.78** | | | |
| 3.Perceived ease of use | 0.81 | 0.51 | 0.57*** | 0.71*** | **0.71** | | |
| 4.Word of mouth | 0.92 | 0.80 | 0.66*** | 0.63*** | 0.81*** | **0.89** | |
| 5.Attitude toward service innovation | 0.88 | 0.65 | 0.77*** | 0.73*** | 0.63*** | 0.77*** | **0.81** |
| Australian non-user sample | | | | | | | |
| 1.Purchase intention | 0.94 | 0.79 | **0.89** | | | | |
| 2.Perceived usefulness | 0.89 | 0.67 | 0.52*** | **0.82** | | | |
| 3.Perceived ease of use | 0.87 | 0.63 | 0.43*** | 0.44*** | **0.79** | | |
| 4.Word of mouth | 0.93 | 0.82 | 0.67*** | 0.42*** | 0.48*** | **0.90** | |
| 5.Attitude toward service innovation | 0.92 | 0.73 | 0.84*** | 0.51*** | 0.39*** | 0.76*** | **0.86** |
| New Zealand user sample | | | | | | | |
| 1.Purchase intention | 0.88 | 0.71 | **0.84** | | | | |
| 2.Perceived usefulness | 0.68 | 0.52 | 0.28* | **0.72** | | | |
| 3.Perceived ease of use | 0.89 | 0.68 | 0.40*** | 0.28* | **0.82** | | |
| 4.Word of mouth | 0.90 | 0.74 | 0.63*** | 0.28* | 0.42*** | **0.86** | |
| 5.Attitude toward service innovation | 0.83 | 0.62 | 0.75*** | 0.24* | 0.42*** | 0.85*** | **0.79** |
| New Zealand non-user sample | | | | | | | |
| 1.Purchase intention | 0.88 | 0.71 | **0.85** | | | | |
| 2.Perceived usefulness | 0.85 | 0.60 | 0.21* | **0.77** | | | |
| 3.Perceived ease of use | 0.85 | 0.59 | 0.37*** | 0.24* | **0.77** | | |
| 4.Word of mouth | 0.91 | 0.76 | 0.56*** | 0.15 | 0.69*** | **0.87** | |
| 5.Attitude toward service innovation | 0.84 | 0.64 | 0.81*** | 0.22* | 0.46*** | 0.74*** | **0.80** |

Figures in the diagonal (values given in bold) are the square root of the Average Variance Extracted (AVE); those below the diagonal are the correlations between the constructs.
Significance Indicators: * $p$ < 0.050, *** $p$ < 0.001.

**Table 7.** Moderating role of attitude toward the advertisement.

| | Relationship | | Path coefficient (β) | | Δ β | P-value for the difference |
|---|---|---|---|---|---|---|
| | | | High AtAd | Low AtAd | | |
| Study 1 | Australia (n = 295) | $H_1$ | 0.106 | 0.303*** | −0.197 | 0.07 |
| | Australia UberX user (n = 145) | $H_3$ | 0.106 | 0.303*** | −0.197 | 0.07 |
| | Australia UberX non-user (n = 150) | $H_1$ | 0.091 | 0.268** | −0.177 | 0.205 |
| Study 2 | New Zealand (n = 278) | $H_1$ | 0.339** | 0.03 | 0.309 | 0.006 |
| | New Zealand UberX user (n = 135) | $H_1$ | 0.436* | −0.161 | 0.597 | 0.004 |
| | | $H_3$ | 0.549** | 0.764*** | −0.215 | 0.074 |
| | New Zealand UberX non-user (n = 143) | $H_1$ | 0.346* | 0.039 | 0.307 | 0.068 |
| | | $H_2$ | 0.28 | −0.261† | 0.540 | 0.125 |
| | | $H_3$ | 0.346* | 0.039 | 0.307 | 0.068 |

Significance Indicators: † $p < 0.100$, * $p < 0.050$, ** $p < 0.010$, *** $p < 0.001$.

# 4. Study 2

## 4.1. Method

Study 2 tests hypothesis 1–5 based on New Zealand samples. The survey questionnaire design, data collection, and data analysis technique followed the same procedure specified in study 1. A total of 278 valid and useable responses were considered completed, valid, and useable for study 2 (Table 1).

## 4.2. Results

An EFA with Principal component method and Varimax rotation assured the unidimensionality of the constructs. Scale item loadings were satisfactory and so all items were retained. The sample adequacy, reliability, and the Bartlett's test of sphericity were satisfactory as well.

In the process of confirmatory factor analysis, two items from perceived usefulness, and one item each from ATSI and purchase intention were removed due to high modification indices. The measurement model resulted in acceptable fit with $\chi^2 = 335.540$, df = 109, $\chi^2/$df = 3.07; RMSEA = 0.08, SRMR = 0.05, CFI = 0.95, and TLI = 0.94. The model further provided satisfactory composite reliabilities, convergent, and discriminant validities for the constructs (Table 2).

The structural model also achieved acceptable fit with $\chi^2 = 346.295$, df = 112, $\chi^2/$df = 3.09; RMSEA = 0.08, SRMR = 0.06, CFI = 0.94, and TLI = 0.93. Consistent with the findings in study 1, the $H_1$, $H_3$, and $H_4$ are supported and $H_2$ is rejected (Table 5).

The moderating influence of AtAd was examined at both model level and path level. The respondents were divided into high and low AtAd samples based on a median score of 4.00. The conceptual model was significantly different between the two sub-samples ($\Delta\chi^2 = 9.446$, $\Delta$df = 4, p = 0.051). The path level comparisons showed that that relationship postulated in $H_1$ (Perceived usefulness → ATSI) was stronger for the sub-sample with high AtAd. The strength of the relationship was invariant for $H_2$, $H_3$, and $H_4$ across two sub-samples.

Following the study 1, the New Zealand sample was divided into user and non-user subsamples. The measurement model provided validities for both subsamples (Table 6). However, the conceptual model was found significantly different (p = 0.092) across the UberX user and non-user in New Zealand. The positive relationship between perceived usefulness and ATSI ($H_1$) was significant (p = 0.064) only for the non-user sample. Similar to study 1, the findings for $H_2$, $H_3$, and $H_4$ were invariant across groups in study 2.

Then, the moderating influence of AtAd was examined for the UberX users in New Zealand. The conceptual model was significantly different between high and low AtAd sub-samples ($\Delta\chi^2$ = 12.816, $\Delta df$ = 4, p = 0.012). In addition, the positive relationship between perceived usefulness and ATSI was stronger for the high AtAd sub-samples. By contrast, the positive relationship between word of mouth and ATSI ($H_3$) was stronger for the low AtAd sub-sample.

The conceptual model was also significantly different between high and low AtAd sub-samples ($\Delta\chi^2$ = 11.299, $\Delta df$ = 4, p = 0.023) within UberX non-users in New Zealand. The path level comparison showed that (i) the positive relationship between perceived usefulness and ATSI ($H_1$) is stronger for high AtAd subsample, (ii) the negative relationship between perceived ease of use and ATSI ($H_2$) was only significant for low AtAd subsample, and (ii) the positive relationship between word of mouth and ATSI ($H_3$) is only significant for low AtAd subsample (Table 7).

## 5. Study 3

### 5.1. Method

Study 3 examines the differences between Australian and New Zealand samples based on hypothesis 1–5. A multigroup SEM was employed to investigate the difference between the two samples. A series of chi-square difference tests were conducted to check the model level and path level differences.

### 5.2. Results

The conceptual model was compared across the samples from Australia and New Zealand. The p-value of the chi-square difference test was not significant at model level ($\Delta\chi^2$ = 5.518, $\Delta df$ = 4, p = 0.238). Following this, path level comparisons were conducted. The positive relationship between perceived usefulness and ATSI ($H_1$) was stronger for the Australian sample. The results for the relationships postulated in $H_2$, $H_3$, and $H_4$ were invariant across two countries.

Next, the model was compared across UberX users in Australia and New Zealand. The model differs significantly across groups ($\Delta\chi^2$ = 10.041, $\Delta df$ = 4, p = 0.04) due to the converse results in $H_2$. The hypothesised relationship between perceived ease of use and ATSI was negative for Australia sample ($\beta$ = −0.268) and positive for New Zealand sample ($\beta$ = 0.077). In addition, the positive relationship between perceived usefulness and ATSI ($H_1$) was stronger for the Australian sample. Results for the relationships hypothesised in $H_3$, and $H_4$ were invariant across the groups.

Finally, the model was compared across the non-user sample for the two countries. The model level comparison showed a non-significant difference ($\Delta\chi^2$ = 8.722, $\Delta df$ = 4, p = 0.068). The path level comparison showed that the positive relationship between perceived usefulness and ATSI ($H_1$) was stronger for Australia's non-user sample. The three other hypotheses were not significantly different across the non-user samples.

## 6. Discussion

This research examines the factors that influence the consumers' attitude toward and intention to use ridesharing (i.e. UberX) services.

### 6.1. Perceived usefulness and ATSI

The results show that consumers' perceived usefulness has a significant positive impact on the consumers' attitude toward UberX. This result is consistent with the findings of similar previous studies on service innovation (e.g. Lee et al., 2018). The benefits provided by UberX services influence the cognitive (e.g. good mobile app) and affective (e.g. feel good) aspects of the consumers' attitude. Park, Baek, Ohm, and Chang (2014) found that a product's perceived usefulness is a direct predictor of behavioural intention to use of the technology of interest. In relation to ridesharing, consumers' perceived usefulness has two primary effects: first, it encourages consumers to take more rides in the point-to-point transport market than they have previously. These rides grow the size of the point-to-point transport market in Australia and New Zealand because consumers are attracted to the services that either offer lower price or the different features that Uber currently offers. Second, price and service differences have seen consumers switch from other point-to-point transport services (such as taxis) to ridesharing, whereby the overall size of the market remains the same, however, there may be net benefits to society because of strong consumer gains (e.g. Rayle et al., 2016). There are several economic features of ridesharing platforms that make them attractive to buyers and sellers (For a review, see Alley, 2016; Einav, Farronato, & Levin, 2016).

### 6.2. Perceived ease of use and ATSI

As a service innovation, Uber has an edge in safety through effective information dissemination, convenience through technological advancements in booking and GPS, and comfort through newer cars and performance conscious drivers (Uber, 2018). This research however does not find any significant positive relationship between the consumers' perceived ease of use and attitude toward UberX. In fact, the study deviates from the theoretical expectation established in the $H_2$ of this research. One plausible explanation to this counterintuitive finding lies in the conceptualisation of the construct. Theoretically, perceived ease of use refers to 'the degree to which a person believes that using a particular system would be free of effort' (Davis et al., 1989, p. 320). Uber operates with mostly the same dynamics as the taxicab, but makes its users feel like they have a personal driver in the safety of their own vehicle, however, do consumers find the usage of UberX services 'free of effort'? Compared to the taxicab and public transports, perhaps 'E-Hail' services such as Uber is perceived as a convenient service but not one that is necessarily 'easy to use'. This suggests that the ridesharing app would require more effort from the users, especially those who have a lower self-efficacy or are risk adverse towards using this type of service innovation. In addition, learning to use the Uber app and its functions (e.g. booking, review ratings, navigation, and payment) can in some cases appear quite cumbersome for both the user and the driver. On the other hand, being a passenger in a traditional taxi is a familiar experience for many around the world, with taxis filling important gaps in public transporting, supporting transport for those with disabilities, alongside participants and workers in the night-time economy. Therefore, within the specific context of this research, perceived ease of use does not result in a positive impact on the consumers' attitude toward UberX.

### 6.3.  WOM and ATSI

Uber's success and its concept of ridesharing have been driven largely by technology and more so by the power and reach of the social network (Breidbach & Brodie, 2017). Of particular importance are the social context and the word of mouth that positively influences the consumers' attitude toward UberX services. Uber's successful referral program is also a strong indication that the word of mouth portal is an extremely important entry point when promoting new or innovative services to customers, where the role of peer recommendations accounts for one-third of new users in trailing Uber services (Rayle et al., 2016). This finding validates the notion that word-of-mouth is a strong catalyst in influencing the consumers' acceptance of a new product or service (Godes & Mayzlin, 2004).

### 6.4.  ATSI and purchase intention

This research further validates the positive relationship between consumer attitude and intention within the context of UberX services. There are numerous past studies that have utilised the Theory of Reasoned Action to explain how consumers' attitude guides their behavioural intention (e.g. Lee, 2012). It is known that attitude influences behavior; hence, the determinants of consumer attitude toward service innovation are key factors influencing consumer's adoption of service innovation, as well as the success of new service. As previously discussed, in the present study, two factors namely perceived usefulness and word of mouth with the service are shown to influence significantly consumer attitude toward UberX as a service innovation.

### 6.5.  Moderating role of attitude toward advertisement

Finally, this research investigates whether the consumers' AtAd has a differential effect on the relationship between ATSI and its antecedents/outcomes. The results show that AtAd moderates the positive relationship between perceived usefulness and ATSI. The result is consistent across study 1 and 2. Perhaps, the moderating role of AtAd might be explained in two ways. First, the survey stimulus used in this research described UberX services as the 'Everyday cars for everyday use. Better, faster, and cheaper than a taxi'. Second, the recent Uber advertisement campaigns such as 'Doors Are Always Opening' (Uber, 2018) promote the benefits offered by the Uber ridesharing services. Therefore, the positive relationship between perceived usefulness and attitude is influenced by the consumers' AtAd.

The moderating role of AtAd on the relationship between word-of-mouth and attitude is supported for UberX user samples in Australia and New Zealand. In particular, the positive relation is statistically significant for the users having a low score in AtAd. This finding complies with the notion that new users receive the promo-code referred by existing Uber users and so the word-of-mouth plays a stronger role than the AtAd does in creating a positive attitude toward the ATAS. In addition, the moderating role of AtAd has been supported for the non-user samples in New Zealand, but the results are not conclusive while compared with the non-user samples in Australia.

## 7. Implications

### 7.1. Theoretical implications

This research contributes to the marketing theory in several ways. First, the findings provide a better understanding of the factor that influences the consumer ATSI within the context of ridesharing services. Second, the relationship between attitude and intention has been validated and the moderating role of AtAd has been examined. Third, the results provide a better understanding on the consumers' attitude toward and purchase intention for service innovation within the context of UberX. These findings are expected to add values into the current scant empirical studies on the ridesharing services. In addition, this research tests and compares the conceptual model across two countries. Furthermore, the relationships are tested and compared between user and non-user samples both within and across the countries. Therefore, this research provides a rigour and robust results supported by relevant theoretical underpinnings.

### 7.2. Managerial implications

The practitioners in UberX and other ridesharing services are expected to benefit from the findings of this research in several ways. First, they can emphasise on the factors that create positive attitude toward the service. Specifically, this research find that perceived usefulness and word-of-mouth are the two key indicators that influence the ATSI. Build on this notion, it is imperative that marketing strategists for UberX and other ridesharing services emphasise on the perceived usefulness of the service. In particular, the benefits offered by their brands need to be integrated and communicated through advertising campaigns. Furthermore, the power of the word of mouth and peer recommendations need to be utilised in promotional strategies. For instance, the interaction between passenger and driver is a potential and interesting one to reflect upon for promotion. Uber themselves have collaborated with Spotify to allow passengers to choose what music to play in the car. Other concepts might include sharing information about drivers to passengers, allowing passengers to request a 'quiet ride' or to request particular routes. Other branding initiatives could see the service provider expand its referral program by increasing the span of promo codes to incentivise existing customers and to target new ones. Furthermore, this marketing strategy will allow for specific efforts to be placed on converting the non-users to users. The ridesharing service managers may also improve the consumers' perceived ease of use of the services. Marketing efforts need to be placed on easing the usage UberX mobile app as well as communicating the perceived ease of use of the app. When designing a service innovation, managers should consider the ease of use of target consumers, including the service process and operation of necessary facilities. This suggests that a better understanding of target consumers and user-oriented process design will be very helpful in determining service innovation usage and adoption (Lee et al., 2018). For instance, in the case of reliance on a credit card for payment that excludes the 'unbanked' could be responded by providing prepaid stored-value money card or gift cards which could be one way of addressing this group. More broadly there are potential ways these services could be used to support the mobility of groups who suffer from low-access to public transport. Furthermore, utilisation of word-of-mouth and personalised e-guides and instructions can form part of the service user interface which would help curb the negative perception around app usage and complexity, and thus increase consumer confidence.

## 8. Limitations and future research

This research has several limitations that need to be acknowledged and might be addressed in future. First, future research may compare the culturally different markets for validating the conceptual model and results. Second, understanding 'inhibitors' of user intention to participate in sharing economy services is also important (Arli, van Esch, & Trittenbach, 2018). While users have perceived participating in sharing economy services more economical, convenient, and enjoyable, potential risks, such as privacy risk and security risk, have deterred them from participating in such services. For instance, participating in the sharing economy often requires users to input detailed personal information which may be used for non-intended commercial activities (Dillahunt & Malone, 2015). In addition, there have been notable cases of rape, vandalism, and theft of using different sharing economy services such as Uber and Airbnb (Bleier, 2015). Therefore, it would be imperative to test whether the conceptual model of this paper varies across gender. Notwithstanding, with the focus of online-based survey and data collection with an app (Uber), future research may include eWOM into the research framework for a better understanding of consumers' ridesharing attitude and intention (Pitt et al., 2019; Zuo et al., 2019). In addition, taking a probabilistic sampling would provide a better understanding of the consumer's intention. Research may also examine the role of perceived value, perceived risk, trust in the platform, economic benefits, boycott/boycott, and consumer advocacy on attitude and intention for using Uber and similar ridesharing services to convert non-users to users. Further studies examining the moderating role of 'consumer innovativeness', 'perceived service quality' 'perceived safety' is also suggested for a better understanding of the consumer–brand relationship. Nonetheless, Uber is facing fierce competitive pressure (Lyft, Olla, Grab, etc.) and has closed its operation in some emerging markets recently (e.g. Singapore). Therefore, further research is warranted on how ridesharing franchises can build a long term and sustainable business model (e.g. Facca, 2013; Thaichon, Weaven, Quach, Baker, & Frazer, 2019; Victoria Bordonaba-Juste & Polo-Redondo, 2008).

## Disclosure Statement

No potential conflict of interest was reported by the author(s).

# References

Ajzen, I. (1991). The theory of planned behavior. *Organizational Behavior and Human Decision Processes, 50*(2), 179–211.

Allen, D. (2015). The sharing economy. *IPA Review, 67*(3), 2527.

Alley, J. K. (2016). *The impact of Uber technologies on the New York city transportation industry* (Unpublished undergraduate project). University of Arkansas, Fayetteville.

Anderson, J. C., & Gerbing, D. W. (1988). Structural equation modeling in practice: A review and recommended two-step approach. *Psychological Bulletin, 103*(3), 411.

Arli, D., van Esch, P., & Trittenbach, M. (2018). Investigating the mediating effect of Uber's sexual harassment case on its brand: Does it matter. *Journal of Retailing and Consumer Services, 43*, 111–118.

Bansal, H. S., Irving, P. G., & Taylor, S. F. (2004). A three-component model of customer to service providers. *Journal of the Academy of Marketing Science, 32*(3), 234–250.

Barabino, B., Deiana, E., & Tilocca, P. (2012). Measuring service quality in urban bus transport: A modified SERVQUAL approach. *International Journal of Quality and Service Sciences, 4*(3), 238–252.

Barrett, P. (2007). Structural equation modelling: Adjudging model fit. *Personality and Individual Differences, 42*(5), 815–824.

Batra, R., & Ray, M. L. (1986). Affective responses mediating acceptance of advertising. *Journal of Consumer Research, 13*(2), 234–249.

Becker-Olsen, K. L., & Hill, R. P. (2006). The impact of sponsor fit on brand equity: The case of non-profit service providers. *Journal of Service Research, 9*(1), 73–83.

Belk, R. W. (2014a). Sharing versus pseudo-sharing in web 2.0. *Anthropologist, 18*(1), 7–23.

Belk, R. W. (2014b). You are what you can access: Sharing and collaborative consumption online. *Journal of Business Research, 67*(8), 1595–1600.

Benkler, Y. (2004). Sharing nicely: On shareable goods and the emergence of sharing as a modality of economic production. *Yale LJ, 114*, 273.

Benkler, Y., & Nissenbaum, H. (2006). Commons-based peer production and virtue. *Journal of Political Philosophy, 14*(4), 394–419.

Benoit, S., Baker, T. L., Bolton, R. N., Gruber, T., & Kandampully, J. (2017). A triadic framework for collaborative consumption (CC): Motives, activities and resources & capabilities of actors. *Journal of Business Research, 79*(October), 219–227.

Biehal, G., Stephens, D., & Curio, E. (1992). Attitude toward the ad and brand choice. *Journal of Advertising, 21*(3), 19–36.

Binninger, A.-S., Ourahmoune, N., & Robert, I. (2015). Collaborative consumption and sustainability: A discursive analysis of consumer representations and collaborative website narratives. *Journal of Applied Business Research, 31*(3), 969–985.

Bleier, E. (2015, August 15). American tourist claims he was held captive and sexually assaulted by his transexual Airbnb host in Spain. *Daily Mail.* Retrieved from https://www.dailymail.co.uk/news/article-3199338/American-tourist-Jacob-Lopez-claims-transexual-Airbnb-host-Madrid-sexually-assaulted-him.html

Breidbach, C. F., & Brodie, R. J. (2017). Engagement platforms in the sharing economy: Conceptual foundations and research directions. *Journal of Service Theory and Practice, 27*(4), 761–777.

Campbell, M. C., & Keller, K. L. (2003). Brand familiarity and advertising repetition effects. *Journal of Consumer Research, 30*(2), 292–304.

Choi, H. R., Cho, M. J., Lee, K., Hong, S. G., & Woo, C. R. (2014). The business model for the sharing economy between SMEs. *WSEAS Transactions on Business and Economics, 11*(2), 625–634.

Cusumano, M. A. (2015). How traditional firms must compete in the sharing economy. *Communications of the ACM, 58*(1), 32–34.

Davidson, A., Habibi, M. R., & Laroche, M. (2018). Materialism and the sharing economy: A cross-cultural study of American and Indian consumers. *Journal of Business Research, 82* (January), 364–372.

Davis, F. D., Bagozzi, R. P., & Warshaw, P. R. (1989). User acceptance of computer technology: A comparison of two theoretical models. *Management Science, 35*(8), 982–1003.

Denning, S. (2014). An economy of access is opening for business: Five strategies for success. *Strategy and Leadership, 42*(4), 14–21.

Dillahunt, T. R., & Malone, A. R. (2015, April 18–23). The promise of the sharing economy among disadvantaged communities. T*he Proceedings of the 33rd Annual ACM Conference on Human Factors in Computing Systems*, Seoul.

Dredge, D., & Gyimóthy, S. (2015). The collaborative economy and tourism: Critical perspectives, questionable claims and silenced voices. *Tourism Recreation Research, 40*(3), 286–302.

Einav, L., Farronato, C., & Levin, J. (2016). Peer-to-peer markets. *Annual Review of Economics, 8*(1), 615–635. doi:10.1146/annurev-economics-080315-015334

Facca, T. M. (2013). Using discriminant analysis to classify satisfaction data to facilitate planning in a franchise context. *Journal of Strategic Marketing, 21*(2), 125–139.

Fishbein, M., & Ajzen, I. (1980). Predicting and understanding consumer behavior: Attitude-behavior correspondence. In I. Ajzen & M. Fishbein (Eds.), *Understanding attitudes and predicting social behavior* (pp. 148–172). Englewood Cliffs, NJ: Prentice-Hall.

Fiske, A. P. (1992). The four elementary forms of sociality: Framework for a unified theory of social relations. *Psychological Review, 99*(4), 689–723.

Gelb, B. D., & Pickett, C. M. (1983). Attitude-toward-the-ad: Links to humor and to advertising effectiveness. *Journal of Advertising, 12*(2), 34–42. doi:10.1080/00913367.1983.10672838

Godes, D., & Mayzlin, D. (2004). Using online conversations to study word-of-mouth communication. *Marketing Science, 23*(4), 545–560.

Hair, J. F., Black, W. C., Babin, B. J., Anderson, R. E., & Tatham, R. L. (2010). *Multivariate data analysis: A global perspective*. Upper Saddle River, NJ: Pearson.

Haley, R. I., & Baldinger, A. L. (1991, April). The ARF copy research validity project. *Journal of Advertising Research, 31*, 11–32.

Hamari, J., Sjöklint, M., & Ukkonen, A. (2015). The sharing economy: Why people participate in collaborative consumption. *Journal of the Association for Information Science and Technology, 67* (9), 2047–2059.

Harman, D. (1967). A single factor test of common method variance. *Journal of Psychology, 35,* 359–378.

Hewett, K., Rand, W., Rust, R. T., & van Heerde, H. J. (2016). Brand buzz in the echoverse. *Journal of Marketing, 80*(3), 1–24.

Hogan, J. E., Lemon, K. N., & Libai, B. (2004). Quantifying the ripple: Word-of-mouth and advertising effectiveness. *Journal of Advertising Research, 44*(3), 271–280.

Horpedahl, J. (2015). Ideology Über Alles economics bloggers on Uber, Lyft, and other transportation network companies. *Econ Journal Watch, 12*(3), 360–374.

Hsu, C. L., & Lu, H. P. (2004). Why do people play on-line games? An extended TAM with social influences and flow experience. *Information and Management, 41*(7), 853–868.

Hsu, M. H., & Chiu, C. M. (2004). Internet self-efficacy and electronic service acceptance. *Decision Support Systems, 38*(3), 369–381.

Hu, L. T., & Bentler, P. M. (1999). Cutoff criteria for fit indexes in covariance structure analysis: Conventional criteria versus new alternatives. *Structural Equation Modeling: A Multidisciplinary Journal, 6*(1), 1–55.

Iyengar, R., Van den Bulte, C., & Lee, J. Y. (2015). Social contagion in new product trial and repeat. *Marketing Science, 34*(3), 408–429.

Keiningham, T. L., Rust, R. T., Lariviere, B., Aksoy, L., & Williams, L. (2018). A roadmap for driving customer word-of-mouth. *Journal of Service Management, 29*(1), 2–38.

Kim, D. J., Ferrin, D. L., & Rao, H. R. (2009). Trust and satisfaction, two stepping stones for successful e-commerce relationships: A longitudinal exploration. *Information Systems Research, 20*(2), 237–257.

Kim, J., Baek, Y., & Choi, Y. H. (2012). The structural effects of metaphor-elicited cognitive and affective elaboration levels on attitude toward the ad. *Journal of Advertising, 41*(2), 77–96.

Kim, J., Yoon, Y., & Zo, H. (2015). *Why people participate in the sharing economy: A social exchange perspective.* PACIS 2015 Proceedings, AISeL, Milan, Italy, 76.

Kim, M. S., & Hunter, J. E. (1993). Relationships among attitudes, behavioral intentions, and behavior: A meta-analysis of past research, part 2. *Communication Research, 20*(3), 331–364.

King, W. R., & He, J. (2006). A meta-analysis of the technology acceptance model. *Information & Management, 43*(6), 740–755.

Kline, R. B. (2011). *Principles and practice of structural equation modelling* (Vol. xvi, 3rd ed.). New York, NY: Guilford Press.

Kraft, P., Rise, J., Sutton, S., & Røysamb, E. (2005). Perceived difficulty in the theory of planned behaviour: Perceived behavioural control or affective attitude. *British Journal of Social Psychology, 44*(3), 479–496.

Kumar, A., Bezawada, R., Rishika, R., Janakiraman, R., & Kannan, P. K. (2016). From social to sale: The effects of firm-generated content in social media on customer behavior. *Journal of Marketing, 80* (1), 7–25.

Lee, B. C. (2012). The determinants of consumer attitude toward service innovation–the evidence of ETC system in Taiwan. *Journal of Services Marketing, 26*(1), 9–19.

Lee, Z. W., Chan, T. K., Balaji, M. S., & Chong, A. Y. L. (2018). Why people participate in the sharing economy: An empirical investigation of Uber. *Internet Research, 28*(3), 829–850.

Libai, B., Muller, E., & Peres, R. (2013). Decomposing the value of word-of-mouth seeding programs: Acceleration versus expansion. *Journal of Marketing Research, 50*(2), 161–176.

MacKenzie, S. B., & Lutz, R. J. (1989). An empirical examination of the structural antecedents of attitude toward the ad in an advertising pretesting context. *Journal of Marketing, 53*(2), 48–65.

MacKenzie, S. B., & Podsakoff, P. M. (2012). Common method bias in marketing: Causes, mechanisms, and procedural remedies. *Journal of Retailing, 88*(4), 542–555.

Malhotra, N. K. (2010). *Marketing research: An applied orientation.* Upper Saddle River, NJ: Pearson.

Mathur, A. (1999). Adoption of technological innovations by the elderly: A consumer socialization perspective. *Journal of Marketing Management, 9*(3), 21–35.

Mitchell, A. A., & Olson, J. C. (1981). Are product attribute beliefs the only mediator of advertising effects on brand attitude. *Journal of Marketing Research, 18*(3), 318–332.

Möhlmann, M. (2015). Collaborative consumption: Determinants of satisfaction and the likelihood of using a sharing economy option again. *Journal of Consumer Behaviour, 14*(3), 193–207.

Moon, J. W., & Kim, Y. G. (2001). Extending the TAM for a World-Wide-Web context. *Information and Management, 38*(4), 217–230.

Münzel, K., Boon, W., Frenken, K., & Vaskelainen, T. (2018). Carsharing business models in Germany: Characteristics, success and future prospects. *Information Systems and E-Business Management, 16* (2), 271–291.

Nica, E., & Potcovaru, A.-M. (2015). The social sustainability of the sharing economy. *Economics, Management and Financial Markets, 10*(4), 69–75.

Nunnally, J. C. (1978). *Psychometric theory* (2nd ed.). New York, NY: McGraw-Hill.

Park, E., Baek, S., Ohm, J., & Chang, H. J. (2014). Determinants of player acceptance of mobile social network games: An application of extended technology acceptance model. *Telematics and Informatics, 31*(1), 3–15. doi:10.1016/j.tele.2013.07.001

Pavlou, P. A., Liang, H., & Xue, Y. (2006). Understanding and mitigating uncertainty in online environments: A principal-agent perspective. *MIS Quarterly, 31*(1), 105–136.

Pitt, C., Eriksson, T., Plangger, K., & Dabirian, A. (2019). Accommodation market labels and customers reviews: An abstract. In P. Rossi & N. Krey (Eds.), *Finding new ways to engage and satisfy global customers. AMSWMC 2018. Developments in Marketing Science: Proceedings of the Academy of Marketing Science.* Cham: Springer.

PricewaterhouseCoopers (PWC). (2015). *The sharing economy: Consumer intelligence series.* Delaware: PricewaterhouseCoopers. Retrieved from www.pwc.com/us/en/technology/publications/assets/pwc-consumer-intelligence-series-the-sharing-economy.pdf

Puschmann, T., & Alt, R. (2016). Sharing economy. *Business & Information Systems Engineering, 58*(1), 93–99.

Rayle, L., Dai, D., Chan, N., Cervero, R., & Shaheen, S. (2016). Just a better taxi? A survey-based comparison of taxis, transit, and ridesourcing services in San Francisco. *Transport Policy, 45*(1), 168–178.

Risselada, H., Verhoef, P. C., & Bijmolt, T. H. (2014). Dynamic effects of social influence and direct marketing on the adoption of high-technology products. *Journal of Marketing, 78*(2), 52–68.

Saaksjarvi, M. (2003). Consumer adoption of technological innovations. *European Journal of Innovation Management, 6*(2), 90–100.

Shimp, T. A. (1981). Attitude toward the ad as a mediator of consumer brand choice. *Journal of Advertising, 10*(2), 9–48.

Standing, C., & Mattsson, J. (2018). Fake it until you make it: Business model conceptualization in digital entrepreneurship. *Journal of Strategic Marketing, 26*(5), 385–399.

Swan, J. E., & Bowers, M. R. (1998). Services quality and satisfaction. *Journal of Services Marketing, 12* (1), 59–72.

Thaichon, P., Weaven, S., Quach, S., Baker, B., & Frazer, L. (2019). What to expect after the honeymoon: Evolutionary psychology of part-time franchising. *Journal of Strategic Marketing*, 1–25. doi:10.1080/0965254x.2019.1570315

Trusov, M., Bucklin, R. E., & Pauwels, K. (2009). Effects of word-of-mouth versus traditional marketing: Findings from an internet social networking site. *Journal of Marketing, 73*(5), 90–102.

Uber. (2018, September 16). Doors Are Always Opening | Uber [Video File]. Retrieved from https://www.youtube.com/watch?v=NiVXmLkcOiA

Van der Heijden, H. (2004). User acceptance of hedonic information systems. *MIS Quarterly, 28*(4), 695–704.

Victoria Bordonaba-Juste, M. V., & Polo-Redondo, Y. (2008). Differences between short and long-term relationships: An empirical analysis in franchise systems. *Journal of Strategic Marketing, 16*, 327–354.

Wallsten, S. (2015). *The competitive effects of the sharing economy: How is Uber changing taxis*. New York, NY: Technology Policy Institute.

Wang, Y. S., Lin, H. H., & Luarn, P. (2006). Predicting consumer intention to use mobile service. *Information Systems Journal, 16*(2), 157–179.

Widianti, T., Sumaedi, S., Bakti, I. G. M. Y., Rakhmawati, T., Astrini, N. J., & Yarmen, M. (2015). Factors influencing the behavioral intention of public transport passengers. *International Journal of Quality & Reliability Management, 32*(7), 666–692.

Yang, S., Song, Y., Chen, S., & Xia, X. (2017). Why are customers loyal in sharing-economy services? A relational benefits perspective. *Journal of Services Marketing, 31*(1), 48–62.

Yang, Y., Liu, Y., Li, H., & Yu, B. (2015). Understanding perceived risks in mobile payment acceptance. *Industrial Management & Data Systems, 115*(2), 253–269.

Zuo, W., Zhu, W., Chen, S., & He, X. (2019). Service quality management of online car-hailing based on PCN in the sharing economy. *Electronic Commerce Research and Applications, 34*, 100827.

# Collaboration, communication, support, and relationships in the context of e-commerce within the franchising sector

Zhanna Kremez, Lorelle Frazer, Sara Quach and Park Thaichon

**ABSTRACT**

This research aims to investigate how ecommerce influences elements of the franchising sector that have adopted an ecommerce strategy. A multiple case-study approach was selected to gain a comprehensive understanding of franchise organisations following implementation in their traditional service or retail businesses. The findings covered, but were not limited to, (a) franchise relationships, (b) franchisor leadership, (c) communication at the franchise network level, (d) collaboration with franchisees, and (e) training and support. The paper offers meaningful outcomes including (a) a framework for franchisee communication and participation, and (b) a model for franchisee acceptance and readiness for change, as well as effective communication in the franchise network. Finally, from the interviews conducted with franchise practitioners, certain practical recommendations have been made that will serve the franchise sector.

## 1. Overview

Ecommerce has become an inherent part of many modern businesses. However, combining the digital interchange of goods or commodities and franchising may encourage a conflict of interest, which requires careful management (Rao & Frazer, 2010; Terry, 2002). While it appears relatively easy for traditional retailers to enter the online transactional space, it is increasingly difficult for franchises to participate due to a number of complicating factors pertaining to potential encroachment and franchisee acceptance (Emerson, 2010); indeed, some franchise networks even resort to litigation to solve their conflicts over digital channels (Knack & Bloodhart, 2001). Therefore, this research aims to investigate the influences of business-to-consumer (B2C) ecommerce on collaboration, communication, franchisee support and franchise relationships.

Conversely, several recent studies in franchising have focused on consumer behaviour (Weaven, Baker, Edwards, Frazer, & Grace, 2018) as well as a range of related issues concerning franchising relationships. This includes expectations after opening a part-time franchising business (Thaichon, Weaven, Quach, Baker, & Frazer, 2019), women in franchisees (Thaichon et al., 2018), self-employment in franchising (Weaven et al., 2019), the effect of learning and development on business performance (Timms, Frazer, Weaven, & Thaichon, 2019), and work–life balance in small businesses (Young, Frazer,

Weaven, Roussety, & Thaichon, 2019). Yet, there remains limited research examining the relational context of ecommerce within the franchising sector. Investigating how successful franchise networks have incorporated ecommerce into their operations and marketing, this paper can otherwise uncover the best practices in the field and develop an ecommerce framework for franchising, where franchisor–franchisee relationships are the cornerstone of any digital marketing strategy. Importantly, reference herein to successful ecommerce implementation is concerned with determining the quality of franchise relationships. Therefore, the definition of success is measured in terms of franchisee acceptance and satisfaction. This approach helps to avoid conflict with franchisees, which can result in a costly and time-consuming process for franchisors and further prove potentially detrimental to the reputation of an entire brand. In addition, this research addresses the role of ecommerce in franchise relationships, specifically regarding how franchisees form effective implementation strategies, as well as their perception of ecommerce in business.

## 2. Literature review

### 2.1. Ecommerce in franchising

Franchising has shown considerable growth in recent years and in developed countries such as the United States (US) (Seo, 2016), France (Cliquet & Voropanova, 2016) and Australia (Young et al., 2019). In fact, several studies highlight the benefits of online platforms and ecommerce in franchising. Notably, Dixon and Quinn, (2004) analysis of franchise websites indicates that many franchisors use online services for communication (with franchisees) and marketing purposes (for customers). Indeed, previous research has shown that network size has a positive effect on implementation as well as subsequent adoption of ecommerce in practice (Perrigot & Pénard, 2013). Some additional benefits include online ordering and payment options (Dixon & Quinn, 2004); cheaper costs and more effective organisational culture (Shah Alam, 2009); favourable relationships between online consumers and e-vendors (Wang, Wang, & Liu, 2016); better function or options for product variety; product customisation, convenience or price (Chaparro-Peláez, Agudo-Peregrina, & Pascual-Miguel, 2016); and more transparent service knowledge and information (Choshin & Ghaffari, 2017). In turn, some of these factors could lead to superior customer satisfaction (Choshin & Ghaffari, 2017); customer commitment, trust and perceived value (Thaichon, Lobo, Prentice, & Quach, 2014); improved service quality and stronger customer loyalty (Quach, Thaichon, & Jebarajakirthy, 2016). Hence, both ecommerce and franchising are considered prominent business strategies.

Moreover, firms franchise their operations to rapidly grow their market, expand business, diversify and improve performance (Wu, 2015). In franchising, there is an established idea or business model franchisors create, which is bought, adopted and operated by franchisees (Peterson & Dant, 1990). Although franchising networks will involve multiple stakeholders, it is necessary for the system to remain consistent across franchise holders (Perrigot & Pénard, 2013). Hence, its operations will require advanced communications between participants to ensure absolute consistency (Cliquet & Voropanova, 2016; Perrigot & Pénard, 2013).

A small group of literature has studied the crossover between franchising and ecommerce, including the strong offline elements of franchising (such as geographical location and the legal system), which affect the implementation of ecommerce in the system. For example, Chau (2003) mentioned ecommerce as a potential 'game changer' in franchising, while Dixon and Quinn (2004) argued that ecommerce is not fully applied in the system since franchisors use only brochure-type websites, cloud storage and online communication systems instead of selling their B2C products online. Recent work by Dorward, Mittermeier, Sandbrook, and Spooner (2017) supports Chau's (2003) prediction by highlighting the augmented reality game Pokémon Go as one example of extending an already successful media and gaming franchise. Despite the extent of ecommerce adoption in franchising, the practice itself supports the franchise system in several aspects.

First, ecommerce leverages communication between parties in a franchising system (Chau, 2003; Perrigot & Pénard, 2013). Franchise firms use websites to deliver information to franchisors, other (and potential) franchisees and individual customers (Chau, 2003; Dixon & Quinn, 2004; Kremez, Frazer, & Thaichon, 2019). For example, world-leading franchisors such as Subway and 7-Eleven offer step-by-step information on their websites detailing how to become a franchisee.

Second, following advanced communications, ecommerce assists in maintaining uniformity in the franchising system (Perrigot & Pénard, 2013). According to the intellectual and industrial property law in most countries, a franchise system is regarded as an intellectual property. Therefore, a franchisee must maintain consistent operating practices that uphold the franchise brand identity. Through an ecommerce system, knowledge (such as price and product information) spreads rapidly in a real time. Indeed, this could assist franchisors in delivering news quickly to franchisees, but there remain concurrent challenges in maintaining operational uniformity due to different resources and (digital) capabilities among network members.

Third, ecommerce plays important roles in customer relationship management. There are two types of customers in a franchise: organisational (franchisee) and individual customers. Ecommerce facilitates communications (Chau, 2003) while the effective knowledge-sharing between franchisor and franchisees improves the latter's satisfaction and compliance (Lee, 2017). Recent research in franchise hotels indicates that ecommerce determines the effect of hotel-customer loyalty programs on room revenue. Given that franchise hotels have comprehensive customer databases, ecommerce can assist in targeting specific market segments with customised product offerings, while maintaining communications between hotels and customers. Collectively, the studies reviewed in this paper seem to suggest a pertinent role of ecommerce in franchising. The evidence presented proposes that its communication feature, in particular, provides additional support in a franchise system and (thus) warrants further investigation.

Yet, how organisations use consumer data underwent change in 2018 following the introduction of a new European privacy law that restricts the way personal data are collected and used (Wachter & Mittelstadt, 2019). The rule, known as the General Data Protection Regulation, focuses on ensuring that users know, understand and consent to the data collected about them. Under this new law, companies must be clear and concise about their collection methods and use of personal data, further spell out why data are being collected and explicate whether that information will be used to create profiles of people's actions and habits. As the law protects only individuals in 28 member countries of the European Union – even if the data were processed elsewhere (Tiku, 2018) – this inevitably affects every company worldwide that deals with European citizens.

## 2.2. Change management: ecommerce in franchising

Change is a constant element that affects all organisations (Todnem By, 2005) including franchise networks. Inevitably, the introduction of ecommerce into franchise systems calls for effective change management and communication within and across organisations. Most literature in both sectors assumes an organisational standpoint, where the main stakeholder groups are managers and employees, which to some extent can inform franchisor–franchisee relations. As such, two dominant models for change management are considered in this section: Lewin (2016) force-field analysis and Kotter's (1996) eight-step change model, along with other literature in the domain.

According to Lewin (2016), any organisation is a system in a dynamic balance ('equilibrium') between two opposing forces: driving forces (those promoting change) and restraining forces (those seeking to maintain the status quo). Successful implementation of change depends on driving forces exceeding restraining forces to shift the equilibrium. Here, force-field analysis would suggest that we investigate the balance of power involved in the situation requiring change and further identify the most important stakeholders, 'target groups', opponents and allies concerned – including the different ways to influence each market (Lewin, 2016. In addition, 1947) argued that during a change process, three stages of unfreezing, moving and refreezing are experienced. Based on this premise, researchers have attempted to identify a set of actions that change agents could take to minimise resistance and help organisations and individuals undergoing transition. For example, Coch and French (1948) explored the effect of employee participation on productivity and satisfaction during organisational change. They found that a greater degree of participation led to higher employee satisfaction, enabling them to adapt more quickly to new production goals (Coch & French, 1948; Holt, Armenakis, Feild, & Harris, 2007). This proposition is further explored in this research.

Similarly, Kotter's (1996) model suggests that eight steps should be taken to ensure successful change. These are as follows: (1) inciting a sense of urgency for change should be increased by inspiring people to move; (2) a team of guiding people with the right emotional commitment and right skills should be brought together to (3) establish a vision and strategy to drive change; (4) emphasis should be placed on involvement and communication, and technological opportunities should be exploited; (5) action needs to be empowered, obstacles removed and managerial support provided; then, (6) visible and attainable goals should be set with corresponding rewards; (7) determination and persistence should also be encouraged, as well as ongoing progress reporting, with future milestones further highlighted; finally, (8) the value of successful change should be reinforced (Kotter, 1995, 1996).

Additionally, Nelissen and van Selm (2008) found that satisfaction with management communication leads to positive responses to organisational change among employees. Indeed, the adequacy of change-related communication was found to be the main predictor of change readiness (McKay, Kuntz, & Näswall, 2013). Therefore, organisations should focus on improving employee satisfaction with how management communicates about objectives and consequences of change, as it is a key determinant of resultant positivity (Nelissen & van Selm, 2008).

In addition, De Ridder (2004) argued that high-quality internal communication may be important in encouraging a supportive attitude towards strategic direction. The author discusses trust in management as a key player in this process. To create trust, managers are required to explicitly communicate the goals of change and remain open about potential issues (De Ridder, 2004). According to Elving (2005) model (used also in this research), communication during the change process can be conducted with two purposes in mind: inform and create community spirit. When undertaken successfully, communication can increase readiness for change and decrease the chance of resistance (Elving, 2005). Thus, it is proposed that defiance in this context can be reduced and, therefore, franchisee acceptance can increase through the broad engagement of franchisees (as key stakeholders), the provision of appropriate education and training, and careful consideration of franchisor relationships. In this framework, clear, consistent and effective communication is the cornerstone for success.

## 3. Methodology

### 3.1. Approach

A multiple case-study approach was selected for this research to gain a comprehensive understanding of several franchise organisations (Eisenhardt, 1989). This enabled the researchers to study their ecommerce strategies from multiple stakeholders' perspectives, including franchisors, franchisees and customers. It further allows for investigation of contemporary phenomena within a real-life, bounded context using multiple sources of evidence (Merriam & Tisdell, 2015; Yin, 2009). Case study research has added use when the research objectives are to explain current situations and to explore the 'why' and 'how' (Yin, 2009) – as in this study. Meanwhile, using multiple examples can enhance precision, validity or generalisability, and stability of the findings (Merriam & Tisdell, 2015; Miles, Huberman, Huberman, & Huberman, 1994). This is because the interaction between a phenomenon and its context is best understood through in-depth case studies (Dubois & Gadde, 2002). As this research is primarily concerned with studying *a* phenomenon – that is, the implications of ecommerce in franchising – and not a particular case as such, a selection of franchise systems were chosen as instrumental cases that collectively provide insight on the issue (Stake, 1994). The examples themselves are of a secondary nature and serve to facilitate understanding of the research problem (Stake, 1994). In addition, the common use of case studies and case analysis in franchising research (e.g. Altinay & Brookes, 2012; Altinay, Brookes, & Aktas, 2013; Altinay, Brookes, Madanoglu, & Aktas, 2014; Brookes, 2014; Brookes & Altinay, 2011; Doherty, 2009; Forte & Carvalho, 2013) could be explained by the limited availability of secondary data, as many of the franchisors and franchisees are private firms.

## 3.2. *Sampling*

The cases selected represent a larger population of examples – that being franchise organisations in Australia employing ecommerce strategies in their traditional service or retail businesses. The best possible explanations of these phenomena were sought and, therefore, viewed as opportunities for close study (Yin, 2009). Thus, purposeful sampling was used (Eisenhardt, 1989; Huberman & Miles, 1994).

The first selection criterion regards the cases' leading position in ecommerce within their industry. Their focus on franchisee satisfaction was important to ensure a collection of franchisors that exhibited best practice in the sector in terms of franchisor–franchisee relations. Additionally, mature systems were chosen since Rao and Frazer (2010) found that mature Australian franchisors (older and larger systems) had better-developed online strategies. The representativeness of these cases within the research context (ecommerce in franchising) was deemed important (Stake, 1994). Therefore, those selected were averaging within the sector 5 per cent of their total sales online (Frazer, Weaven, & Bodey, 2012; Frazer, Weaven, & Grace, 2014) and had not experienced a dramatic increase in returns through their digital channel (e.g. Dominos) or were not purely trading online (e.g. Aussie Farmers Direct). Table 1 details and explains the criteria used for selecting cases for this research.

The data acquired for each case consist of interviews with four franchisees and one or two interviews with the franchisor. In total, five interviews were conducted for Case 1, and six were conducted for Case 2. The franchisor representatives were selected in both cases for their involvement in project managing ecommerce implementation – that is, acting as change agents and communicating with franchisees about introducing ecommerce into the system. Interviewees were also actively participating in the training and support of franchisees as an ecommerce strategy was being integrated into their marketing channels and instore environments.

**Table 1.** Criteria for case selection and characteristics of chosen cases.

| Criteria for case selection | Description | Case 1 | Case 2 |
|---|---|---|---|
| System age | Mature systems (over 10 years) | Founded in 1993 | Founded in 1992 |
| System size | Large systems (more than 50 total units) | 106 retail service centres (self-reported data, 2012) | 70 retail centres and 250 mobile (self-reported data, 2013) |
| Plural form or pure-form franchises | Franchise organisations with a minimal percentage of company-owned units | One company-owned unit | No company-owned units, 100% franchised |
| Level of franchisee involvement | Prior interviews identified sophisticated methods of franchisee involvement | High | High |
| Industry | Mixed service and retail | Transport, postal and warehousing | Administration and support services |
| Percentage of online sales | Percentage of sales through an online channel from the total number of sales | Approximately 5% | Approximately 5% |
| Level of ecommerce development and strategy success | Established and successful ecommerce strategy | Yes | Yes |
| Brand recognition | Established brand in its industry | Yes | Yes |
| International operations | Franchising outside of Australia | Yes (NZ and UK) | Yes (NZ and US) |

New Zealand (NZ).

**Table 2.** Criteria for franchisee selection.

| Criteria for selecting franchisees | Description |
| --- | --- |
| One FAC member (currently) | A current FAC member involved with the brand and actively takes part in FAC's life; they are also familiar with the FAC structure and processes |
| One FAC member (at the time of ecommerce implementation) | A FAC member at the time of ecommerce strategy implementation (very involved and knowledgeable about the process) |
| Number of years in the system | Not just experienced franchisees or new franchisees |
| MUF | At least one SUF must be included in the sample |
| SUF | At least one MUF must be included in the sample |
| Variety in territorial position | Diversity as to different states in Australia as well as demographic density (CBD, suburban, rural) |
| One that embraced ecommerce | A participant that embraced ecommerce initially |
| One that was sceptical of ecommerce | A participant that did not embrace ecommerce initially and was sceptical about its benefits for the system |
| One that was undecided about ecommerce | A participant that was neither for nor against ecommerce, and did not have a strong opinion about the practice |

Next, interviews were conducted with four franchisees in each case, with participants selected according to specific criteria (see Table 2). The goal for including these benchmarks was to achieve as much variability as possible between the franchisees interviewed. Participants were a mixture of single-unit franchisees (SUFs) and multi-unit franchisees (MUFs), with half of the total sample in both cases currently serving on the Franchise Advisory Council (FAC). Their geographical location varied from CBDs and suburban areas to regional areas located across different states in Australia.

An additional dimension was achieved through interviewing sector experts regarding ecommerce in franchising. Participants were asked to reflect on their experiences with franchisor clients when their franchise set forth to incorporate ecommerce strategies into their traditional business model. The interviews were unstructured and respondents were prompted to explain further on areas of interest to the research. In total, seven experts were interviewed, including three franchise consultants, two internet and digital media consultants (with experience in franchising), and two franchise lawyers.

## 4. Results and discussion

### 4.1. Franchise relationships

#### 4.1.1. Franchisor: franchisee relationships

Although franchise relationships constitute a central part of this research, participants, when asked directly about the influence of this change/innovation on franchisor–franchisee relations, mostly agreed that it had no direct effect. In general, they did not discuss these affiliations when prompted, but rather spoke on other underlying concepts *relating* to relationships, such as trust, franchisor leadership and the challenge of introducing innovation (i.e. ecommerce) into their networks. This included their perspectives on change in their own sphere and in the business world in general.

Trust in franchisor integrity and franchisor competence is a determinant of healthy franchising relationships (Altinay & Brookes, 2012; Altinay et al., 2014; Davies, Lassar, Manolis, Prince, & Winsor, 2011; Rosado-Serrano & Paul, 2018; Rosado-Serrano, Paul, & Dikova, 2018). Davies et al. (2011) explained the contingencies that arise from trust in franchise systems due to the mutual interdependence of a franchisor and its franchisees and asymmetrical control. In this bond, franchisees rely on their franchisor for both promotional support and managerial support, which together relates to training and process design (Davies et al., 2011). Therefore, trust is created when a franchisor can demonstrate both the competence to deliver these expectations and the ability to do so with integrity.

The findings of this research show that franchisor competence is demonstrated in both cases, with evidence from franchisee interviews supporting a high level of trust in franchisor competence. For example, one participant noted that their franchisor 'is very strong on the online side, and marketing in general' (CS2 Franchisor 3). However, with regard to franchisor integrity, the findings show that both cases could improve in this area. In particular, meeting time lines relates to integrity and influences trust negatively when they are exceeded (as has occurred according to respondents in both cases). Further, from prior research (Kremez, 2015) it was evident that the design and enactment of ecommerce usually involved more time than initially estimated. Therefore, it is proposed that allowing sufficient time for ecommerce implementation and keeping to agreed schedules would successfully mediate the risk of trust being affected.

Relationships are also based on the confidence that a franchisor has the sufficient knowledge to act in the best interest of a system. Competence can be demonstrated through leadership, which was another prominent theme discussed during interview.

### 4.1.2. Franchisor leadership

The concept of franchisor leadership emerged following discussion with franchisors, and was further explored with franchisees in both cases. Franchisee participants described leadership with words such as 'forward vision', 'innovative', 'trying to keep ahead of the game', 'progressive', 'thinking outside the square' and being 'right at the front when it comes to introducing these new sorts of technology' (CS2 Franchisor 4). Conversely, franchisors characterised the concept as 'showing … leadership and maturity' and 'strategic direction', and bringing with it 'an expectation … to come up with the initiatives, the strategies and then go back to them' (CS2 Franchisor 2). According to one participant:

> I think franchisees join the systems to be led and to be, hopefully, better than their competitors … So taking a position of leadership in an area that they possibly do not have expertise or knowledge in, but certainly have strong views about (i.e. e-commerce), was important to get buy-in … And if you are showing your leadership and maturity to launch something that is going to grow the market and not erode it, I don't think you will get too many franchise partners that will stand in the way. (CS2 Franchisor 1)

Further, experts in this study consistently supported the contention that strong leadership was needed to further develop innovations of a strategic nature, such as ecommerce integration into a traditional franchise system. One expert noted that franchisees would expect a franchisor 'to provide that leadership, but sometimes it is just not forthcoming' (Expert 1). In addition, he explained that in cases where the franchisor did not have the resources to implement ecommerce or had not prioritised this matter, the franchisees had decided to take their actions regarding ecommerce and go 'off and [do] their own thing, with their little websites here and there, and Gumtree and eBay, and things like that' (Expert 1). However, this can ultimately damage the integrity of the franchise brand.

## 4.2. Communication and collaboration with franchisees

Communication was another important theme in this study noted to reduce fear and anxiety in franchisees (thus, supporting the findings of prior research) (Kremez, 2015). Clarity and consistency of communication were also highlighted as important factors for reducing franchisees' fear of the unknown and for gaining franchisee acceptance of change strategies. Indeed, extant research findings suggest that several elements influence the quality of the franchise relationship, including effective communication, which is critical for ensuring both trust and commitment, in turn (Watson & Johnson, 2010).

Different strategies and media were sought within franchise networks to communicate with franchisees when introducing ecommerce on two distinct levels: (a) the FAC level and (b) the whole franchise network level. Here, FAC was regarded as a representative body of franchisees with substantial power in the franchisor–franchisee relationship. At this level, the communication style was more collaborative and inclusive, whereas at the network level, a power imbalance was more evident and the communication strategy followed a top-down approach. That said, franchisees still had their questions answered and concerns clarified in both Cases 1 and 2 (see Table 3).

One of the franchisees interviewed described different modes and media of communication:

> Oh, you know, [the franchisor] had meetings and I think I flew to [name of city] for one of them. They had consultations. They talked about it at the conference. They networked with a selected group of the franchisees, the FAC. So they do communicate what they wanted to do. We might not always understand the full picture. You might not always believe that it's gonna work. You might think, 'oh my God, that's gonna take all our business'. But it hasn't. (CS1 Franchisee 2)

In both cases, the strategy went through an extended process of negotiation and refinement, with franchisees 'involved in that process right from the beginning through to the end' (CS1 Franchisee 3). However, respondents who were also proactive business owners were not always seeking participation. For example, CS1 Franchisor 4 stated that they 'generally go with the flow, to be perfectly honest', and further explained that he trusted the CEO and that his work was confined to the local level – here, the franchisor's responsibility was instead designated to tackling the global perspective. In contrast, other franchisees expressed that more input from a wider selection of fellow stakeholders should have been sought to optimise the change process.

### 4.2.1. Communication at the franchise network level

One of the strategies for communication at the whole network level (with supposed effect in both cases) regarded a special process during a national franchise conference. This provided

**Table 3.** Summary of communication methods.

|  | Case 1 | Case 2 |
|---|---|---|
| (a) FAC/selected group of franchisees | Regional/national meetings Consultations/workshops Experience working with FAC | FAC meetings and special meetings |
| (b) The whole franchise network | National conference Intranet Ongoing support | National convention Intranet Ongoing support |

an efficient way to present and gather information in a large group setting (i.e. containing more than 100 people in one room). The process involved encouraging franchisees to ask questions, writing them down as a record and then providing a response. This practice helped the franchisees feel safer about change and reduced their fears.

In both cases, the launch of an ecommerce strategy to franchisees occurred at the national conference, and was described similarly by participating franchisors:

> There were a lot of questions based on the fact that they did not understand entirely what was proposed. We spent a lot of time clarifying how exactly it was meant to work ... So what we did is we collated all [the] questions from franchisees, which ended up being about 41 questions, I think. And the questions were about the strategy, operational questions, the rationale for the [financial] model ... All those sorts of questions. It was all about clarifying the model and how it would work in reality – just enabling them to ask all the questions about 'why this' and 'why that'. (CS1 Franchisor)

Similarly, Case 2 also used the national conference to inform franchisees about the new ecommerce system:

> Once a year we bring all of our franchise partners together for our annual convention where we are very much focused on education and other initiatives. But we made a dedicated session on how we were going to tackle ecommerce. So, [in an] open forum any questions could be asked: 'here is the website, here are the products, here is the pricing, this is how the model works, this is how an order will work, and this is how your dollars will redistribute back to you'. So, we actually took it one step further than our advisory council and addressed each of our franchise partners directly at our national convention. (CS2 Franchisor 1)

Evidently, communication, as a key component of any relationship, is a vital component of any change process. A framework for franchisee engagement in change is proposed where communication forms an integral part therein. The framework best describes how communication can be practically applied to achieve goals for franchisor–franchisee collaboration and subsequently foster healthy relationships in a system with asymmetrical control.

### 4.2.2. Communication at the FAC level: FAC's crucial role in the consultation process

When important strategic decisions are made that affect customers and franchisees, considering the latter's perspective is of paramount importance because (first and foremost) the ecommerce model must work operationally for both business owners and staff at the shopfront. Obtaining feedback from franchisees was critical for the success of this innovation, as they are interfacing with customers daily. Therefore, there must be a mechanism in place to assist franchisor and franchisee collaboration and create solutions that benefit the system as a whole. One way of enacting partnership was through the FACs, which are advisory bodies of elected franchisees that large and mature franchise networks normally have in place. However, as expert bodies on operational aspects, and not marketing or finance, they may not be suited to address complex issues such as ecommerce.

A prominent theme that emerged during research was that FACs were instrumental in ensuring that franchisees were heard and their feedback was considered, and that franchisees at large were represented when important strategic matters were being decided within the group. Both cases had a strong and an effective FAC. According to the Franchising

Australia 2012 survey (Frazer et al., 2012), only 48 per cent of Australian franchise networks had an advisory council, and not all of them were set-up to work at their best capacity in serving a brand and franchisor–franchisee relations. Therefore, the cases presented here, although not typical, represent exemplars in the franchising community in terms of the nature and operation of their FACs. They also exercised the choice to showcase their FAC structure and processes in this research. For example, according to one franchisor:

> our advisory council is a group of five or six elected representatives that we use to bounce new ideas, discuss concerns, etc. And for us, it means hearing the voice of the collective as opposed to hearing the voice of an individual. It changes every year in terms of membership, and it also matured over the years in terms of its value to both franchise partners and the organisation. (CS2 Franchisor 1)

Evidently, an advisory council confronts the general business overview and its expertise is mainly within the operational domain. Ecommerce crosses over operations, marketing, logistics, finance and IT. Therefore, it requires additional knowledge in those other areas, which FAC may not possess. There are mechanisms of engaging experts in fields beyond council expertise, and they may be called either from the pool of franchisees or from the franchisor staff, *or* be an external expert with no affiliation. Hence, a prominent theme that emerged was the strength of the FAC in general, as well as its key role in forming strategy decisions, such as those investigated in this research:

> I'm a strong believer of the Advisory Council … [but] some of the franchisees think that the FAC is purely there to rubber stamp something that the franchisor has put in front of us – but it's not the case. There is quite a bit of debate that goes on, and sometimes heated debate. (CS1 Franchisee 3)

However, there did appear to be a 'disconnect' or information gap between FAC-level franchisees and general franchisee-level owners who had never participated in council meetings:

> Look, for me it was okay because I was – I'm on the Advisory Council, so I was quite privy to quite a lot of it. So I had a very good idea of what was happening. Sometimes it could be confusing for other people, and they may not have a full understanding of what sort of rigorous debate took place in the meeting. (CS2 Franchisee 2)

Both franchise companies had an FAC. Table 4 below summarises the descriptions of each advisory council in Cases 1 and 2.

### 4.2.3. Framework for franchisee communication and participation

In relation to franchisee engagement in change and innovation projects, both cases followed a multi-level process in which franchisees were involved in every stage of ecommerce implementation. Participation was implemented through each respondents' respective FAC. Although none of the cases utilised a project team for working on development and implementation of ecommerce into the business model, in both cases the franchisors and some franchisees reflected that a special purpose group would be a preferable instrument. Interviewees concurred that such a group would have been more effective and efficient in supporting an innovation project, particularly when its scope was beyond the FAC's competence (outside general day-to-day business and beyond the

**Table 4.** Description of the FAC for Case 1 and Case 2.

| | FAC Case 1 | FAC Case 2 |
|---|---|---|
| Year founded | 2006 | 2000 |
| Number of franchisee members | 8–10 members | 5–6 members |
| Term of service | Two years | Two years (by rotation) |
| Number of meetings each year and their format | • Annual meetings and additional meetings over teleconference, if required | • Meets face to face four times a year; meets every month by telephone (1–2 hour meetings) |
| Level of FAC | • Only national-level council; no regional structures in place | • Regional-level council<br>• National-level council (each with its chair) |
| Process and inclusion of voices from the general franchisee community | • Agenda goes out to the whole group<br>• Any franchisee can put forward a discussion point for the agenda<br>• Any franchisee can contact their FAC member to discuss their ideas for submission at an upcoming FAC meeting | • Each council meets once a month; between two levels they have fortnightly meetings<br>• When expertise is needed beyond the FAC, knowledge is sought from either the pool of franchisees, HO staff or external experts |

operations area). The participants described this group of people working together as an 'innovation team', a 'dedicated group of franchisees' or a 'special committee'.

This idea also confirms the findings from previous studies in which some of the franchise networks used project teams to work on ecommerce arrangements in the system (Kremez, 2015). This was generally reported as a very effective way of engaging interested and competent franchisees and other stakeholders or external advisors.

In this case study research, some franchisees suggested involving more parties, and not just the FAC members, in developing an ecommerce model. Accordingly, this would have facilitated early identification of certain issues in the process, thus, streamlining implementation. In addition, the framework that relies heavily on FAC support would only work if there were an effective advisory council in place. Since not all networks have an operational FAC (Frazer et al., 2012), it is important that the framework not only considers this discrepancy, but also proves effective, regardless of council presence. Moreover, smaller networks generally do not have an FAC but still require a process for seeking franchisee input into their decisions.

The experts interviewed also agreed that the use of a special group, referred hereafter as the project team, is most appropriate for addressing system-level problems of a strategic nature beyond the operational area of knowledge:

> FACs are often very operationally focused. So, they will talk about how they can do Process A better or how they can get ... Supplier B to deliver on time, and things like that. They can also have significant input into marketing initiatives. And, of course, ecommerce crosses several of those things – it involves marketing, it involves operations, and it involves logistics. And that becomes a little bit complicated for an FAC to deal with. So, the FAC may say that we want to know what the franchisor wants to propose with regard to ecommerce, but the FAC will not have the answer. (Expert 1)

Further, inherent difficulties are still encountered with FAC support. Primarily, these councils may not be set-up to operate for the benefit of the system and, second, proper guidelines regulating FAC operation often have not been established, thus, preventing councils from efficiently fulfilling their role. Three experts in franchise consulting suggested that a project team should be used to address complex issues of this nature. They referred to this special purpose group in different ways, either as a 'working group' (Expert 1), 'taskforce' (Expert 2) or a 'subcommittee' (Expert 5). The rationale for using a project team concerns a situation in which the issue under consideration is beyond FAC expertise and requires knowledge in several areas other than operations. The composition of a project team will also depend on the nature of a project and may involve franchisees, franchisor staff, external experts and even clients. According to Expert 1, 'this working group will consist of franchisees who are more savvy in these things than others'. The life span of the project team then depends on achieving the goals created prior to commencement:

> I'd make it a taskforce. I think bringing it to FAC meetings is a bit general. I think a taskforce would work better, as people are focused on a specific question. (Expert 2)

In situations in which a franchise network has an FAC in place, a project team would be formed with council assistance and endorsement. One expert in this study was involved in a project team and chaired the 'subcommittee' dedicated to the creation of an ecommerce strategy. He described the case, as follows:

> In one case, part of the strategy was [that] there was a very progressive franchisor [and] the issue was raised; it was discussed, it was broken down to a working party: a subcommittee. The subcommittee went and got other franchisees involved. Certain research was done. Certain modelling was undertaken. And then it was brought back to the FAC who had several discussions around what it should be. So it was a very good sort of structure ... When the FAC endorsed the final one, basically it went out for comment to the larger group and several state meetings were held to explain in detail how it was going to go. (Expert 5)

In summary, based on the interview results, the researchers developed a framework for optimal franchisee engagement in change and innovation projects. Consistent with the main findings presented in previous sections, the framework highlights the key role of advisory councils and further presents the process on different levels – from the franchisor level to the FAC level, and through to an individual franchisee level, including how and at what stage those levels have input towards the end goal (see Figure 1). More specifically, we identify eight steps that are crucial for setting up an effective process for franchisee engagement in change and innovation:

(1) Identify the issue for the system, where 'issue' denotes the strategic and ongoing nature of engagement, which is associated with change and innovation of some sort that is not purely operational. (Ongoing strategic matters that are limited to operations can be dealt with by the FAC, provided it is effective.)

(2) The franchisor develops a basic strategy line (or several strategies or approaches) for discussion with franchisees.

(3) Rigorous dialogue of the strategy or strategies is guided between the FAC and franchisor, where franchisee FAC members lead the discussion. Various tools can be used to maintain a constructive tone. If there is no FAC or if the FAC is dysfunctional, then the project teams can be created at this point.

(4) Decisions are made around the composition of a project team (if deemed necessary), including evaluation of the need to involve external experts.

(5) The project team is formed and consists of franchisees with expertise in the subject matter, franchisor staff members with relevant knowledge and experts

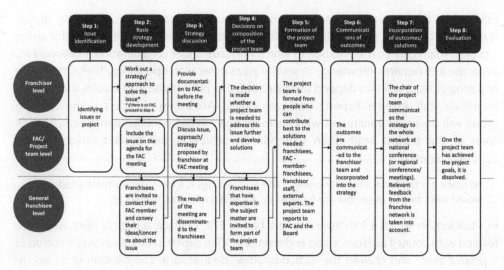

**Figure 1.** Framework for franchisee engagement in change and innovation.

(if needed). This group works on the relevant issue and forms one or several solutions.

(6) Outcomes of the project team's work are communicated to the entire network (after gaining approval from the franchisor). These are presented by the chair of the project team (preferably a franchisee rather than a member of the franchisor's team).

(7) Outcomes and solutions are incorporated into the initial strategy, provided there is adequate feedback from the franchise group as a whole.

(8) The project team is dissolved if there is unanimous agreement that its goals have been achieved and no further work and refinement are required.

Essentially, this framework builds on the reflective process from leading franchise groups in Australia that are constantly improving their systems and innovating to ensure a high level of franchisee satisfaction and quality franchisor–franchisee relationships. Also, it reflects expert opinion on successful franchisee engagement, informed by practical consulting experience. The framework crosses over communication, participation and franchise relations, which represent concepts that are cornerstone elements of this research. The approach adopted in this structure – wherein franchisee input is sought for creating an ecommerce strategy or in making another important decision within the franchise network – reinforces arguments in the existing literature. Indeed, White (2010) maintained that the basis of franchise relationships as a whole is determined by the culture of the franchise system towards franchisee participation in decision-making, as well as leadership in the franchisee community. Although the unique relational structure between franchisees and franchisors does lend itself to difficulties in strategy creation (White, 1998, 2010), those systems that build the foundations for constructive relations with franchisees (and further include their input into the strategy) have a higher chance of succeeding in the long term.

### 4.3. Training and support

Training is an integral part of the change initiative in any organisation, and – especially in a franchise system – serves to make sure that it is disseminated and implemented correctly throughout the network. However, should franchisees not receive adequate training, any innovation, however beneficial it may be for the system, may contribute to failure. Therefore, it is important to ensure that the relevant training and support structures are in place before introducing change in a franchise network. As such, this section discusses the findings on both cases' training and support initiatives for franchisees when ecommerce was introduced into their respective business model.

#### 4.3.1. Case 1

In Case 1, the franchisor used a training night to introduce a basic overview of the online service system. The support structure was created, and any questions could be fielded with individual concerns resolved. The support structure included (1) a comprehensive intranet website with all the procedures arranged, (2) a dedicated customer service staff member to help with the 'online' side of the franchisees' businesses, and (3) field support managers assisting franchisees with this aspect of operation.

As CS1 Franchisor explained, the purpose of the training and support structures helped franchisees to learn about the ecommerce system:

> We had a training night where they learned the new system, the way it fitted the business model and into the marketing. So we trained them on the product positioning, marketing, as well as being able to help, transact and deal with customers about it all. We knew it was not going to be enough, but it gave them an overview.

Second, support structures were implemented to assist franchisees if they had questions pertaining to the ecommerce system:

> We then turned these things into procedures to put on our intranet, and we also have in the office here a dedicated customer service person to help with 'online' ... We also have our field support managers that have assisted them as well. (CS1 Franchisor)

Franchisors indicated that the technology was easy to use and all the relevant information was provided through the intranet to franchisees. However, there were still some who needed extra assistance: 'It's just those who have not embraced it; we still need to hold their hands' (CS1 Franchisor).

There was diversity between franchisees' perspectives on the adequacy and appropriateness of training and support provided around the time of launching an ecommerce system into their network. Some felt that the training was insufficient: 'It was there; it was basic. It was just the evening session: "This is what it is?" A few screenshots, and "go ahead and try it out". Do you know what I mean? It could have been much better' (CS1 Franchisee 1). Others confirmed that the support structure was there when needed:

> In my view, [franchisor] does provide a really good support structure. They're not a franchisor who will be knocking on your door every day or every week, but if you need them they're there, and they've got the right people to help you through any issues you have. (CS1 Franchisee 3)

### 4.3.2. Case 2

Similar to Case 1, the ecommerce platform in Case 2 was launched at an annual conference where the details were explained to all franchisees. However, technical features were not discussed at that point. A strong support structure was also provided, which included (1) an intranet website with procedures, and (2) support staff members at the franchisor's office to guide franchisees through an online transaction.

Although during the launch the franchisor did not delve into technical details about the system, strong support structures were provided to facilitate the franchisees' learning. The franchisor was able to provide 'one-on-one hand-holding' (CS2 Franchisor 1) in the training process, as franchisees would not usually receive online orders every day:

> So when a franchise partner received an order, we would call them and take them through. Because it is their first time in doing an order like this, we would refresh their memory, remind them what the deal was, and remind them how they needed to handle the transaction. So, in effect, we trained them on the fly, would be the best way to describe it. (CS2 Franchisor 1)

Importantly, individualised support was kept in place two years after implementation of the ecommerce platform to alleviate any concerns arising from the management of online orders. As CS2 Franchisor 2 explained, 'I generally will follow up a franchise partner with a phone call if it's a big order or if it's an unusual order, just to make sure that we're seeing the customer through that journey in the right way'.

From the franchisee point of view, there was certainty that support was there when needed as well as information on the intranet: 'Definitely plenty of people in the head office that we can always talk to if we've got questions or go with our concerns. Definitely easy to find the information if we wanted, or speak with someone' (CS2 Franchisor 3). However, the system was not fully automated, which had associated disadvantages. For example, orders were not being forwarded to the nearest franchisee promptly, for which the support staff at the franchisor's office were made responsible (Table 5).

### 4.4. Proposed model

A conceptual model for introducing change into franchise networks was developed, based on this research (see Figure 2). This can serve for further study and hypothesis testing. The model proposes that resistance to change, change readiness and franchise acceptance are important determinants of success, consistent with existing literature on organisational change (Elving, 2005). Essentially, two main factors can affect change outcomes: franchise relationships and communications.

First, it is proposed that a healthy franchise relationship (Davies et al., 2011; White, 2010; Wright & Grace, 2011) can decrease resistance to change and contribute to franchisee acceptance and overall readiness. In fact, Grace, Frazer, Weaven, and Dant (2016) found that the quality of the franchise relationship is influenced by positive organisational culture and perception of franchisor competence and integrity. These factors are particularly critical for ensuring trust- and commitment-based partnerships between franchisors and franchisees in the long term.

Second, clear, consistent and effective communication is the cornerstone for success. When undertaken successfully, communication can increase readiness for change, decrease resistance to change and enhance franchise acceptance. Communication during

**Table 5.** Summary of training and support for Case 1 and Case 2.

| | Case 1 | Case 2 |
|---|---|---|
| Overall description | • Franchisor used a training night where a basic overview of the online service system was given<br>• The support structure was created and included:<br>(1) a comprehensive intranet website with all the procedures<br>(2) a dedicated customer service staff member to help with the 'online' side of franchisees' businesses<br>(3) field support managers assisting franchisees with this aspect of their business. | • Ecommerce was launched at an annual conference<br>• Technical details were not discussed at that point<br>• A strong support structure was provided and included:<br>(1) intranet website with procedures<br>(2) a support staff member at the franchisor's office to guide franchisees through online transactions. |
| Franchisor perspective | • Adequate training and information was provided during the training night<br>• Relevant support structures were provided as a follow-up<br>• Franchisees who need ongoing support with the system are those who have not yet embraced it | • Basic training about the system at the annual conference<br>• Strong one-on-one support during the first online transaction, as well as some subsequent unusual ones |
| Franchisee perspective | • Training was basic but sufficient<br>• A support structure was provided | • Training was adequate<br>• The support structure was adequate and highly individualised<br>• Disadvantages of the manual system were evident in some orders not being passed on promptly |

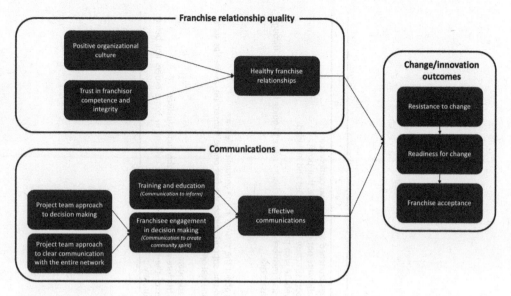

**Figure 2.** A model for franchisee acceptance, readiness for change and effective communication in the franchise network.

the change process can also be conducted with two purposes in mind: inform (through the provision of training and education) and create community spirit (through engagement in decision-making) (Elving, 2005). In other words, effective communication in this framework refers to communication that prioritises relationships with franchisees by engaging them in decision-making, and providing appropriate and adequate training and education regarding the subject of change. The two core aspects of franchisee engagement within strategy-making are (1) using the project team approach to seek franchisee input, and (2) maintaining clear and consistent communication with the entire franchise network about change.

## 5. Implications and future research directions

### 5.1. Implications for the franchise sector

This research has reinforced the literature on franchise relationships and further found that franchisees generally perceive franchisor leadership as one of the key aspects in facilitating the transition required for implementing ecommerce in their networks. Indeed, Watson & Johnson (2010) found evidence that 'listening and mutual respect between franchisor and franchisees provide the foundation for a successful franchise system' (p. 63); thus, they suggest that this can be achieved through a compassionate leadership style.

Moreover, franchisees in this research specifically alluded to the personality, experience or the skill set of their CEO or another senior franchisor team member involved in the development and implementation of an ecommerce strategy, where leadership (in this sense) seemed to influence franchisee perceptions about the relationship in general. This finding augments the literature, affirming that franchisor–franchisee relations seem to be an individual-to-individual (franchisor, CEO, etc.) relationship, rather than an individual-to-collective (franchise firm, franchisor team) relationship. Indeed, this is unsurprising because franchisors play a key role in evolving organisational culture and communicating the franchise vision. Although Watson & Johnson (2010) found this to be true in small franchise firms – proposing that it may not be the case for bigger businesses because of the organisational complexity pertinent to large systems – this study noted the same perceptions from franchisees (regarding franchisor leadership), where the role of the franchisor remains very important in motivating franchisees and communicating organisational vision.

Franchising professionals could also learn several key lessons from this research. First, franchisors should involve franchisees in developing their system's ecommerce strategies. Second, communication about forthcoming change and implementation should be timely, clear, consistent and regular, and underpinned by transparency and mutual benefit of the franchisor and the franchisees involved, *while* maintaining realistic time lines.

Both groups' perspectives need also be considered if a franchising relationship is to work as a genuine partnership. As encroachment is a sensitive issue and ecommerce embodies such an important strategic decision, unilateral action by the franchisor could potentially limit cooperation and have an overall negative effect on franchisor–franchisee relations (Hellriegel & Vincent, 2000). For franchisors integrating ecommerce into an existing system (that was not initially designed to incorporate the effect of online sales on franchisee territories), the optimal approach for developing a successful policy and strategy is to work collaboratively with franchisees (Terry, 2002). Their involvement in this development process can also benefit franchisor–franchisee relations in general (Abell & Scott, 2000; Hellriegel & Vincent, 2000). Alternatively, franchisors who exclude franchisees entirely from decisions around ecommerce could even face legal action if they are violating franchise or competition laws (Abell & Scott, 2000).

In summary, from the interviews conducted with franchise practitioners, certain practical recommendations can be made that will service the franchise sector:

(1) For any innovation in the franchise network, involve the franchisees as early as possible in the process of generating ideas. Franchisors may need to pay closer attention to the collegial structures, such as FACs and project teams that allow for franchisee input into strategy creation. Participation of franchisees in the strategy may be beneficial and necessary to ensure successful implementation of change in general. Such a process may also assist in fostering franchisee trust (Grace et al., 2016). Having an effective process in place in which franchisee feedback can be sought, analysed and actioned may support franchise networks to be more resilient and further promote superior franchisor–franchisee relations.

(2) It is important to be as clear and consistent as possible in franchisor-to-franchisee communication. This may be helpful to use a big event, such as an annual franchise conference, to explain a new strategy or innovation to franchisees. Clarity and consistency of communication were found to be important factors in reducing franchisees' fear of the unknown and for gaining franchisee acceptance of the strategy. Problems in franchisee–franchisor relationships are often located in the area of perceived rights and expectations; therefore, clearer communication (including the language used in legal documents) may help to avoid potential conflict.

(3) The language in a franchise agreement has to be unambiguous, and franchisee rights have to be stated very specifically. This can alleviate misunderstandings and conflicts that arise between parties in the future. Franchisors and franchisees might consider using relational contracts that are 'constructed incomplete intentionally so the contracting parties have room to manoeuvre', but remain 'very clear on how the contract begins and how to back out from it' (Rosado-Serrano & Paul, 2018, p. 4). Indeed, they might be more suitable to regulate trust- and commitment-based franchise relationships.

(4) The value of quality training and support services to franchisees is supported by extant research, where such services as staff training, software ordering, telephone assistance, point of sale and franchise councils were associated with less disruption to a system's functioning (Grünhagen, Di Pietro, Stassen, & Frazer, 2008). Here, Watson & Johnson (2010) also found a link between the quality of training and support services offered by the franchisor and overall company success.

## 5.2. Further research directions

Although this paper focused on franchisor ecommerce, the framework and model developed here can be applied beyond these settings, such as to any major change initiatives occurring within a franchise or when a key decision is to be made. The underlying principles can be effected broadly to the area of franchise relationships. Further research can also attempt to address issues related to other stakeholders such as franchisee unions. In addition, it is recommended that future studies extend the research by exploring the findings through different theoretical lenses, such as the application of relational contract theory in franchise agreements (e.g. Rosado-Serrano & Paul, 2018). This could lead to a theoretical contribution to the body of literature about the nexus between ecommerce and franchising, where scholars agree that empirical research remains limited.

## Disclosure Statement

No potential conflict of interest was reported by the author(s).

## References

Abell, M., & Scott, A. (2000). The e-commerce challenge for franchising. *Managing Intellectual Property, 1*(101), 34–37.

Altinay, L., & Brookes, M. (2012). Factors influencing relationship development in franchise partnerships. *Journal of Services Marketing, 26*(4), 278–292.

Altinay, L, Brookes, M, & Aktas, G. (2013). Selecting franchise partners: Tourism franchisee approaches, processes and criteria. *Tourism Management, 37*, 176–185. doi:10.1016/j.tourman.2013.01.016

Altinay, L., Brookes, M., Madanoglu, M., & Aktas, G. (2014). Franchisees' trust in and satisfaction with franchise partnerships. *Journal of Business Research, 67*(5), 722–728.

Brookes, M. (2014). The dynamics and evolution of knowledge transfer in international master franchise agreements. *International Journal of Hospitality Management, 36*, 52–62. doi:10.1016/j.ijhm.2013.07.005

Brookes, M., & Altinay, L. (2011). Franchise partner selection: perspectives of franchisors and franchisees. *Journal of Services Marketing, 25*(5), 336–348. doi:10.1108/08876041111149694

Chaparro-Peláez, J., Agudo-Peregrina, Á. F., & Pascual-Miguel, F. J. (2016). Conjoint analysis of drivers and inhibitors of e-commerce adoption. *Journal of Business Research, 69*(4), 1277–1282.

Chau, S. (2003). The use of e-commerce amongst thirty-four Australian SMEs: An experiment or a strategic business tool? *Journal of Systems and Information Technology, 7*(1/2), 49–66.

Choshin, M., & Ghaffari, A. (2017). An investigation of the impact of effective factors on the success of e-commerce in small-and medium-sized companies. *Computers in Human Behavior, 66*, 67–74.

Cliquet, G., & Voropanova, E. (2016). E-commerce and encroachment: Evidence from French franchise networks. *Journal of Marketing Channels, 23*(3), 114–128.

Coch, L., & French, J. R., Jr. (1948). Overcoming resistance to change. *Human Relations, 1*(4), 512–532.

Davies, M. A., Lassar, W., Manolis, C., Prince, M., & Winsor, R. D. (2011). A model of trust and compliance in franchise relationships. *Journal of Business Venturing, 26*(3), 321–340.

De Ridder, J. A. (2004). Organisational communication and supportive employees. *Human Resource Management Journal, 14*(3), 20–30.

Dixon, H., & Quinn, B. (2004). Franchising and the internet: An exploratory study of franchisor web sites. *Internet Research, 14*(4), 311–322.

Doherty, A. M. (2009). Market and partner selection processes in international retail franchising. *Journal of Business Research, 62*(5), 528–534. doi:10.1016/j.jbusres.2008.06.011

Dorward, L. J., Mittermeier, J. C., Sandbrook, C., & Spooner, F. (2017). Pokémon Go: Benefits, costs, and lessons for the conservation movement. *Conservation Letters, 10*(1), 160–165.

Dubois, A., & Gadde, L. E. (2002). Systematic combining: An abductive approach to case research. *Journal of Business Research, 55*(7), 553–560.

Eisenhardt, K. M. (1989). Building theories from case study research. *Academy of Management Review, 14*(4), 532–550.

Elving, W. (2005). The role of communication in organisational change. Corporate communications. *An International Journal, 10*(2), 129–138.

Emerson, R. W. (2010). Franchise encroachment. *American Business Law Journal, 47*(2), 191–290.

Forte, R., & Carvalho, J. (2013). Internationalisation through franchising: The Parfois case study. *International Journal of Retail & Distribution Management, 41*(5), 380–395. doi:10.1108/IJRDM-03-2013-0063

Frazer, L., Weaven, S., & Bodey, K. (2012). *Franchising Australia 2012*. Brisbane: Griffith University.

Frazer, L., Weaven, S., & Grace, A. (2014). *Franchising Australia 2014*. Brisbane,Australia: Asia–Pacific Centre for Franchising Excellence, Griffith University.

Grace, A. R., Frazer, L., Weaven, S. K., & Dant, R. P. (2016). Building franchisee trust in their franchisor: Insights from the franchise sector. *Qualitative Market Research: An International Journal, 19*(1), 65–83.

Grünhagen, M., Di Pietro, R. B., Stassen, R. E., & Frazer, L. (2008). The effective delivery of franchisor services: A comparison of U.S. and German support practices for franchisees. *Journal of Marketing Channels, 15*(4), 315–335.

Hellriegel, J. E., & Vincent, W. S. (2000). The encroachment handbook, the problem, the history, *the solution. Paper presented at the 14th conference of the international society of franchising*, San Diego.

Holt, D. T., Armenakis, A. A., Feild, H. S., & Harris, S. G. (2007). Readiness for organizational change: The systematic development of a scale. *The Journal of Applied Behavioral Science, 43*(2), 232–255.

Huberman, A. M., & Miles, M. B. (1994). Data management and analysis methods. In N. K. Denzin & Y. S. Lincoln (Eds.), *Handbook of qualitative research* (pp. 428–444). Thousand Oaks, CA: SAGE Publications.

Knack, G. L., & Bloodhart, A. K. (2001). Do franchisors need to rechart the course to internet success. *Franchise Law Journal 20*(1), 133–147.

Kotter, J. P. (1995). Leading change: Why transformation efforts fail. *Harvard Business Review, 73*, 59–67.

Kotter, J. P. (1996). *Leading change*. Boston, MA: Harvard Business School Press.

Kremez, Z. (2015). The effects of e-commerce on franchising: An exploratory Australian-based study. *Paper presented at the International Society of Franchising (ISoF) conference*, Oviedo, Spain.

Kremez, Z., Frazer, L., & Thaichon, P. (2019). The effects of e-commerce on franchising: Practical implications and models. *Australasian Marketing Journal (AMJ)*, *27*, 158–168.

Lee, K. J. (2017). Knowledge sharing in franchise system: Franchisee self-leadership, satisfaction, and compliance. *International Journal of Contemporary Hospitality Management*, *29*(12), 3101–3118.

Lewin, K. (1947). Group decision and social change. *Readings in Social Psychology*, *3*(1), 197–211.

Lewin, K. (2016). Frontiers in group dynamics: Concept, method and reality in social science; social equilibria and social change. *Human Relations*, *1*, 3–41.

McKay, K., Kuntz, J. R., & Näswall, K. (2013). The effect of affective commitment, communication and participation on resistance to change: The role of change readiness. *New Zealand Journal of Psychology (Online)*, *42*(2), 29–40.

Merriam, S. B., & Tisdell, E. J. (2015). *Qualitative research: A guide to design and implementation*. NJ, USA: John Wiley and Sons.

Miles, M. B., Huberman, A. M., Huberman, M. A., & Huberman, M. (1994). *Qualitative data analysis: An expanded sourcebook*. CA, USA: SAGE.

Nelissen, P., & van Selm, M. (2008). Surviving organizational change: How management communication helps balance mixed feelings. *Corporate Communications: An International Journal*, *13*(3), 306–318.

Perrigot, R., & Pénard, T. (2013). Determinants of e-commerce strategy in franchising: A resource-based view. *International Journal of Electronic Commerce*, *17*(3), 109–130.

Peterson, A., & Dant, R. P. (1990). Perceived advantages of the franchise option from the franchisee perspective: Empirical insights from a service franchise. *Journal of Small Business Management*, *28*(3), 46.

Quach, T. N., Thaichon, P., & Jebarajakirthy, C. (2016). Internet service providers' service quality and its effect on customer loyalty of different usage patterns. *Journal of Retailing and Consumer Services*, *29*, 104–113.

Rao, S., & Frazer, L. (2010). The use of internet-based technologies in Australian franchise systems: A preliminary study. *Journal of Internet Business*, *2*, 1–35.

Rosado-Serrano, A., & Paul, J. (2018). A new conceptual model for international franchising. *International Journal of Hospitality Management*, *75*, 179–188.

Rosado-Serrano, A., Paul, J., & Dikova, D. (2018). International franchising: A literature review and research agenda. *Journal of Business Research*, *85*, 238–257.

Seo, K. (2016). The effect of franchising on debt maturity in the US restaurant industry. *Tourism Economics*, *22*(6), 1404–1422. doi:10.1177/1354816616672802

Shah Alam, S. (2009). Adoption of internet in Malaysian SMEs. *Journal of Small Business and Enterprise Development*, *16*(2), 240–255.

Stake, R. E. (1994). Case studies. In N. K. Denzin & Y. S. Lincoln (Eds.), *Handbook of Qualitative Research* (pp. 236–247). Thousand Oaks: SAGE Publications.

Terry, A. (2002). The e-business challenge to franchising. *Australian Business Law Review*, *30*(3), 227–241.

Thaichon, P., Lobo, A., Prentice, C., & Quach, T. N. (2014). The development of service quality dimensions for internet service providers: Retaining customers of different usage patterns. *Journal of Retailing and Consumer Services*, *21*(6), 1047–1058.

Thaichon, P., Weaven, S., Quach, S., Baker, B., & Frazer, L. (2019). What to expect after the honeymoon: Evolutionary psychology of part-time franchising. *Journal of Strategic Marketing*, 1–25. doi:10.1080/0965254X.2019.1570315

Thaichon, P., Weaven, S., Quach, S., Bodey, K., Merrilees, B., & Frazer, L. (2018). Female franchisees; a lost opportunity for franchising sector growth? *Journal of Strategic Marketing*, 1–16. doi:10.1080/0965254X.2018.1482946.

Tiku, N. (2018). Europe's new privacy law will change the web and more. *Wired Magazine*, 30.

Timms, J., Frazer, L., Weaven, S., & Thaichon, P. (2019). Stay ahead of a game or stay still: The impact of learning and development on business performance. In V. Ratten (Ed.). *Subsistence entrepreneurship* (pp. 215–237). Cham: Springer.

Todnem By, R. (2005). Organisational change management: A critical review. *Journal of Change Management*, *5*(4), 369–380.

Wachter, S., & Mittelstadt, B. (2019). *A right to reasonable inferences: Re-thinking data protection law in the age of big data and AI*. Columbia Business Law Review, 494.

Wang, W. T., Wang, Y. S., & Liu, E. R. (2016). The stickiness intention of group-buying websites: The integration of the commitment–trust theory and e-commerce success model. *Information and Management, 53*(5), 625–642.

Watson, A., & Johnson, R. (2010). Managing the franchisor–franchisee relationship: A relationship marketing perspective. *Journal of Marketing Channels, 17*(1), 51–68.

Weaven, S., Baker, B. L., Edwards, C., Frazer, L., & Grace, D. (2018). Predicting organizational form choice from pre-entry characteristics of franchisees. *Australasian Marketing Journal (AMJ), 26*(1), 49–58.

Weaven, S., Frazer, L., Brimble, M., Bodle, K., Roussety, M., & Thaichon, P. (2019). Encouraging indigenous self-employment in franchising. In V. Ratten (Ed.). *Subsistence entrepreneurship* (pp. 69–87). Cham: Springer.

White, D. W. (1998). The impact of environmental uncertainty on strategy creation style in a franchise channel setting. *Journal of Strategic Marketing Review, 6*(4), 273–304.

White, D. W. (2010). The impact of marketing strategy creation style on the formation of a climate of trust in a retail franchise setting. *European Journal of Marketing, 44*(1/2), 162–179.

Wright, O., & Grace, A. (2011). Trust and commitment within franchise systems: An Australian and New Zealand perspective. *Asia Pacific Journal of Marketing and Logistics, 23*(4), 486–500.

Wu, C. W. (2015). Antecedents of franchise strategy and performance. *Journal of Business Research, 68*(7), 1581–1588.

Yin, R. K. (2009). *Case study research: Design and methods*. California: SAGE Publications.

Young, R., Frazer, L., Weaven, S., Roussety, M., & Thaichon, P. (2019). Work hard, play hard: Work-life balance in small business. In V. Ratten (Ed.). *Subsistence entrepreneurship* (pp. 195–213). Cham: Springer.

# Franchisees with multiple stakeholder roles: perceptions and conflict in franchise networks

Aveed Raha &#9415; and Ilir Hajdini &#9415;

**ABSTRACT**

Although the causes of conflict in networks and interorganizational relationships have long been investigated, scholars have overlooked the importance of stakeholders with multiple roles in eliciting managerial (mis)perceptions and potential for conflict. We find that franchisees take on multiple stakeholder roles, as customers, employees, investors, and business partners. Drawing from agency and stakeholder theories, we empirically demonstrate that the franchisor's perception of franchisees' multiple stakeholder roles affects managerial support and conflict outcomes in franchisor-franchisee relationships. The primary data support our claims that when franchisees are viewed as investors and business partners, franchisors increase the level of support offered and franchise systems experience less conflict.

## Introduction

Franchising is a system of relational exchanges wherein the hub firm (franchisor) and the local entrepreneurs (franchisees) cooperate to mutually promote a brand and co-create value (Kaufmann & Stern, 1988; Palmatier et al., 2006). Entrepreneurs who choose franchising expect to receive managerial support, whilst retaining some level of managerial autonomy. However, the franchisor's goal is to expand its business by retaining service uniformity, even at the expense of franchisee autonomy. As a result, tensions and disputes may arise between franchisees and franchisors (Altinay et al., 2014). The literature suggests that a lack of franchisee experience and autonomy, franchisor support, and efficient communication weakens network ties and heightens conflict (Blut et al., 2011; Frazer et al., 2012; Grace et al., 2013; Kidwell et al., 2007; Pondy & Huff, 1985; Spinelli & Birley, 1998; Weaven et al., 2010). Conflict typifies destructive relational sentiments, resulting in opportunistic behavior that undermines the franchisor-franchisee relationship and harms the overall franchise brand image (Blut et al., 2011; Gaski, 1984; Pondy, 1992; Rosenberg & Stern, 1970). Hence, the success of franchise networks depends, in part, on minimizing conflict in franchisor-franchisee relationships (Altinay et al., 2014; O. E. Omar, 1998).

The literature is replete with studies investigating the existence, antecedents, and consequences of conflict in franchisor-franchisee relationships (Frazer, 2001; Frazer et al., 2012; Grace et al., 2013; Grünhagen & Dorsch, 2003; Kaufmann & Lafontaine, 1994; Spinelli & Birley, 1998; Victoria Bordonaba-Juste & Polo-Redondo, 2008; Weaven et al., 2010). However, there is a paucity of research that examines how the franchisor's perceptions of franchisees' roles and goals may lead to differing expectations and, therefore, conflict. For instance, Top management's perceptions have been shown to be the primary drivers of managerial effort and organizational outcomes (Falbe & Welsh, 1998; Hambrick & Mason, 1984; O. Omar & Blankson, 2000; Petrenko et al., 2016). The lack of research in this field is surprising, given that, in franchising, the franchisor may view the roles of its franchisees as that of customers, employees, investors, and business partners. For instance, the franchisor may view its franchisees as taking on the role of its customers owing to the fact that they may repeatedly purchase from the franchisor's appointed suppliers (e.g. Davies et al., 2011; Hajdini & Raha, 2018; Michael, 2000). Similarly, the franchisor may view the role of its franchisees as that of investors, who make specific investments (Brickley, 2002; Dant & Berger, 1996) or may even invest in the franchisor's stock (Justis et al., 1991). Hence, role perceptions are important for relationship cultivation (Brown & Peterson, 1993; Grace et al., 2013) because, depending on how the franchisor perceives its franchisees' stakeholder roles (i.e. as customers, employees, investors, or business partners), it may adjust the level of support it provides to them, which can increase or decrease the level of conflict in its relationships with franchisees.

Agency theory views the franchisor (i.e. principal) and franchisees (i.e. agents) as intentionally and unintentionally pursuing divergent goals (Barney & Ouchi, 1986; Doherty & Quinn, 1999). Franchise partners design organizational structures, contracts, monitoring mechanisms, and other incentives to mitigate risks of opportunism and conflict that arise from goal divergence. The theory encompasses how principals' perceptions of agents' behavior influences the quality of the principal-agent relationship (Cruz, Gómez-Mejia, & Becerra, 2010). More specifically, the principal's decision to exercise or delegate control and provide support depends on its subjective assessment of agents' behavior. This implies that the franchisor's subjective assessment of its franchisees' behavior influences the franchisor's level of provided support and the quality of the franchisor-franchisee relationship.

Stakeholder theory emphasizes, however, the important role of all primary stakeholders (i.e. customers, shareholders, employees, suppliers, and the local community) that affect and/or are affected by the achievement of a firm's objectives (Clarkson, 1995; Freeman, 1984; Parmar et al., 2010; Savage et al., 1991). Primary stakeholders are viewed to be of critical importance to the survival of the firm; therefore, their claims and interests are to be attended to accordingly in order to improve stakeholder relationships and organizational performance. Mitchell et al. (1997) argue that the level of salience that certain stakeholders attract from managers depends on the attributes they possess; in particular, their power, legitimacy, and urgency.

Although proponents of both agency and stakeholder theory acknowledge the existence of conflicting agents' goals and demands and the existence of more salient stakeholders, they do not address relationship quality between the principal and agents with multiple stakeholder roles, such as franchisees. There is a lack of research concerning the amount of attention and support that agents with multiple stakeholder roles attract from their principals (Agle et al., 1999). Consequently, the literature does not sufficiently address the following research questions: *Does the franchisor view its franchisees as taking on the multiple stakeholder roles of customers, investors, employees, or business partners? If yes, is the level of the franchisor's provided support adjusted according to its perceptions of the respective stakeholder roles that the franchisees might take on? Furthermore, eventually, how does the adjustment to the level of support provided influence the level of conflict?*

Answering such questions is important because agents who may be viewed to take on multiple stakeholder roles may warrant higher attention, have more complex demands, or even pursue more divergent goals than their principals. Drawing from agency and stakeholder theories, this paper represents the first attempt to reveal franchisor perceptions of franchisees with multiple stakeholder roles, which may enhance franchise partners' ability to cultivate healthier franchisor-franchisee relationships and minimize agency costs and potential conflict.

The objective of this paper is to empirically demonstrate how franchisors' perception of franchisees' multiple stakeholder roles affects the level of provided support and conflict potential in franchising networks. We contribute to the literature on franchising and alliance relationships (Davies, 1994; Grace et al., 2013) by demonstrating that the level of support and conflict is contingent on franchisors' perception of franchisees' multiple stakeholder roles as customers, employees, investors, and business partners. Further, this study provides important implications for agency and stakeholder theories because it sheds new light on the fact that some agents can take on multiple stakeholder roles, thereby requiring higher managerial attention and support. These findings suggest that the franchisor perceptions of franchisee stakeholder roles are a determinant of the quality of the relationship between franchise partners.

We next explore the related literature. Then, we develop four hypotheses, describe our data collection method, and present our main findings. We conclude by discussing the study's main inferences.

## Theoretical background

### Agency theory

Agency theory regards agency relationships, which, under a cooperative schema, describe how one individual or group of individuals (i.e. a principal) allows another individual or group (i.e. agents) to perform business activities on their behalf (Barney & Ouchi, 1986; Eisenhardt, 1989). The theory relies on two main assumptions (Jensen & Meckling, 1976). First, the goals of agents barely converge with those of the principal. The principal pursues shareholders' goals, while an agent may, at the same time, pursue its own goals. Disagreement on goals between principals and agents result in agency costs (e.g. costs of monitoring and conflict). Second, the attitudes of principals and agents toward risk differ: the principal is risk-neutral, whereas agents are risk-averse in order to preserve their own wealth. Contracts serve as a governance mechanism to ensure efficient alignment of interests between the principal and agents (Shankman, 1999). Thus, agency theory views firms as a nexus of contracts between principals and agents (Hill & Jones, 1992). However, contract incompleteness, asymmetric information, and goal divergences prevent perfect convergence between the goals of principals and agents (Wright et al., 2001).

Several studies in the franchising literature examine franchise relationships from a principal-agent perspective (Combs et al., 2004). Lafontaine (1992) and Bhattacharyya and Lafontaine (1995) show empirically that a double-sided moral hazard (e.g. franchisor-franchisee bidirectional free riding) exists in franchise relationships owing to the existence of shared contracts that affect the franchisor's propensity to franchise (Grünhagen et al., 2017). Falbe and Welsh (1998) posit that agency theory can explain how the decision on the proportion of franchised-outlets compared with company-owned outlets affects the quality of communication in franchise relationships. Doherty and Quinn (1999) explain key elements of relationship development in international retail franchising. Michael (1999) finds that cooperative advertising in franchise systems can generate conflicts if several franchisees operate under a common brand. Grünhagen and Dorsch (2003) find that, compared with multi-unit operators, single-unit franchisees have stronger tendencies to nurture positive perceptions of the value of their franchisor's business model. Roh and Yoon (2009) classify franchisor's provided support into pre-opening support (e.g. initial training) and ongoing support (e.g. central purchasing, communication, and business assistance), and show that less conflict exists when franchisors provide ongoing support. Investigating the relational constructs of support and conflict in franchising in China, Doherty et al. (2014) find that non-compliance and counterfeits by franchisees are among the most prominent reasons for conflict. Building on agency theory, López-Fernández and López-Bayón (2018) examine the antecedents of early franchise relationship terminations, finding that franchisees' entrepreneurial autonomy reduces terminations.

### Stakeholder theory

Stakeholder theory acknowledges the interests and well-being of any individual or group who affects or is affected by the achievement of organizational objectives beyond shareholder wealth (Boatright, 1994; Freeman, 1984; Phillips et al., 2003). The underlying assumption of stakeholder theory is that firms' stakeholders are its constituents who, in supplying the firm with vital resources, expect the firm to satisfy their individual interests (Hill & Jones, 1992; Tantalo & Priem, 2016). Stakeholder theory provides the basis for exploring the nature of relationships as a way of managing various stakeholders' interests in relation to joint value creation (Donaldson & Preston, 1995; Freeman, 2010; Jones & Wicks, 1999). Stakeholders are grouped according to their importance and contribution to the firm's survival and durability: *primary* stakeholders directly impact the firm's survival, while *secondary* stakeholders have no direct influence. Customers, employees, suppliers, the local community, and shareholders are typically considered primary stakeholders, while the media, government, activists, and interest groups are secondary stakeholders (Clarkson, 1995; Parmar et al., 2010).

The literature regarding the explicit application of stakeholder theory to franchising systems is scarce. Weaven et al. (2014) present an integrative model of knowledge management across the franchisor–franchisees and customers triad. They show that each franchise partner's knowledge influences their own interests as well as that of customers. Perrigot et al. (2012) investigate the antecedents of using social media networks such as Facebook to communicate with stakeholders in franchise systems. In a case study of the hotel industry, Altinay and Miles (2006) use the stakeholder salience framework to explain the selection process of international franchisees. Welsh et al. (2006) examine international franchising in emerging markets, and identify some of the most important stakeholders in these markets.

According to stakeholder theory, the nature of resources that stakeholders possess and their contribution to firms' overall value creation enable stakeholders to influence firms' managerial perceptions (Agle et al., 1999; Mitchell et al., 1997). However, this theory has still not been applied to explain the influence of the multiple roles of such stakeholders on the perceptions franchisors may have of them. Similarly, agency theory has not addressed stakeholders with multiple roles. Such stakeholders may have more complex require- ments, warrant higher attention, or even have goals with greater divergence from those of the principal, thereby exacerbating potential agency costs and conflicts. Thus, in the next section, building upon agency and stakeholder theories, we illustrate our conceptual model and develop our hypotheses concerning the effects of franchisor perceptions of franchisees' multifaceted stakeholder roles on the level of conflict through the mediating effect of franchisor's provided support. We next discuss franchisee stakeholder roles, and then posit the hypotheses.

## Hypotheses

### Franchisors' perceived roles of franchisees as customers and employees

The franchising literature implicitly views franchisees as customers and employees. Some authors argue that franchisees should be perceived as customers because franchisors sell business formats to them (e.g. Davies et al., 2011). Indeed, franchisees may repeatedly purchase products from franchisor-appointed suppliers or directly from franchisors (Michael, 2000) and pay additional fees to renew their contracts or become multi-unit franchisees (Blair & Lafontaine, 2005). The franchisor may additionally perceive its fran- chisees as customers who supply an ongoing stream of revenues.

Drawing from agency theory, the franchisor is advised to exercise tighter control over franchisees operations to mitigate potential vertical and horizontal agency problems (Lafontaine, 1992; Rubin, 1978). When the franchisor views its franchisees as customers, a *vertical* agency problem may arise as franchisees bargain for lower supply prices or royalty fees, acquire inputs from suppliers other than the franchisor's appointed suppliers, or free ride by reducing product/service quality. Such problems eventually harm the franchisor's brand image and income. To protect its interests against the costs of such vertical agency problems, the franchisor might specify more detailed contracts and use monitoring mechanisms at the expense of more provided support.

Franchisors might also view franchisees as employees. United States labor and employ- ment regulations expand the scope of franchisor liability by potentially treating a franchisee's employees as 'joint' or 'related' employees of the franchisor (Hagedorn et al., 2017). This may affect how the franchisor perceives its franchisees and how it monitors their treatment of their own employees (i.e. in our case, managers of company- owned outlets) to avoid litigation. When the franchisor's employees are promoted to franchisee consultant positions or hired by other multi-unit franchisees, the franchisor may perceive its franchisees and employees interchangeably (Bradach, 1997). Accordingly, the role of a franchisee resembles that of a quasi-employee in terms of its relationship with the franchisor, as they willingly or unwillingly relinquish part of their own identity to adopt that of the franchisor's (Caves & Murphy, 1976; Lawrence & Kaufmann, 2011).

When the franchisor views its franchisees as employees, a *horizontal* agency problem may prevail because the franchise network is a hybrid form of business comprising both franchised and company-owned outlets. The managers of company-owned outlets are the franchisor's employees who are in charge of the same business operations as franchisees. They may shirk because of the weak incentives that are tied to their job performance, thereby imposing high monitoring costs on the franchisor and franchisees (Bradach, 1997; Rubin, 1978). The franchisor may therefore enforce high level of control and monitoring at the expense of more provided support.

The possibility that 'customer franchisees' or 'employee franchisees' may free ride or shirk may fuel the potential for heightened conflict by encouraging the franchisor and franchisees to behave opportunistically (Piercy, 1998). Therefore, when the franchisor perceives its franchisees as its customers or employees, it may design franchise contracts that favor the franchisor (Storholm & Scheuing, 1994), even using termination clauses to fire negligent 'employed franchisees.' In addition, franchisors may exercise contract termination clauses or violate franchisees' territorial exclusivity by placing their own outlets close to those of franchisees in an attempt to impose a higher level of control, increasing the likelihood of franchisee retaliation with non-compliance to system standards or fee arrangements (Hajdini & Raha, 2018; Hajdini & Windsperger, 2019). Thus, when the franchisor perceives its franchisees as customers or employees, it may adopt an arms-length relationship that results in higher levels of administrative control.

An arms-length relationship is based on contractual agreements, and results in interactions between a firm and its stakeholders being strictly grounded in bargaining power (Bridoux & Stoelhorst, 2014). When the franchisor adopts an arms-length approach, it relies on economic and legal sanctions to enforce obligations specified in formal contracts, including detailed performance standards and requirements (Chiles & McMackin, 1996; Dyer & Singh, 1998; Rousseau, 1989; Zhao & Wang, 2011). However, the adoption of an arms-length customer-business approach may discourage the franchisor from offering additional support, possibly resulting in greater potential for conflict (Davies et al., 2011; Falbe et al., 1999; Grace et al., 2013; Grünhagen & Dorsch, 2003; Spinelli & Birley, 1998). Accordingly, we propose the following hypotheses:

**H1a:** *When the franchisor perceives franchisees as customers, a lower level of support is provided to them, which causes a higher level of conflict between the franchisor and its franchisees.*

**H1b**: *When the franchisor perceives franchisees as employees, a lower level of support is provided to franchisees, which causes a higher level of conflict between the franchisor and its franchisees.*

### Franchisors' perceived roles of franchisees as investors and business partners

Franchisees may also be perceived as investors who own the outlet by investing specific resources and becoming members of a cooperative network (Barthélemy, 2011; El Akremi et al., 2011). Franchisees pay upfront fees, royalties (Brickley, 2002), and advertising fees (Dant & Berger, 1996), and may invest in franchisor stock (Justis et al., 1991).

As highlighted by stakeholder theory, primary stakeholders can benefit a firm by providing access to vital resources (Freeman, 1984; Parmar et al., 2010). To expand, the franchisor needs capital resources from franchisees (Windsperger & Dant, 2006). In order to effectively compete against established rivals in the market, franchisors strive to achieve economies of scales in areas of purchasing and advertising by increasing their number of franchisees (Caves & Murphy, 1976). Because franchisees are required to make specific investments, such as payment of fees upfront, designing the outlet, and training employees, they are viewed as quasi–investors that provide the means for expansion (Norton, 1995). Unlike lenders who may diversify their investment portfolio to reduce risk, franchisees put all their investments into one or a small number of outlets. Franchisees with quasi–investor roles can enable the franchisor to accomplish its growth objectives by providing access to vital resources such as capital (Barney, 2018). If franchisors view franchisees as quasi–investors, they may decide that franchisees deserve more support, which can motivate 'investor franchisees' to continue investing and cooperating.

Franchisees can also play the role of business partner with franchisors. Business partner franchisees enable franchisors to expand in return for the right to operate a proven business concept (Altinay et al., 2014; Bennett et al., 2010). According to Spinelli and Birley (1996), the franchisor and franchisees are distinct entities, and franchisees enjoy autonomy while enabling the franchisor to grow and prosper (Dant & Gundlach, 1999). Franchisees are reliable business partners because they possess local market knowledge, which is exceedingly important for the franchisor to enter and succeed in new markets (Windsperger, 2004).

Franchisees' local market knowledge regarding customer tastes, local procurement, labor market conditions, or legislation facilitates chain expansion. These resources, according to the stakeholder theory, provide franchisees with greater power to attract franchisor attention (Agle et al., 1999; Mitchell et al., 1997). Consequently, when the franchisor perceives its franchisees as business partners, it provides higher support to boost franchisees' entrepreneurial spirit and encourage them to behave more cooperatively. Accordingly, mutual understanding and alignment of interests are more probable, which decreases the potential for conflict between partners. When the franchisor views capital provided by franchisees as essential to growth, the 'investor franchisees' and 'business partner franchisees' receive more support, thereby reducing conflicts. Formally,

**H2a:** *When the franchisor perceives franchisees as investors, the franchisor provides a higher level of support to franchisees, which causes a lower level of conflict between franchisors and its franchisees.*

**H2b:** *When the franchisor perceives franchisees as business partners, the franchisor provides a higher level of support to franchisees, which causes a lower level of conflict between franchisors and its franchisees.*

## Methods

To test the hypotheses, we conducted a survey of franchises in Austria, the Czech Republic, Germany, and Slovakia: four neighboring countries known as the Central European Union states, with an interdependent franchising market. The countries engage in high degree of economic and political exchange, which affects business interactions. There are strong cultural and economic ties between the Czech Republic and Slovakia as these countries were unified in the past. According to the European Franchise Federation

(2012), over 60% of German and Austrian domestic brands have expanded to the markets of the other two Central European countries, i.e. the Czech Republic and Slovakia.

The survey questionnaire was developed from several interviews with franchise experts from franchise associations. From the interviews, we identified 1,245 franchise systems in the four countries. We then mailed the questionnaire to 374 Austrian, 165 Czech, 577 German, and 129 Slovak franchise systems. To maximize the number of respondents who would receive the questionnaires, we sent emails containing a link to an electronic version of the questionnaire. We attached a cover letter explaining the study's objectives and assuring respondent anonymity. The target persons for filling out the questionnaire were key informant personnel such as franchise expansion managers or franchisors' CEOs. To increase the response rate, we sent a reminder email and carried out one round of telephone calls to remind respondents to return the questionnaires.

A total of 221 questionnaires were returned by recipients during the survey period, which corresponded to a response rate of 17.7 percent. We received 63 responses from franchisors in Germany (29%), 69 from those in Austria (31%), 35 from those in Slovakia (16%), and 54 from the franchisors in the Czech Republic (24%). We excluded 58 questionnaires owing to missing responses to some items, resulting in a final sample of 168 questionnaires.

To check for non-response bias, we compared early versus late respondents with respect to various aspects of the franchisors' size and age. The ANOVA test showed no significant difference between these two groups. We also included age and size of the franchise systems in our analysis as control variables. Age is a proxy for interorganizational experience and was measured as the number of years the respondent reported being in business (Roome & Wijen, 2006). The inclusion of age allows us to examine whether level of conflict is influenced by length or duration of franchise relationship. We also controlled for the effect of franchise system size. Larger franchisors differ in their resources and capabilities to deal with their franchisees (Reuer & Ariño, 2007). For this purpose, respondents were asked to provide the number of employees in their headquarters, allowing us to check whether size influences the level of conflict within franchise systems.

### Analyses of measurement models

Our hypotheses were tested using structural equation modeling with LISREL 8.80. Prior to running the structural model, we conducted a series of confirmatory factor analyses (CFA) to check the reliability and validity of constructs in the measurement models. First, in regard to the dependent variable *conflict*, we included four items adopted from Grace et al. (2013). However, one of the four original items was excluded from the final measurement model because it did not significantly load on the construct (t-value = 0.89), and its standardized loading was below the recommended cut-off threshold of 0.50 (Hair et al., 2006). Second, in regard to *support*, we included five items adopted from Grace et al. (2013) to create the construct of interest. The CFA results showed that all indicators did significantly load on the construct (see Table 1). The final two-factor multi–item measurement models including both *conflict* and *support* indicated decent fit by chi-square = 36.47, degrees of freedom = 19, p-value = 0.00923, RMSEA = 0.07, NFI = 0.96, GFI = 0.95, CFI = 0.98, and SRMR = 0.04. Table 1 shows the item framing and standardized loadings.

**Table 1.** Measurement models: item scales and convergent validity.

| Measurement Items | Standardized Loadings | T-values | AVE | CR |
|---|---|---|---|---|
| **Conflict** | | | | |
| There is a lot of conflict in the relationship between me and my franchisees. | 0.81 | 11.67 | 0.66 | 0.85 |
| I frequently disagree with my franchisees. | 0.79 | 11.30 | | |
| The disagreements I have with my franchisees are usually quite intense. | 0.84 | 12.38 | | |
| **Support** | | | | |
| We strongly consider our franchisees goals and values. | 0.70 | 10.17 | 0.88 | 0.90 |
| We help our franchisees out, no matter what. | 0.75 | 11.07 | | |
| We understand and accommodate franchisees problems and needs. | 0.94 | 15.93 | | |
| We support franchisees whenever possible. | 0.88 | 14.24 | | |
| Help is readily available for my franchisees when they have a problem. | 0.74 | 10.87 | | |

We conducted several tests to check for convergent validity, discriminant validity, and common method bias. In relation to convergent validity, we calculated the average variance extracted (AVEs) and the composite reliability of *support* and *conflict* (Bagozzi & Heatherton, 1994). Results showed that AVEs were greater than the recommended threshold of 0.50 (Fornell & Larcker, 1981) and composite reliabilities were greater than 0.60, demonstrating that the convergent validity of *support* and *conflict* constructs is supported (see Table 1 and Figure 1).

To check discriminant validity between *conflict* and *support*, we conducted a chi-square difference test as recommended by Bagozzi et al. (1991). We compared the difference in chi-squared values between two nested models: one model was constrained with covariance of one between *conflict* and *support*; the second model was unconstrained, allowing the two constructs to covary freely. Results showed that the difference between the chi-squared values for the nested models were significantly different from zero, indicating that the constructs are distinct and capture different concepts ($\Delta\chi^2 = 199.23, \Delta df = 1, p < 0.005$).

To test whether common method variance affects the validity of our results, we conducted a chi-square difference test between two measurement models as recommended by Podsakoff et al. (2003). In the first model, we created a one-factor construct that reflects all measurement items; we call this construct *common*. Then, we compared this model through a chi-squared difference test with a two-factor measurement model, in which *conflict* and *support* were measured separately. The results showed that the hypothesized model is superior to the one-factor measurement model (COMMON), indicating that common method bias does not bias our findings ($\Delta\chi^2 = 277.08, \Delta df = 35, p < 0.005$).

Third, the independent variables that capture how the franchisor perceives its franchisees were derived by asking respondents to rate the following: 'We perceive franchisees as our ...' '... customers,' '... employees,' '... investors,' or '... business partners' (1 = strongly disagree to 7 = strongly agree). The development of these measures was inspired from the literature in which managerial perception is viewed as a strong factor affecting organizational decisions and outcomes (Falbe & Welsh, 1998; Hambrick & Mason, 1984). The franchisor may perceive the role of its franchisees as those of customers, employees, investors, or business partners. Thus, the independent variables of our model are franchisor perceptions, which impact the organizational outcomes of support and conflict in franchise networks.

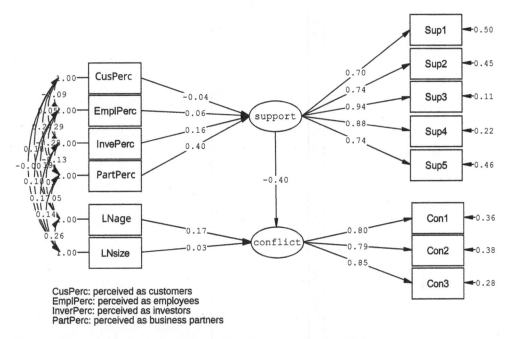

CusPerc: perceived as customers
EmplPerc: perceived as employees
InverPerc: perceived as investors
PartPerc: perceived as business partners

**Figure 1.** Measurement and structural models with standardized coefficients.

## Results

Table 2 shows descriptive statistics and correlations between variables. Franchisees take on the roles of business partners ($\bar{x}$ = 6.55), customers ($\bar{x}$ = 5.17), investors ($\bar{x}$ = 3.56), and employees ($\bar{x}$ = 1.88). Franchisees are mostly perceived as customers and business partners.

However, our SEM analysis indicates mixed results in regard to the influence of franchisor perceptions on support and conflict. Although franchisees are strongly perceived as customers (Table 2), this perception has no significant effect on the level of provided support or level of conflict (Table 3).

The overall goodness of fit of the structural model indicates that the data fits to the hypothesized model reasonably well (Chi-Square = 75.96, df = 61, p-value = 0.09; RMSEA = 0.03; NFI = 0.94; GFI = 0.94; CFI = 0.98; SRMR = 0.05). Figure 1 illustrates the path analysis of the measurement and structural models. Table 3 shows direct effects and indirect mediation effects. Surprisingly, H1a and H1b are not supported. However, the results provide support to H2a and H2b, inferring that when the franchisor views the role of its franchisees as those of investors and business partners, it provides higher levels of support, which in turn lead to lower levels of conflict. Further, we controlled for the effect of franchise systems age ($\bar{x}$ = 15.45) and size ($\bar{x}$ = 47.36) on the level of conflict. The results show that older franchisors are more likely to engage in conflicts with their franchisees than younger ones due to their inflexibility to cope with market dynamics (Sorenson & Sørensen, 2001). However, the size of franchise systems showed no significant influence on the level of conflict.

To cross check the robustness of our estimation results, we conducted two-stage regression analysis using STATA version 14.1. In line with our model specification, we first regressed the four perceived franchisee roles (customers, employees, investors, and

**Table 2.** Descriptive statistics.

| Variables | Mean | CustomerPercep | EmployeePercep | InvestorPercep | PartnerPercep | Support | Conflict | SIZE | AGE |
|---|---|---|---|---|---|---|---|---|---|
| CustomerPercep[a] | 5.17 | 1 | | | | | | | |
| EmployeePercep | 1.87 | -.093 | 1 | | | | | | |
| InvestorPercep | 3.26 | .053 | .290** | 1 | | | | | |
| PartnerPercep | 6.55 | .243** | -.284** | -.127 | 1 | | | | |
| Support | 5.93 | .046 | -.017 | .131 | .320** | 1 | | | |
| Conflict | 2.54 | -.056 | -.012 | .070 | -.288** | -.325** | 1 | | |
| SIZE | 47.36 | .006 | .079 | .102 | .086 | .109 | .022 | 1 | |
| AGE | 15.45 | .093 | -.130 | .106 | .040 | .024 | .170* | .322** | 1 |

[a]Pecept = Perception.
**Correlation is significant at the 0.01 level (2-tailed).
*Correlation is significant at the 0.05 level (2-tailed).

**Table 3.** Structural model results.

| Path | Beta coefficient (standardized) | t-value | Sig* |
|---|---|---|---|
| **Direct Effects** | | | |
| Perceived as customers→Support | −0.04 | −0.52 | No |
| Perceived as employees→Support | 0.06 | 0.73 | No |
| Perceived as investors→Support | 0.16 | 1.97 | Yes |
| Perceived as partners→Support | 0.40 | 4.66 | Yes |
| Support→Conflict | −0.40 | −4.47 | Yes |
| **Mediation Effects** | | | |
| Perceived as customers→Support→Conflict (H1a) | 0.02 | | Not supported |
| Perceived as employees→Support→Conflict (H1b) | −0.02 | | Not supported |
| Perceived as investors→Support→Conflict (H2a) | −0.06 | | Supported |
| Perceived as partners→Support→Conflict (H2b) | −0.16 | | Supported |

**Fit of model**: Chi-Square = 75.96, df = 61, p-value = 0.09; RMSEA = 0.03; NFI = 0.94; GFI = 0.94; CFI = 0.98; SRMR = 0.05.
*Sig = significant at 5%.

partners) on *support*. We retained the calculated fitted values of support. In the next step, we regressed support and control variables of age and size on *conflict*. We used the robust standard estimation technique to mitigate possible heteroscedasticity from the data obtained from the four different European countries.

We find that the results are consistent with the reported SEM results, indicating that perceived stakeholder roles of franchisees as customers and employees have no significant influence on support or conflict. The other two perceived franchisee roles as investors and partners have significant positive impact on the level of provided support to franchisees and reduce the level of conflict. The VIF test for multicollinearity shows that multicollinearity is unlikely to bias our estimation results (VIF is between 1.06 and 1.17).

## Discussion

This study shows that the amount of attention and support franchisees receive from franchisors depends on franchisor perceptions of the stakeholder roles that franchisees play. In response to the first research question (i.e. does the franchisor view its franchisees as taking on the multiple stakeholder roles of customers, investors, employees, or business partners?), we show that, in practice, franchisees are multifaceted stakeholders with multiple roles as customers, employees, investors, and business partners. Empirical results show that franchisees are perceived mostly as customers and business partners and, to a lesser extent, as investors and employees.

The second and third research questions (i.e. is the level of the franchisor's provided support adjusted according to its perceptions of the respective stakeholder roles that the franchisees might take on? And, how does the adjustment to the level of support provided influence the level of conflict?) draw from agency and stakeholder theories and investigate the influence of franchisees' perceived roles on the level of provided support and conflict. First, we find that franchisor perceptions of franchisees' stakeholder roles as that of customers and employees have no significant influence on the level of conflict, because the mediating influence of the provided support to franchisees does not significantly differ. One explanation for this finding is that, when franchisees are perceived as customers or employees, the franchisor is still aware of their crucial role in the overall performance of the franchise system, and does not change the level of support provided. Maintaining support at a certain level, even if franchisees are perceived as customers or employees, can imply that the franchisor views the franchising network as a collaborative enterprise (Halal, 2001). From the franchisor's point of view, value can be created jointly by providing support to franchisees, irrespective of their specific stakeholder role (Tantalo & Priem, 2016).

The empirical results, however, confirm that when franchisees' roles are perceived to be as those of investors or business partners, the franchisor can successfully mitigate the level of conflict by increasing the level of support to franchisees. Increased support can encourage cooperation and commitment from franchisees to contribute more to overall performance of the franchise network by, for instance, encouraging current and prospective franchisees to make more specific investments (Grace et al., 2013). Perceiving franchisees as investors, the franchisor provides higher support to signal protection of franchisees' specific investments (Solis-Rodriguez & Gonzalez-Diaz, 2012). Similarly, franchisor perception of franchisees as business partners is positively associated with higher levels of franchisor-provided support and lessened conflict. The expansion of the franchising network into new markets by means of issuing additional licensees to increased numbers of franchisees is a strategic goal for every franchisor. In new markets, the franchisor has little knowledge of local market conditions. This obliges the franchisor to rely on crucial local market know-how that local franchisees possess (Mumdžiev & Windsperger, 2011). As a result, the perceived business partnering role of franchisees is very important for achieving expansion goals and justifies the increased level of support and reduced levels of conflict.

### Theoretical and managerial implications

Our results support prior research findings that companies' performance is influenced by their response to environmental conditions on the basis of their executive managerial perceptions rather than on the objective characteristics of the environment (Hambrick & Mason, 1984; Miles, Snow, & Pfeffer, 1974). However, prior franchising and alliance literature has ignored the role of perceptions in determining the quality of relationships (Combs et al., 2011; Falbe & Welsh, 1998). The extant literature in franchise relationships has explored franchising as a form of agency relationship (Barthélemy, 2008); however, fewer studies have drawn on stakeholder theory (Combs et al., 2011). Agency theory emphasizes the existence of *horizontal* and *vertical* agency costs, while stakeholder theory highlights the existence of more salient stakeholders (Barthélemy, 2008; Mitchell et al., 1997); however, neither theory explains the influence of role perceptions on conflict with multifaceted agents (Agle et al., 1999). Studies informed by these theories highlight the importance of stakeholder demands and supportive mechanisms in promoting a more productive and trustful environment (Dada, Watson, & Kirby, 2012; Frazer, Merrilees, & Bodey, 2007; Pizanti & Lerner, 2003).

This study adds to the literature on marketing channels and franchise relationships by applying a combined stakeholder and agency perspective to show that conflict is mitigated when the franchisor adjusts its managerial support in accordance with the competing claims of franchisees with multiple stakeholder roles (Combs et al., 2011; Dant et al., 2011). In other words, this study tackles an overlooked aspect of how franchisor's perceptions contingent on the nature of franchisees' characteristics are followed by adjusted managerial support to mitigate conflict.

On the managerial front, the findings suggest that franchisee practitioners may invest resources, time, and effort in activities that are more associated with the roles of investors or business partners if they aim to receive higher support and experience lower levels of conflicts during the course of the franchise agreement. For instance, by acquiring from franchisor's appointed suppliers, investing in franchisor's stock, or becoming multi-unit franchisees, franchisees may be perceived as investors or business partners and, accordingly, viewed as more salient and important for the success of the franchisor's chain.

The results also suggest how franchisors can provide support to franchisees in a more purposeful manner. The franchisor can therefore mitigate conflict by designing purposeful support, which encourages franchisees to make specific investments and cooperate as they take on perceived roles as investors or business partners.

### Limitations and future research

This study has several limitations. First, because the data was collected from multiple countries, the unique cultural backgrounds of franchisors may have affected their perceptions of franchisee stakeholder roles. An analysis based on cross-cultural comparison in future studies would enrich our findings. Our study may also encourage future research to consider other cognitive aspects of the franchisor that affects their perceptions of franchisees' multiple roles.

Second, we could not control for the effect of franchising governance mode (single vs multi-unit franchisees) on franchisor perceptions and level of conflict. Future research could shed light on how single and multi-unit franchisees differ in terms of perceived stakeholder roles and levels of received support.

Third, our conceptual model does not explain the performance implications of franchisees with multiple stakeholder roles. Future work could examine the influence of simultaneous multiple stakeholders' roles on franchisor attention, network relationship quality, and system performance.

Fourth, future research could examine the importance of stakeholders with multiple roles in attracting managerial attention and support in different industry settings and alliance relationships, such as joint ventures or licensing arrangements. Certain stakeholder roles can have amplifying or even moderating effects in warranting managerial attention or relationship cultivation in conjunction with other stakeholder roles.

Finally, future empirical studies may address the limitation of single-item measures for multiple perceived franchisee roles by developing new multi–item measures.

In sum, adopting a stakeholder-agency theoretical approach might represent a fruitful avenue of research to explore the role of agents with multiple stakeholder roles, while accounting for the influence of all other agent-stakeholders in relationship cultivation and joint value co-creation.

### Disclosure statement

No potential conflict of interest was reported by the author(s).

## Funding

This work was supported by the Austrian National Bank under Grant number [18056].

## ORCID

Aveed Raha (iD) http://orcid.org/0000-0002-5174-2632
Ilir Hajdini (iD) http://orcid.org/0000-0002-9521-4372

## References

Agle, B. R., Mitchell, R. K., & Sonnenfeld, J. A. (1999). Who matters to CEOs? An investigation of stakeholder attributes and salience, corporate performance, and CEO values. *Academy of Management Journal, 42*(5), 507–525. https://doi.org/10.5465/256973

Altinay, L., Brookes, M., Madanoglu, M., & Aktas, G. (2014). Franchisees' trust in and satisfaction with franchise partnerships. *Journal of Business Research, 67*(5), 722–728. https://doi.org/10.1016/j.jbusres.2013.11.034

Altinay, L., & Miles, S. (2006). International franchising decision-making: An application of stake-holder theory. *The Service Industries Journal, 26*(4), 421–436. https://doi.org/10.1080/02642060600621613

Bagozzi, R. P., & Heatherton, T. F. (1994). A general approach to representing multifaceted person-ality constructs: Application to state self-esteem. *Structural Equation Modeling: A Multidisciplinary Journal, 1*(1), 35–67. https://doi.org/10.1080/10705519409539961

Bagozzi, R. P., Yi, Y., & Phillips, L. W. (1991). Assessing construct validity in organizational research. *Administrative Science Quarterly, 36*(3), 421–458. https://doi.org/10.2307/2393203

Barney, J. B. (2018). Why resource-based theory's model of profit appropriation must incorporate a stakeholder perspective. *Strategic Management Journal, 39*(13), 3305–3325. https://doi.org/10.1002/smj.2949

Barney, J. B., & Ouchi, W. G. (1986). *Organizational economics*. Jossey-Bass.

Barthélemy, J. (2008). Opportunism, knowledge, and the performance of franchise chains. *Strategic Management Journal, 29*(13), 1451–1463. https://doi.org/10.1002/smj.719

Barthélemy, J. (2011). Agency and institutional influences on franchising decisions. *Journal of Business Venturing, 26*(1), 93–103. https://doi.org/10.1016/j.jbusvent.2009.05.002

Bennett, S., Frazer, L., & Weaven, S. (2010). What prospective franchisees are seeking? *Journal of Marketing Channels, 17*(1), 69–87. https://doi.org/10.1080/10466690903436313

Bhattacharyya, S., & Lafontaine, F. (1995). Double-sided moral hazard and the nature of share contracts. *The Rand Journal of Economics, 26*(4), 761–781. https://doi.org/10.2307/2556017

Blair, R. D., & Lafontaine, F. (2005). *The economics of franchising*. Cambridge University Press.

Blut, M., Backhaus, C., Heussler, T., Woisetschläger, D. M., Evanschitzky, H., & Ahlert, D. (2011). What to expect after the honeymoon: Testing a lifecycle theory of franchise relationships. *Journal of Retailing, 87*(3), 306–319. https://doi.org/10.1016/j.jretai.2010.06.003

Boatright, J. R. (1994). Fiduciary duties and the shareholder-management relation: Or, what's so special about shareholders? *Business Ethics Quarterly, 4*(4), 393–407. https://doi.org/10.2307/3857339

Bradach, J. L. (1997). Using the plural form in the management of restaurant chains. *Administrative Science Quarterly, 42*(2), 276–303. https://doi.org/10.2307/2393921

Brickley, J. A. (2002). Royalty rates and upfront fees in share contracts: Evidence from franchising. *Journal of Law, Economics, and Organization, 18*(2), 511–535. https://doi.org/10.1093/jleo/18.2.511

Bridoux, F., & Stoelhorst, J. W. (2014). Microfoundations for stakeholder theory: Managing stake-holders with heterogeneous motives. *Strategic Management Journal, 35*(1), 107–125. https://doi.org/10.1002/smj.2089

Brown, S. P., & Peterson, R. A. (1993). Antecedents and consequences of salesperson job satisfaction: Meta-analysis and assessment of causal effects. *Journal of Marketing Research, 30*(1), 63–77. https://doi.org/10.1177/002224379303000106

Caves, R. E., & Murphy, W. F. (1976). Franchising: Firms, markets, and intangible assets. *Southern Economic Journal, 42*(4), 572–586. https://doi.org/10.2307/1056250

Chiles, T. H., & McMackin, J. F. (1996). Integrating variable risk preferences, trust, and transaction cost economics. *Academy of Management Review, 21*(1), 73–99. https://doi.org/10.5465/amr.1996.9602161566

Clarkson, M. E. (1995). A stakeholder framework for analyzing and evaluating corporate social performance. *Academy of Management Review, 20*(1), 92–117. https://doi.org/10.5465/amr.1995.9503271994

Combs, J. G., Ketchen, D. J., Jr, Shook, C. L., & Short, J. C. (2011). Antecedents and consequences of franchising: Past accomplishments and future challenges. *Journal of Management, 37*(1), 99–126. https://doi.org/10.1177/0149206310386963

Combs, J. G., Michael, S. C., & Castrogiovanni, G. J. (2004). Franchising: A review and avenues to greater theoretical diversity. *Journal of Management, 30*(6), 907–931. https://doi.org/10.1016/j.jm.2004.06.006

Cruz, C. C., Gómez-Mejia, L. R., & Becerra, M. (2010). Perceptions of benevolence and the design of agency contracts: CEO-TMT relationships in family firms. *Academy of Management Journal, 53*(1), 69–89. https://doi.org/10.5465/amj.2010.48036975

Dada, O., Watson, A., & Kirby, D. A. (2012). Toward a model of franchisee entrepreneurship. *International Small Business Journal, 30*(5), 559–583. https://doi.org/10.1177/0266242610376078

Dant, R. P., & Berger, P. D. (1996). Modelling cooperative advertising decisions in franchising. *Journal of the Operational Research Society, 47*(9), 1120–1136. https://doi.org/10.1057/jors.1996.141

Dant, R. P., Grünhagen, M., & Windsperger, J. (2011). Franchising research frontiers for the twenty-first century. *Journal of Retailing, 87*(3), 253–268. https://doi.org/10.1016/j.jretai.2011.08.002

Dant, R. P., & Gundlach, G. T. (1999). The challenge of autonomy and dependence in franchised channels of distribution. *Journal of Business Venturing, 14*(1), 35–67. https://doi.org/10.1016/S0883-9026(97)00096-7

Davies, G. (1994). Maintaining relationships with retailers. *Journal of Strategic Marketing, 2*(3), 189–210. https://doi.org/10.1080/09652549400000010

Davies, M. A., Lassar, W., Manolis, C., Prince, M., & Winsor, R. D. (2011). A model of trust and compliance in franchise relationships. *Journal of Business Venturing, 26*(3), 321–340. https://doi.org/10.1016/j.jbusvent.2009.09.005

Doherty, A. M., Chen, X., & Alexander, N. (2014). The franchise relationship in China: Agency and institutional theory perspectives. European. *Journal of Marketing, 48*(9/10), 1664–1689. https://doi.org/10.1108/EJM-04-2012-0199

Doherty, A. M., & Quinn, B. (1999). International retail franchising: An agency theory perspective. *International Journal of Retail & Distribution Management, 27*(6), 224–237. https://doi.org/10.1108/09590559910278588

Donaldson, T., & Preston, L. E. (1995). The stakeholder theory of the corporation: Concepts, evidence, and implications. *Academy of Management Review, 20*(1), 65–91. https://doi.org/10.5465/amr.1995.9503271992

Dyer, J. H., & Singh, H. (1998). The relational view: Cooperative strategy and sources of interorganizational competitive advantage. *Academy of Management Review, 23*(4), 660–679. https://doi.org/10.5465/amr.1998.1255632

Eisenhardt, K. M. (1989). Making fast strategic decisions in high-velocity environments. *Academy of Management Journal, 32*(3), 543–576. https://doi.org/10.5465/256434

El Akremi, A., Mignonac, K., & Perrigot, R. (2011). Opportunistic behaviors in franchise chains: The role of cohesion among franchisees. *Strategic Management Journal, 32*(9), 930–948. https://doi.org/10.1002/smj.912

European Franchise Report. (2012). http://www.eff-franchise.com/Data/PUBLICATION%202012%20EFF%20FRANCHISE%20REPORT.pdf

Falbe, C. M., Dandridge, T. C., & Kumar, A. (1999). The effect of organizational context on entrepre-neurial strategies in franchising. *Journal of Business Venturing*, *14*(1), 125–140. https://doi.org/10.1016/S0883-9026(97)00099-2

Falbe, C. M., & Welsh, D. H. (1998). NAFTA and franchising: A comparison of franchisor perceptions of characteristics associated with franchisee success and failure in Canada, Mexico, and the United States. *Journal of Business Venturing*, *13*(2), 151–171. https://doi.org/10.1016/S0883-9026(97)00068-2

Fornell, C., & Larcker, D. F. (1981). Structural equation models with unobservable variables and measurement error: Algebra and statistics. *Journal of Marketing Research*, *18*(3), 382–388. https://doi.org/10.1177/002224378101800313

Frazer, L. (2001). Causes of disruption to franchise operations. *Journal of Business Research*, *54*(3), 227–234. https://doi.org/10.1016/S0148-2963(00)00118-1

Frazer, L., Merrilees, B., & Bodey, K. (2007). Franchisors do their homework before entering interna-tional markets: Experiences from the Australian franchising sector. *International Entrepreneurship and Management Journal*, *3*(4), 437–452. https://doi.org/10.1007/s11365-007-0054-z

Frazer, L., Weaven, S., Giddings, J., & Grace, D. (2012). What went wrong? Franchisors and franchisees disclose the causes of conflict in franchising. *Qualitative Market Research: An International Journal*, *15*(1), 87–103. https://doi.org/10.1108/13522751211192017

Freeman, R. E. (1984). *Strategic management: A stakeholder approach*. Boston: Pitman.

Freeman, R. E. (2010). Managing for stakeholders: Trade-offs or value creation. *Journal of Business Ethics*, *96*(1), 7–9. https://doi.org/10.1007/s10551-011-0935-5

Gaski, J. F. (1984). The theory of power and conflict in channels of distribution. *Journal of Marketing*, *48*(3), 9–29. https://doi.org/10.1177/002224298404800303

Grace, D., Weaven, S., Frazer, L., & Giddings, J. (2013). Examining the role of franchisee normative expectations in relationship evaluation. *Journal of Retailing*, *89*(2), 219–230. https://doi.org/10.1016/j.jretai.2012.12.002

Grünhagen, M., & Dorsch, M. J. (2003). Does the franchisor provide value to franchisees? Past, current, and future value assessments of two franchisee types. *Journal of Small Business Management*, *41*(4), 366–384. https://doi.org/10.1111/1540-627X.00088

Grünhagen, M., Zheng, X. V., & Wang, J. J. (2017). When the music stops playing: Post-litigation relationship dissolution in franchising. *Journal of Retailing*, *93*(2), 138–153. https://doi.org/10.1016/j.jretai.2016.10.002

Hagedorn, M., Law, T. H., & Manovskii, I. (2017). Identifying equilibrium models of labor market sorting. *Econometrica*, *85*(1), 29–65. https://doi.org/10.3982/ECTA11301

Hair, J. F., Black, W. C., Babin, B. J., Anderson, R. E., & Tatham, R. L. (2006). *Multivariate data analysis* (6th ed.). Pearson Prentice Hall.

Hajdini, I., & Raha, A. (2018). Determinants of contractual restraints in franchise contracting. *Managerial and Decision Economics*, *39*(7), 781–791. https://doi.org/10.1002/mde.2961

Hajdini, I., & Windsperger, J. (2019, October). Contractual restraints and performance in franchise networks. *Industrial Marketing Management*, *82*, 96–105. https://doi.org/10.1016/j.indmarman.2019.02.011

Halal, W. (2001). The collaborative enterprise: A stakeholder model uniting profitability and responsibility. *Journal of Corporate Citizenship*, *2*, 27–42. http://www.jstor.org/stable/jcorpciti.2.27Hope that helps

Hambrick, D. C., & Mason, P. A. (1984). Upper echelons: The organization as a reflection of its top managers. *Academy of Management Review*, *9*(2), 193–206. https://doi.org/10.5465/amr.1984.4277628

Hill, C. W., & Jones, T. M. (1992). Stakeholder-agency theory. *Journal of Management Studies*, *29*(2), 131–154. https://doi.org/10.1111/j.1467-6486.1992.tb00657.x

Jensen, M. C., & Meckling, W. H. (1976). Theory of the firm: Managerial behavior, agency costs and ownership structure. *Journal of Financial Economics*, *3*(4), 305–360. https://doi.org/10.1007/978-94-009-9257-3_8

Jones, T. M., & Wicks, A. C. (1999). Convergent stakeholder theory. *Academy of Management Review*, *24*(2), 206–221. https://doi.org/10.5465/amr.1999.1893929

Justis, R. T., Chan, P. S., & Werbel, J. D. (1991). Reward strategies for franchising organizations. *Journal of Small Business Strategy*, *2*(2), 16–23. https://libjournals.mtsu.edu/index.php/jsbs/article/view/249

Kaufmann, P. J., & Lafontaine, F. (1994). Costs of control: The source of economic rents for McDonald's franchisees. *The Journal of Law and Economics*, *37*(2), 417–453. https://doi.org/10.1086/467319

Kaufmann, P. J., & Stern, L. W. (1988). Relational exchange norms, perceptions of unfairness, and retained hostility in commercial litigation. *Journal of Conflict Resolution*, *32*(3), 534–552. https://doi.org/10.1177/0022002788032003007

Kidwell, R. E., Nygaard, A., & Silkoset, R. (2007). Antecedents and effects of free riding in the franchisor–franchisee relationship. *Journal of Business Venturing*, *22*(4), 522–544. https://doi.org/10.1016/j.jbusvent.2006.06.002

Lafontaine, F. (1992). Agency theory and franchising: Some empirical results. *The Rand Journal of Economics*, *23*(2), 263–283. https://doi.org/10.2307/2555988

Lawrence, B., & Kaufmann, P. J. (2011). Identity in franchise systems: The role of franchisee associations. *Journal of Retailing*, *87*(3), 285–305. https://doi.org/10.1016/j.jretai.2010.11.003

López-Fernández, B., & López-Bayón, S. (2018). Antecedents of early terminations in franchising: Franchisor versus franchisee cancelations. *Small Business Economics*, *50*(4), 677–695. https://doi.org/10.1007/s11187-017-9889-z

Michael, S. C. (1999). The elasticity of franchising. *Small Business Economics*, *12*(4), 313–320. https://doi.org/10.1023/A:1008019418231

Michael, S. C. (2000). Investments to create bargaining power: The case of franchising. *Strategic Management Journal*, *21*(4), 497–514. https://doi.org/10.1002/(SICI)1097-0266(200004)21:4<497::AID-SMJ87>3.0.CO;2-%23

Miles, R. E., Snow, C. C., & Pfeffer, J. (1974). Organization-environment: Concepts and issues. *Industrial Relations: A Journal of Economy and Society*, *13*(3), 244-264. https://doi.org/10.1111/j.1468-232X.1974.tb00581.x

Mitchell, R. K., Agle, B. R., & Wood, D. J. (1997). Toward a theory of stakeholder identification and salience: Defining the principle of who and what really counts. *Academy of Management Review*, *22*(4), 853–886. https://doi.org/10.5465/amr.1997.9711022105

Mumdžiev, N., & Windsperger, J. (2011). The structure of decision rights in franchising networks: A property rights perspective. *Entrepreneurship Theory and Practice*, *35*(3), 449–465. https://doi.org/10.1111/j.1540-6520.2011.00440.x

Norton, S. W. (1995). Is franchising a capital structure issue? *Journal of Corporate Finance*, *2*(1–2), 75–101. https://doi.org/10.1016/0929-1199(95)00005-S

Omar, O., & Blankson, C. (2000). New car retailing: An assessment of car manufacturers' fairness on main dealers. *Journal of Strategic Marketing*, *8*(3), 261–275. https://doi.org/10.1080/09652540050110002

Omar, O. E. (1998). Strategic collaboration: A beneficial retail marketing strategy for car manufacturers and dealers. *Journal of Strategic Marketing*, *6*(1), 65–78. https://doi.org/10.1080/096525498346702

Palmatier, R. W., Dant, R. P., Grewal, D., & Evans, K. R. (2006). Factors influencing the effectiveness of relationship marketing: A meta-analysis. *Journal of Marketing*, *70*(4), 136–153. https://doi.org/10.1509/jmkg.70.4.136

Parmar, B. L., Freeman, R. E., Harrison, J. S., Wicks, A. C., Purnell, L., & De Colle, S. (2010). Stakeholder theory: The state of the art. *Academy of Management Annals*, *4*(1), 403–445. https://doi.org/10.1080/19416520.2010.495581

Perrigot, R., Kacker, M., Basset, G., & Cliquet, G. (2012). Antecedents of early adoption and use of social media networks for stakeholder communications: Evidence from franchising. *Journal of Small Business Management*, *50*(4), 539–565. https://doi.org/10.1111/j.1540-627X.2012.00366.x

Petrenko, O. V., Aime, F., Ridge, J., & Hill, A. (2016). Corporate social responsibility or CEO narcissism? CSR motivations and organizational performance. *Strategic Management Journal*, *37*(2), 262–279. https://doi.org/10.1002/smj.2348

Phillips, R., Freeman, R. E., & Wicks, A. C. (2003). What stakeholder theory is not? *Business Ethics Quarterly*, *13*(4), 479–502. https://doi.org/10.5840/beq200313434

Piercy, N. F. (1998). Barriers to implementing relationship marketing: Analysing the internal market-place. *Journal of Strategic Marketing*, *6*(3), 209–222. https://doi.org/10.1080/096525498346630

Pizanti, I., & Lerner, M. (2003). Examining control and autonomy in the franchisor-franchisee relationship. *International Small Business Journal*, *21*(2), 131–159. https://doi.org/10.1177/0266242603021002001

Podsakoff, P. M., MacKenzie, S. B., Lee, J. Y., & Podsakoff, N. P. (2003). Common method biases in behavioral research: A critical review of the literature and recommended remedies. *Journal of Applied Psychology*, *88*(5), 879. https://doi.org/10.1037/0021-9010.88.5.879

Pondy, L. R. (1992). Overview of organizational conflict: Concepts and models. *Journal of Organizational Behavior*, *13*(3), 255. https://doi.org/10.1002/job.4030130304

Pondy, L. R., & Huff, A. S. (1985). Achieving routine in organizational change. *Journal of Management*, *11*(2), 103–116. https://doi.org/10.1177/014920638501100215

Reuer, J. J., & Ariño, A. (2007). Strategic alliance contracts: Dimensions and determinants of contractual complexity. *Strategic Management Journal*, *28*(3), 313–330. https://doi.org/10.1002/smj.581

Roh, E. Y., & Yoon, J. H. (2009). Franchisor's ongoing support and franchisee's satisfaction: A case of ice cream franchising in Korea. *International Journal of Contemporary Hospitality Management*, *21*(1), 85–99. https://doi.org/10.1108/09596110910930205

Roome, N., & Wijen, F. (2006). Stakeholder power and organizational learning in corporate environmental management. *Organization Studies*, *27*(2), 235–263. https://doi.org/10.1177/0170840605057669

Rosenberg, L. J., & Stern, L. W. (1970). Toward the analysis of conflict in distribution channels: A descriptive model. *The Journal of Marketing*, *34*(4), 40–46. https://doi.org/10.1177/002224297003400407

Rousseau, D. M. (1989). Psychological and implied contracts in organizations. *Employee Responsibilities and Rights Journal*, *2*(2), 121–139. https://doi.org/10.1007/BF01384942

Rubin, P. H. (1978). The theory of the firm and the structure of the franchise contract. *The Journal of Law and Economics*, *21*(1), 223–233. https://doi.org/10.1086/466918

Savage, G. T., Nix, T. W., Whitehead, C. J., & Blair, J. D. (1991). Strategies for assessing and managing organizational stakeholders. *The Executive*, *5*(2), 61–75. https://doi.org/10.1097/CCM.0000000000003964

Shankman, N. A. (1999). Reframing the debate between agency and stakeholder theories of the firm. *Journal of Business Ethics*, *19*(4), 319–334. https://doi.org/10.1023/A:1005880031427

Solis-Rodriguez, V., & Gonzalez-Diaz, M. (2012). How to design franchise contracts: The role of contractual hazards and experience. *Journal of Small Business Management*, *50*(4), 652–677. https://doi.org/10.1111/j.1540-627X.2012.00370.x

Sorenson, O., & Sørensen, J. B. (2001). Finding the right mix: Franchising, organizational learning, and chain performance. *Strategic Management Journal*, *22*(6-7), 713–724. https://doi.org/10.1002/smj.185

Spinelli, S., & Birley, S. (1996). Toward a theory of conflict in the franchise system. *Journal of Business Venturing*, *11*(5), 329–342. https://doi.org/10.1016/0883-9026(96)00049-3

Spinelli, S., & Birley, S. (1998). An empirical evaluation of conflict in the franchise system. *British Journal of Management*, *9*(4), 301–325. https://doi.org/10.1111/1467-8551.00101

Storholm, G., & Scheuing, E. E. (1994). Ethical implications of business format franchising. *Journal of Business Ethics*, *13*(3), 181–188. https://doi.org/10.1007/BF02074817

Tantalo, C., & Priem, R. L. (2016). Value creation through stakeholder synergy. *Strategic Management Journal*, *37*(2), 314–329. https://doi.org/10.1002/smj.2337

Victoria Bordonaba-Juste, M., & Polo-Redondo, Y. (2008). Differences between short and long-term relationships: An empirical analysis in franchise systems. *Journal of Strategic Marketing*, *16*(4), 327–354. https://doi.org/10.1080/09652540802264033

Weaven, S., Frazer, L., & Giddings, J. (2010). New perspectives on the causes of franchising conflict in Australia. *Asia Pacific Journal of Marketing and Logistics*, *22*(2), 135–155. https://doi.org/10.1108/13555851011026917

Weaven, S., Grace, D., Dant, R., & Brown, J. R. (2014). Value creation through knowledge management in franchising: A multi-level conceptual framework. *Journal of Services Marketing*, *28*(2), 97–104. https://doi.org/10.1108/JSM-09-2013-0251

Welsh, D. H., Alon, I., & Falbe, C. M. (2006). An examination of international retail franchising in emerging markets. *Journal of Small Business Management*, *44*(1), 130–149. https://doi.org/10.1111/j.1540-627X.2006.00158.x

Windsperger, J. (2004). Centralization of franchising networks: Evidence from the Austrian franchise sector. *Journal of Business Research*, *57*(12), 1361–1369. https://doi.org/10.1016/S0148-2963(03)00068-7

Windsperger, J., & Dant, R. P. (2006). Contractibility and ownership redirection in franchising: A property rights view. *Journal of Retailing*, *82*(3), 259–272. https://doi.org/10.1016/j.jretai.2006.06.001

Wright, P., Mukherji, A., & Kroll, M. J. (2001). A reexamination of agency theory assumptions: Extensions and extrapolations. *The Journal of Socio-economics*, *30*(5), 413–429. https://doi.org/10.1016/S1053-5357(01)00102-0

Zhao, Y., & Wang, G. (2011). The impact of relation-specific investment on channel relationship performance: Evidence from China. *Journal of Strategic Marketing*, *19*(1), 57–71. https://doi.org/10.1080/0965254X.2010.537763

# Why franchisors recruit franchisees from the ranks of their employees

Peter Balsarini ⓘD, Claire Lambert ⓘD and Marie M. Ryan ⓘD

**ABSTRACT**
A shortage of suitable franchisees has long plagued the Australian franchise industry impacting franchisors' capacity to grow their chains. This exploratory research identifies, defines and examines an unresearched category of franchisees that of internally recruited franchisees, who prior to their franchise recruitment were employees of the franchisor. This category has previously been ignored by the literature even though estimates of some chains place the proportion of internally recruited franchisees at over 40 per cent. Employing qualitative interviews with key franchisor decision makers this research begins to address this gap. This study investigates what factors drive franchisors to recruit franchisees from the ranks of their employees and how they perceive this impacts on the achievement of franchising's four strategic imperatives of unit growth, system uniformity, local responsiveness and system-wide adaption. Seven drivers for the internal recruiting of franchisees were identified: company owned units, significant system hierarchy, larger unit scale, unit viability, system maturity, capital freedom and strong growth in unit numbers. A preliminary model of factors influencing the propensity of franchise systems to recruit franchisees internally is presented. This research provides the first contribution to the franchise literature on the internally recruited franchisee phenomenon. In a practical sense this study should influence the recruitment practices of franchisors.

## 1. Introduction

Worldwide, franchising representing the fastest growing form of retailing (Hizam-Hanafiah & Li, 2014) accounting for 32 per cent of retail sales in Germany, 40 per cent in the USA and 52 per cent in Australia (Dant, Grunhagen, & Windsperger, 2011). In Australia, franchising constitutes a significant and growing sector of the economy with franchised units having increased from 43,800 in 1999 to 79,000 in 2016, directly employing almost 500,00 people (Frazer, Weaven, Grace, & Selvanathan, 2016). Nevertheless, this growth is now under threat with some major Australian franchise groups experiencing more than a 50 per cent reduction in franchise enquiries in 2017–18 (Bailey, 2018). While some of this reduction is undoubtedly due to negative publicity surrounding the 2018 Australian Senate inquiry into the Franchising Code of Conduct (Inside Franchise Business, 2018), a lack of suitable franchisees has long been a key constraint facing franchisors in their quest for growth

(Bradach, 1997). Even prior to this recent reduction, a national survey found over 70 per cent of franchisors rated a lack of suitable franchisees as their major ongoing challenge (Frazer, Weaven, & Grace, 2014). It has been an enduring industry problem, with an earlier survey finding that almost half of Australian franchisors believed the availability of prospective franchisees was insufficient to meet their growth needs (Frazer, Weaven, & Bodey, 2012). Indeed, the recent trend towards part-time franchising in some sectors may be in reaction to the difficulty in finding full-time potential franchisees (Thaichon, Weaven, Quach, Baker, & Frazer, 2019). Arguably this franchisee shortage has also been exacerbated by a lack of female participation in franchising (Thaichon et al., 2018).

One reaction by franchisors to a shortage of suitable new franchisees has simply been to grant more franchises to existing franchisees. Known as multiple unit franchising, this expansionary strategy has been extensively researched (Bradach, 1995; Garg, Priem, & Rasheed, 2013; Hussain, Sreckovic, & Windsperger, 2018; Kaufmann & Dant, 1996; Weaven & Frazer, 2007). However, another potential reaction is to recruit franchisees internally from the ranks of the franchisors' own employees. Recently this has been indicated as a possible solution by numerous franchising trade publications. Articles with titles such as *On the hunt for a franchisee? Take a look at your own employees* (Syed & Syed, 2019); *Four Reasons Why Former Employees Make the Best Franchisees* (Bisio, 2015); *Crossing over: why employees make great franchisees* (Russell, 2014) and *From head office employee to franchisee* (Camplin, 2013) have emerged in trade publications citing the internal recruiting of franchisees as a viable solution to the franchisee shortage.

Despite the prevalence of recruiting internally in franchise industry articles and its apparent widespread practice, the literature on internally recruited franchisees remains scant, with no academic studies examining internally recruited franchisees. The current research contributes to filling this gap by identifying, defining and exploring the emerging, yet under researched category of internally recruited franchisees. It presents valuable insight into the opportunities that internally recruited franchisees can provide to help alleviate the franchisee shortage prevalent in todays' marketplace, and thereby facilitate growth that may otherwise be stymied. The current study contributes to the existing franchise literature that has been totally predicated on externally recruited franchisees, by specifically initiating research into the franchisee category of internally recruited franchisees. Accordingly, this research addresses two research questions:

RQ1. What factors drive franchisors to recruit franchisees from the ranks of their employees?

RQ2. What impact do franchisors perceive that the internal recruiting of franchisees will have on franchise systems achieving the four franchising strategic imperatives of unit growth, system uniformity, local responsiveness and system-wide adaption?

## 2. Literature review

### 2.1 Franchising formats

Business format franchising, as the preeminent form of franchising (Storholm & Scheuing, 1994) is the focus of this research. It involves the franchisor's provision of a complete business system including brand-name, training, marketing and site selection (Bender, 2015). Generally, it entails the franchisee agreeing to conform to the franchisor's standards and paying a franchise fee with an ongoing royalty, which is often a percentage of sales (Croonen, Brand, & Huizingh, 2016).

## 2.2  Main theories for franchising research

Traditionally, franchising research has focused on the three theories of resource scarcity, agency theory and plural form symbiosis (Combs, Ketchen, & Short, 2011; Gillis & Castrogiovanni, 2012). Resource scarcity has its nexus in the causal connection between resources and competitive advantage (Barney, 1991; Sirmon, Hitt, Ireland, & Gilbert, 2011). It suggests a major reason for franchisors franchising is franchising provides access to franchisees' capital, as well as their managerial, entrepreneurial and local knowledge (Caves & Murphy, 1976; Combs, Michael, & Castrogiovanni, 2009; Ketchen, Ireland, & Snow, 2007; Norton, 1988a; Oxenfeldt & Kelly, 1969; Perryman & Combs, 2012).

Agency theory contends that company employed managers may supply less than their best efforts [*shirking*] and choose actions that lead to lower wealth for the principals (Alchian & Demsetz, 1972; Alon, 2001; Eisenhardt, 1989; Lafontaine, 1992). Franchising circumvents this outcome by giving franchisees residual claims to their store's profits, thereby encouraging franchisees to work harder and reducing the monitoring costs of the franchisor (Bradach, 1997; Norton, 1988a; Perryman & Combs, 2012; Rubin, 1978).

Bradach and Eccles (1989) coined the term 'plural form symbiosis' to describe the franchising phenomena where franchisors maintain some company-owned outlets but also franchise outlets. Later studies confirmed the symbiotic advantages conferred on a franchise system that maintained both forms (i.e. company owned outlets and franchise outlets), with franchisees deemed to foster the entrepreneurial characteristics of innovation and local market adaption, while company-owned outlets promote standardization (Combs et al., 2011; Darr, Argote, & Epple, 1995; Kaufmann & Eroglu, 1999; Meiseberg, 2013; Perrigot & Herrbach, 2012).

## 2.3  Categories of franchisees

Prototypically a franchisee has been characterised as an individual external to the organisation who is prepared to apply their accumulated financial, entrepreneurial, and managerial capital to owning and running a single franchise outlet (Kaufmann & Dant, 1996). Therefore, for many years the generally accepted view of a franchise system was that it comprised a franchisor and a conglomeration of single unit franchisees. From the early 1990 s researchers began to focus on the growing phenomenon of multiple unit franchisees. Specifically, this involved instances where multiple franchise units in the same chain are owned by the same franchisee. This has subsequently been acknowledged as a common form of expansion for many franchise systems (Garg et al., 2013; Hussain et al., 2018) with multiple unit franchisees also controlling a significant percentage of franchise units (Weaven & Frazer, 2007).

## 2.4  Externally recruited franchisees v internally recruited franchisees

In stark contrast to the attention paid to multiple unit franchising over the past 25 years, no studies were found which focused on the distinctions between two other categories of franchisees, that of externally recruited franchisees (ERFs) and internally recruited franchisees (IRFs). ERFs represent the more conventional view of a franchisee involving the traditional approach of recruiting franchisees externally with the franchisee offering their capital, entrepreneurial spirit, and business knowledge often from diverse fields (Norton, 1988b). Indeed, the entire concept of franchising is based on a franchisee being an independent businessperson who lacks the requisite expertise within the new field of endeavor, but obtains that expertise through the dyadic experience of acquiring a franchise from a franchisor, hence the description 'being in business for yourself but not by yourself' (Kaufmann, 1999, p. 345). The franchisor finds this business relationship attractive, as they gain an injection of capital without requiring the issuing of shares or borrowing of funds, they also gain the entrepreneurial oversight of someone who has *skin in the game* (Frazer & Roussety, 2017). Agency theory suggests that because the franchisee shares in the unit's growth upside, in both a profit and capital sense the franchisee has far more incentive than employee management to improve results (Rubin, 1978).

In this research an internally recruited franchisee is defined as a franchisee who, prior to their franchise recruitment, was an employee of the franchisor or an employee of one of its franchisees. Most often, IRFs were previously employed within the operations side of the franchisor's business as unit managers or above, and thus 'were proven operators' (Bradach, 1997, p. 292) who had displayed operational aptitude over a prolonged period. Indeed, in his 1977 biography McDonald's founder Ray Kroc acknowledged that in franchisee selection McDonald's gave preference to long serving employees (Kroc & Anderson, 1977). This 'long preexisting relationship' (Bradach, 1997, p. 292) added to the level of trust between the franchisor and the IRF. In a similar way to multiple unit franchisees, IRFs' operational knowledge circumvents the need for the standard training period, which means the gestation period for an IRF from initial recruitment to being active within an outlet is significantly less than an ERF (Lashley & Morrison, 2000). Due to their required years of franchisor employee service, logically this leaves IRFs with less opportunity for broad business experience from other industries when compared with ERFs. IRFs also often possess less financial capital than their ERF counterparts with Bradach observing 'while company people rarely had the required capital, the chain ... often assisted them in buying the franchise' (1997, p. 292).

While IRFs have been acknowledged frequently in recent trade publications (Bisio, 2015; Camplin, 2013; Russell, 2014; Syed & Syed, 2019), the category of IRFs has received little research attention in the academic literature. Indeed, Lashley and Morrison's (2000) book is primarily about franchising hospitality services and devotes just two of its 274 pages to sourcing franchisees from company employees. While Bradach's (1997) study assigns just four of its 76 paragraphs to the same topic. Though dated, both these works place the prevalence of IRFs in major chains such as Jack-in-a-Box and McDonald's at above 40 per cent (Bradach, 1997; Lashley & Morrison, 2000). Remarkably, despite this reported prevalence no prior research has focused on IRFs.

### 2.5 *The four franchising strategic imperatives as a conceptual framework*

The first research question is almost completely inductive and consequently imposes no existing conceptual framework. The second research question uses an accepted conceptual framework from the franchising literature of franchising's four strategic imperatives as the lens through which to conduct the exploration (Creswell, 2014). Bradach's pioneering (1995) study on multiple unit franchising identified four key factors for system success known as the four franchising strategic imperatives. Specifically they include unit growth, system uniformity, local responsiveness and system-wide adaption. These imperatives have subsequently provided the conceptual framework for numerous franchising studies, including Boulay, Caemmerer, Evanschitzky and Duniach's (2016) recent investigation into the links between multiple unit franchising and the attainment of the four franchising strategic imperatives. The four strategic imperatives have also been used to explain why franchisors choose between the various governance models of franchising (Bodey, Weaven, & Grace, 2011, 2013). Two separate studies, Cliquet and Penard (2012) and Meiseberg (2013) found that plural forms generally enhanced a franchise systems chance of attaining the imperatives. Given these four franchising strategic imperatives are utilised as the conceptual framework in this research to address the second research question, a description of each imperative is now presented.

For franchisors, *unit growth* (growth in the number of units) is an imperative as it facilitates economies of scale through bulk purchasing, as well as the diffusion of marketing and administrative costs over a greater number of individual outlets (Garg, Rasheed, & Priem, 2005). As most franchise chains operate as a plural form, with both company-owned and franchised outlets, unit growth can develop from three sources: (1) adding a company-owned outlet, (2) granting a new outlet to an existing franchisee, or (3) adding a new franchisee and a new outlet (Bradach, 1995; Garg et al., 2005; Meiseberg, 2013). If the latter source is selected a further decision is required, whether to recruit an IRF or an ERF as the new franchisee for the new outlet.

The second imperative of *system uniformity* refers to the franchise system having standardised methods of operation that have little variation from unit to unit (Bodey et al., 2013). As many franchise systems are founded on brand name capital, consistency becomes very important for the sustainability of the franchise chain (Bodey et al., 2011; Nelson, Loken, & Bennett, 2009). A sustainable competitive advantage can be significantly eroded if a lack of uniformity leads to the dilution and weakening of the brand (Boulay et al., 2016).

The third imperative of *local responsiveness* signifies the need to be flexible enough to understand customer needs and adapt to heterogeneous markets. The successful spread of franchise chains has meant individual units may compete in diverse local markets (Bradach, 1995). Generally, franchisees have been considered more responsive to local needs than managers of company-owned units, with franchisees' local market knowledge forming a critical part of a chain's resources (Boulay et al., 2016). This knowledge, coupled with franchisees' strong unit profit motivation (Rubin, 1978), provides the springboard for a competitive advantage at the local level (Minkler, 1992).

Bradach (1995, p. 78) suggested *system-wide adaption* involved four components: '(1) generating new ideas, (2) testing and evaluating ideas, (3) deciding which to pursue, and (4) implementing them'. To be successful franchise systems need to implement a strategic marketing management process, whereby adaption involves responses to changes in marketing, competitive environments, and customer tastes (Bodey et al., 2011). Inherent here, is the notion these adaptions are appropriate system-wide, hence this imperative has some association with the concept of system uniformity discussed earlier (Bodey et al., 2011). While some adaptions to the system are inspired by the franchisor, there are numerous examples where franchisees' new ideas and innovations have proven crucial for success in franchise systems (Dada, Watson, & Kirby, 2015; Meiseberg, 2013; Watson, Dada, Grünhagen, & Wollan, 2016). Such co-created value meets the criteria for entrepreneurial marketing (Whalen et al., 2016) thereby fostering an opportunity for a competitive advantage.

## 3. Research methodology

Given the scarcity of literature on IRFs as a franchisee recruitment option, a qualitative methodology was employed for this exploratory study (Eisenhardt, 1989; Saunders, Lewis, & Thornhill, 2009). Aaker, Kumar, and Day (1997) describe exploratory studies as 'research that usually is designed to generate ideas where the hypotheses are vague or ill-defined' (p. 759). Qualitative research is appropriate when the focus is on gaining an in-depth understanding to facilitate the development of 'interpretations of phenomena of interest without numerical measurement' (Zikmund, Ward, Lowe, Winzar, & Babin, 2011, p. 65). For the first research question given no previous academic inquiry had been made into the drivers behind the internal recruiting of franchisees, an inductive approach was employed (Creswell, 2014). The aim was to allow the data gathered to identify and develop the theory (Corbin, 2017). Respondents were simply asked 'Why franchisors may decide to recruit franchisees from the ranks of their employees'. For research question two, the theoretical lens (Creswell, 2014) of the four strategic franchising imperatives was used to explore the perceived impact of IRFs on franchise systems. While this lens shaped the questions asked (Creswell, 2014), the approach remained inductive with no propositions developed in advance as to what the ultimate impacts could be. Semi-structured interviews were conducted one-to-one to gain rich insights into the research questions (Saunders et al., 2009). At the commencement of the interview, demographic and career history data was captured which was later triangulated with more comprehensive information from the participants' LinkedIn profiles and franchisor websites. A list of topics was then explored relating to the research questions and the participants' experiences in making franchisee recruitment decisions. The process was adaptive, with the researchers fine tuning and adjusting between interviews (Dick, 2016). The interviews were recorded and lasted a duration of up to one hour.

Thematic analysis is principally concerned with identifying, organizing, and interpreting themes in textual data. It is now ubiquitous in qualitative organisational research (King & Brooks, 2018), and used in recent franchising research (Grace, Frazer, Weaven, & Dant, 2016). Accordingly, the six phases of thematic analysis (Braun & Clarke, 2006) were employed for this study: data familiarisation, coding, generating initial themes, reviewing themes, theme definition and naming, writing results. Familiarization began during transcription, as this was undertaken by the researchers rather than being outsourced (Frazer, 2004). Further, familiarisation occurred via the transcripts being initially examined with notes of first impressions made. Transcripts were then read and re-read in detail, further immersing the researchers in the data. Initial coding then followed, with the labeling of information deemed relevant to the first research question. These codes were then scrutinized to identify broader patterns and organized into potential themes (Attride-Stirling, 2001). The more grounded approach to research question one meant these themes were generated without reference to theory. For added rigour, the data was also analyzed using Leximancer V4.51 (Wilk, Soutar, & Harrigan, 2019) with no additional meaningful themes emerging. All candidate themes were then discussed and reviewed until intercoder agreement (MacPhail, Khoza, Abler, & Ranganathan, 2016) was achieved as to their pertinence to the first research question (Denzin & Lincoln, 2005). Significant themes were defined and named, with their relationships to research question one conceptualized and developed [see Figure 1]. Direct quotes were used in the writing up of the results to provide raw data that encapsulates participants' views (Labuschagne, 2003). A similar sequence was followed for the second research question however, codes were first generated relative to the theoretical framework of the four strategic franchising imperatives, and then organized into themes under each imperative.

## 3.1 Sampling

Purposive sampling involves 'selecting units ... based on specific purposes associated with answering a research study's questions' (Teddlie & Yu, 2007, p. 77). In order to explore the major reasons for the internal recruiting of franchisees, it was critical decision makers responsible for or exposed to the strategic reasoning for such recruitment practices within franchise chains, were recruited for the in-depth interviews. Since the entry of the major US fast food chains into Australian in the late 1960 s (Schaper & Buchan, 2014), the fast food industry has been synonymous with franchising (Grünhagen & Mittelstaedt, 2005) and is estimated to encompass almost A\$20 billion per annum in sales (Vuong, 2017). Thus, a purposive sample of current and former Australian fast food franchisor executives whose roles had been integrally involved in their organizations' franchising policy, decisions and outcomes was obtained. To achieve this, snowball sampling was utilized and recruiting occurred until sufficient saturation was achieved

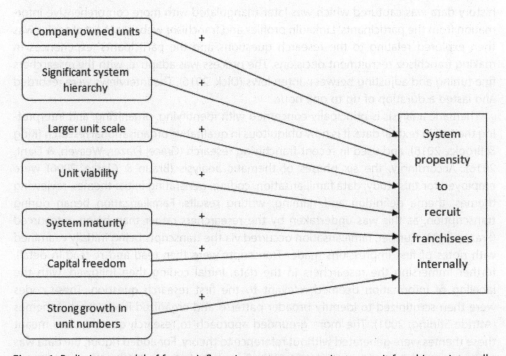

**Figure 1.** Preliminary model of factors influencing system propensity to recruit franchisees internally.

(Guest, Bunce, & Johnson, 2006). Ultimately, interviews were conducted with nine franchise executives. As endorsed by previous qualitative franchising research (Kaufmann,
1999; Weaven, Isaac, & Herington, 2007) a cross-sectional perspective across levels of
management was sought. Three participants falling into the Top-level [Managing
Director], three falling into the Mid-level [Regional/State Manager] and three falling into
the Lower-level [Operations Manager, Franchise Coordinator]. Validity was enhanced by
way of six of these executives having exposure to more than one franchise chain, and all
having exposure to at least one franchise chain where internal recruiting of franchisees
had occurred. Indeed, nearly half (four) provided somewhat unique perspectives as they
had gone on to become internally recruited franchisees themselves, after their corporate
careers. A total of 224 years' experience in the field of franchising was tapped in to
(ranging from six to 38 years) with the sample, the average being 25.6 years.
Characteristics of the sample are presented in Table 1.

## 4. Results

### 4.1 Drivers for internal recruiting of franchisees

In relation to the first research question exploring the drivers for a franchisor to recruit
franchisees internally, the results revealed several factors were evident in raising the
overall propensity of a franchise system to recruit internally. These factors are presented
in Figure 1 and are expanded upon below with references made to existing literature.

### 4.1.1. Company owned units

Bradach (1997, p. 291–292) observed 'a key constraint facing chains as they sought to grow
was finding interested and qualified franchisees. The plural form offered a means of escaping
this constraint by utilizing company people as franchisees'. Consequently, systems that do not
have company-owned stores have a greatly reduced potential to recruit internally. The
prototypical IRF has already run an outlet giving them the critical operations knowledge
required to be a franchisee. Indeed, respondent FE4 commented that almost all IRFs 'have
been trained in operations or been a ... unit manager'. Thus, by having a proportion of

**Table 1.** Australian fast food executive characteristics.

| Executive Level | Franchise Executive | Highest position in a franchise chain | Highest units responsible for | Number of chains involved with | Subsequently became a franchisee (IRF) | Years in franchising |
|---|---|---|---|---|---|---|
| Top | FE1 | Managing Director | 700+ | 2 | No | 27 |
| Top | FE2 | Managing Director | 250+ | 2 | No | 34 |
| Top | FE3 | Managing Director | NA* | 10+ | No | 19 |
| Mid | FE4 | Regional Manager | 100+ | 1 | Yes | 33 |
| Mid | FE5 | Regional Manager | 50+ | 3 | No | 10 |
| Mid | FE6 | Managing Director# | 40+ | 2 | No | 6 |
| Lower | FE7 | Operations Manager | 15+ | 2 | Yes | 38 |
| Lower | FE8 | Franchise Coordinator | 15+ | 1 | Yes | 35 |
| Lower | FE9 | Franchise Coordinator | 15+ | 1 | Yes | 28 |

* consults to many chains
# chain operates in one state only

company-owned stores franchise chains have a fertile source from which to recruit internal candidates. The definition of IRF also encompasses employees of franchisees. Recent research has found employees of franchisees may be positively influenced by support provided by the franchisor (Ramaseshan, Rabbanee, & Burford, 2018). However, this avenue for recruitment may be limited by lack of support from franchisees. FE3 noting that where a franchisor is actively seeking IRFs 'some franchisees don't like to communicate that to their staff because they feel they are going to lose their staff ... and have to recruit again'.

### 4.1.2. Significant system hierarchy

Systems that have a significant system hierarchy possess a greater opportunity to recruit internally. Larger systems require a much greater head office infrastructure facilitating a career path for employees beyond the store level. This point and the first point on the extent of company owned units are interrelated. Chains that operate company-owned stores require more significant system hierarchies to provide greater oversight of these units, with up to 10 times more monitoring costs being spent on the company-owned outlets versus outlets that are franchised (Bradach, 1997; Perryman & Combs, 2012). Commenting on a large system that had over 250 Australian stores, FE2 stated that IRFs represented 'at least half' of the franchisee cohort and comprised mainly of former 'store managers or corporate head office persons'. In contrast, when asked about the extent of internal recruiting in their chain of just over 40 stores with a very lean corporate staffing structure, FE6 stated 'as we are all franchised ... there is little of that happening and because of our scale we do not have a lot of progression'.

Organisations with a larger system hierarchy also often encounter the need to manage, motivate and turnover that hierarchy. In today's litigious world, this can pose difficulties with Australian unfair dismissal legislation applying to employees earning below A\$148,700 annually (Fair Work Commission, 2019). FE7 had experience with a large chain that some-times resolved such issues by offering the outgoing employee a franchise, what became known internally as 'the golden handshake'. Indeed, FE7 recalled specific instances where an internal franchise candidate was chosen 'because we had another corporate person coming up to take their (employee) role'. However, the prospect of receiving a franchise opportunity was also used as a tool to motivate and 'for rewarding and recognizing loyal and long serving employees' FE4. When asked if this approach was used by franchisors as a motivational tool for some employees, FE9 who ultimately became a franchisee commen-ted, 'it always was for me, one hundred per cent'. Merely witnessing other employees become franchisees also had a positive effect. 'From a motivational perspective I think it was the greatest thing for someone in a corporate situation to see their boss get *promoted* into becoming a franchisee' FE9.

### 4.1.3. Larger unit scale

Systems that have a smaller scale at the unit level and therefore fewer employee managers, tended to be less able to recruit internally. Commenting on their franchise system's lack of IRFs, FE6 observed:

> ... it is a scale related thing, because in our franchise model they (the franchisees) have a fairly low level of staff ... so they are the managers, the franchisees. They have a lot of casual staff who by default do not work full-time and so do not have aspirations to go on and develop a career in the business.

Inherent in this quote is the system's small scale at the individual unit level, which meant franchisees usually acted as the unit managers themselves rather than employing managers, thus shrinking the pool for potential IRFs. This contrasted markedly with the much larger unit scale of one international franchise chain that had over 500 Australian stores and recruited IRFs extensively. According to FE3, the average store in this chain 'has about 140 staff, 15 managers and a store manager sitting at the top of the tree'. Further, FE4 who has a 31-year history with this same chain observed, this chain had 'no shortage of employees at all levels wanting to become their own boss (franchisees)'.

### 4.1.4. Unit viability

Respondents indicated that franchise chains struggling for viability at the unit level find it difficult to recruit internally. While external recruits were driven by return on investment, internal recruits' frame of reference was related to the company salary that they would forego to become a franchisee. Thus for internal recruits, expected franchise unit viability needed to match or exceed their corporate exit salary. In clarifying this point, FE4 pronounced that internal recruits needed to foresee the likelihood that they would earn more as a franchisee, 'even if they were earning just a bit more than what they had been previously'.

Commenting on a number of their chain's head office staff who had recently decided against acquiring a franchise due to lack of unit viability, respondent FE6 stated 'to be honest I think they would be looking at it and saying, in the current climate it is a lot of work for little return'. Conversely, FE2 mentioned in regards to one large international chain with an annual EBITDA profit of A$800,000 per store, 'it is not hard to find someone to go into just about any store in Australia now ... they have got 80 people (employees) in the office that want stores'. This point contrasted with the chain where FE2 was managing director, which had 'lots of franchisees working 60 hours a week for A$50,000 per annum per annum take-home pay' and was consequently struggling with recruiting franchisees. Even though this franchise was a large international brand, it was 'probably dying a slow death' FE2. Indeed, several respondents identified that for any franchise system, profitability at an individual unit level is a key overarching ingredient, not just a requisite for IRFs. FE5 stating 'I think any successful franchisor has, number one, got to be committed to making their franchisees successful. I think that is the difference between a good and bad franchisor'.

### 4.1.5. System maturity

Early in a system's life cycle the opportunity for internal recruiting appears limited for three reasons. Firstly, there are limited internal candidates to choose from as corporate headcounts for chains in their infancy are typically small. Secondly, as observed by FE5 prior to their recruitment as a franchisee 'in most cases IRFs have clocked up 15 years in the system they were working in', which precludes their early availability. Thirdly, in their early years franchise systems are usually extremely reliant on the financial capital provided by franchisees (Caves & Murphy, 1976). IRFs tend to have less capital when compared with ERFs, 'internally ... there is a bit less capital because franchisors are not the greatest of (salary) payors' FE9.

Thus, franchise chains entering system adolescence may have an advantage in being be able to sustain unit growth by utilising some of their experienced system employees to become IRFs. Indeed, commenting on the maturity of a chain which started in 2006 and where they now hold a senior role, FE1 stated 'I think these next 10 years are our (the franchise system's) teenage years'. Further, they saw such systems as being increasingly reliant on some of their maturing pool of system employees becoming IRFs to facilitate future growth. Indeed, regarding this chain's prevalence of IRFs FE1 observed, 'it is just starting to happen, I think we started franchising to internal employees in the 10th year about three years ago'.

### 4.1.6. Capital freedom

When contemplating why do organizations franchise, FE4 remarked 'for a lot of new brands ... it's because they do not have the capital, so they need the (franchisees) capital'. FE2 observed, that particularly in the early years 'franchisors want some people with good equity and that is usually not an (internal) employee'. Chains that reach a unit count of over 50 outlets are viewed as attaining a critical threshold where the need for franchisees' capital reduces, 'you have got this big gap ... and these are the guys that do it really well, they have best practice' FE3. Indeed because they have greater access to financial capital, more established chains become less reliant on franchisee's capital for growth (Oxenfeldt & Kelly, 1969). Ostensibly, this provides the capital freedom to generate more creative franchise structures that make it easier for internal recruits, who possess less financial capital, to acquire a franchise. Such established chains are often more focused on acquiring franchisee's human capital as identified by agency theory, which suggests franchisees will outperform company managers (Norton, 1988a; Rubin, 1978). Indeed, FE1 and FE7 cited the modification of their franchise system's standard franchise structure, was key to facilitating the entry of numerous IRFs who had less capital than ERFs. This modified arrangement allowed the franchisee 'to put in less money and the franchisor shared more of the profit pie ... because they were putting in more money' FE1. Now involved at a senior level with a subsequent chain, FE1 believes such schemes are so crucial in fostering internal recruits and growth, they are encouraging their current chain to develop a similar mechanism. This is particularly prescient as this chain now has over 10 years of operation, has just reached over 100 stores, and has recently receive a capital injection from a private equity firm, thus it is primed for growth.

### 4.1.7. Strong growth in unit numbers

Unit numbers tend to increase the most on a percentage basis, in the early years of operation of a franchise system. However on an absolute unit numbers basis, the greatest growth often occurs some time beyond 10 years of operation. FE1 reflecting on the evolution of a large chain where they had been managing director noted, that the zenith of recruiting IRFs coincided with peak growth in store numbers. At that point, this chain was adding 'nearly one store a week' FE1. From around year 15 to year 25 of its Australian presence this chain more than doubled in size, 'so we went through huge growth ... and it was (driven by) predominantly long serving employees becoming franchisees' FE5.

During such times of high growth, a prevalent factor in recruiting IRFs appeared to be expediency due to the overwhelming requirement to satisfy the system's unit growth objectives within the imposed time horizons. Expediency was expressed most often by the mid-level interviewees (regional managers) who felt the direct pressure to meet growth targets dictated from management above. As a regional manager FE5 commented on the difficultly of coordinating many conflicting demands:

> that was very difficult ... you would have planning issues on one side ... delays in terms of the store development plan, equally on the other side you would have the (trainee) franchisee's own development, their level of proficiency, their level of capability ... and you have a candidate (external) potentially saying, well I do not want that store ... so therefore I needed to consider a company employee to fill the gap.

The expediency provided by an IRF was directly related to them not needing the recruiting and training time required to on-board an external candidate, which could be up to 9 months duration. Furthermore, not all ERF candidates made it through the training process with Bradach (1995) estimating that only '1% –2% of the people who made initial inquiries were approved' (p. 74). Consequently, the perceived 'risk profile became greater with an external franchisee' FE5. IRFs were perceived as significantly less risky and considered 'ready to go' (FE4). With 'internal people for a franchise you have had 15 years to interview them and you really, really know what you are getting' FE1. 'It takes away your risk by recruiting internally because you have already done your due diligence on those people. You have sort of done the psychometric testing because you have worked with them' FE2. This was also consistent with Bordonaba-Juste and Polo-Redondo's (2008) findings on relationship duration, trust, and commitment in a franchise setting.

## 4.2 Perceived impact of IRF on the four franchising strategic imperatives

The second research question explored what impact franchisors perceived IRFs had on the franchise system achieving the four franchising strategic imperatives. The results indicate IRFs are perceived to confer system advantages for unit growth and system uniformity. Table 2 presents these results which are now expanded upon.

### 4.2.1. Unit growth

It was evident IRFs can have a positive impact on a franchising system achieving their growth imperatives. For some chains, as evidenced by several respondent quotes previously cited, IRFs represented a significant additional source of qualified potential franchisees. This was particularly apparent for chains that had: their own stores, significant system hierarchy, scale at the unit level, unit viability, attained a level of system maturity, and some capital freedom. Indeed, numerous interviewees outlined the importance the capacity to recruit internally provided in meeting growth targets. The vagaries of external franchisee recruitment did not always align with the unit growth schedules imposed from top management. Consequently when timing became an issue,

**Table 2.** Perceived impact on the four franchising strategic imperatives.

| Strategic Franchising Imperative | Internally Recruited Franchisees | Externally Recruited Franchisees |
|---|---|---|
| Growth | ✓✓ | |
| Uniformity | ✓✓ | |
| Local Responsiveness | | ✓ |
| Systemwide Adaption | | ✓✓ |

✓✓ = Strong positive relationship ✓ = Moderate positive relationship the expediency provided by IRFs came to the forefront of the decision process, 'to attract people it is probably easier to recruit ... internally ... (IRFs are) always what I call the emergency requirement" FE4. 'In most cases of the internal people that ended up with a store ... it was because a situation arose, and we said who is the right individual to fill that hole for us' FE7. When asked how often internal recruits ended up being the fallback option to expedite growth targets, FE5 a regional manager responded, 'that happened a lot'.

### 4.2.2.  System uniformity

All but one respondent acknowledged IRFs' superiority delivering system uniformity and achieving system standards. FE7 stated:

> I tended to find an internal person maintained the standards a lot higher because they had been exposed to it a lot more ... I found people who came from totally different industries (ERFs) ... needed to be coaxed a lot more in that area to understand that this industry needed those high standards.

FE4 saw IRF's strengths in system uniformity and standards as 'one of the reasons that they are attractive to the franchisor'. In fact, most respondents acknowledged IRFs were a superior option in respect to system uniformity:

> the standards were always better from IRFs mostly because they just knew what to do and often the people that came from internal were operations people, so the positive you had with them was that they knew the standards, they could run great operations (FE2).

### 4.2.3.  Local responsiveness

When it came to local responsiveness, two thirds of respondents believed IRFs were less likely than ERFs to be truly responsive to local market demands. The other third perceived there was little difference. According to FE5 'external franchisees were far more agile in adjusting to local market conditions and more consumer aware. There was an inherent robotic reliance on the system in the case of the internal franchisee. So, chalk and cheese on that one'. While FE1 observed, as a franchisee:

> you have got to understand ... the community and the surrounds you operate in. An internally recruited franchisee probably does not get that as much as an external one does ... (ERFs) would be a lot better in the community than the internal franchisees. They (ERFs) would ... be able to engage with the local community, local politicians, local charities in a way that most internal franchisees during their employee career were really not that much exposed to.

### 4.2.4.  System-wide adaption

A clear difference was evident between the franchise executives' perceptions of IRFs competencies in respect to system-wide adaption and generating new ideas and innovation. ERFs were perceived as far more adept than IRFs in generating new ideas and innovations. As stated by FE4 'IRFs were more conservative ... a lot of them only knew what they knew ... they were good at following the formula but then sometimes did not cope well with change'. Further, as FE5 acknowledged in respect to system-wide adaption:

my experience was that the former company employees were a lot more restrained and a lot more silent and stood back when it came to challenging the status quo ... if there was a new initiative, I think you would have external candidates driving it.

Consistently, ERFs were perceived as offering more to franchise systems in situations where 'you are looking to innovate and think differently, and when you are facing challenges that you cannot draw on your history to solve' FE6. A point further elaborated upon by FE5, 'in terms of challenging the status quo, challenging the way we go to market, challenging how the brand is represented, clearly external franchisees were so much more talented than internal'.

As IRFs have accumulated many years of institutionalized thinking concentrating on the organisational compliance and execution issues of the franchisor, their entrepreneurial and innovative skills were perceived as underdeveloped when compared with ERFs. This view was encapsulated by FE7's observation:

> an internal person thought what they were taught was right ... whereas an external person would say, well why does it have to be that way ... I can think of a different way of doing it that might achieve that faster or more economically. So, I think the external person (ERF) in many cases came up with a lot of our ideas.

A view was expressed, that too high a proportion of internally recruited franchisees could see a chain become incestuous, engage in groupthink and ultimately lack the business diversity required for success. FE5 characterized this 'as the gene pool that you bring to the business, how diverse you are (ERFs) and how insular you are (IRFs)'. FE1 who started with one chain at 15 and went on to become Managing Director stated, 'I think the internal person has been indoctrinated into the company, believes in the company, probably does not question the company as much'. FE1 subsequently commented that maintaining a proportion of ERFs was the preventive solution to this:

> ... questioning of the company's decision-making was always a lot more forthright from external people than it was from internal people ... they had this demeanor about them (the ERFs), about being absolutely frank ... if you asked me who would tell you without mixing words exactly what they thought about the company and the errors that we were making, it was the externals.

## 5. Discussion

This study's results suggest the exploration of IRFs has been a worthwhile line of enquiry. This deduction is perhaps not surprising given the origin of the topic was predicated on the disparity between coverage of IRFs in industry publications, versus their noticeable absence in academic literature.

The first research question identified multiple drivers for a system's propensity to recruit franchisees internally which include the presence of company owned stores, significant system hierarchy, larger unit scale, unit viability, system maturity, capital freedom and strong unit growth in numbers. While these IRF drivers are preliminary, they have never been identified in any previous research and warrant further examination.

Regarding the second research question which explored the perceived impact of IRFs on the franchise system achieving the four franchising strategic imperatives, the internal recruiting of franchisees appears to confer significant advantages in achieving the unit growth imperative, particularly given the acknowledged industry scarcity of qualified ERFs. The imperative for system uniformity also seems to be enhanced by IRFs. However, IRFs are not as favorable as ERFs in respect to the imperatives of local responsiveness and system-wide adaption.

With reported rates of IRFs prevalent in some franchise systems within this study's sample approaching 50 per cent, IRFs provide a catalyst for a significant new avenue of franchising behaviour to be researched. In fact, this could mirror the extent of the impetus provided to franchising studies by multiple unit franchising, from the mid-1990 s to the late 2000's (Bradach, 1995; Kaufmann & Dant, 1996). Indeed, Weaven and Frazer's (2007, p. 194) observation that 'the paucity of prior research concerned with multiple unit franchising adoption appears at odds with this expansionary strategy' may prove just as apt for IRFs.

The results of the current study strongly suggest IRFs provide one solution to franchisors' resource scarcity needs, however rather than being for financial capital it is for human capital. IRFs appear to be consistent with, and predicated on agency theory in its purest form, as it assumes that the same individual will provide superior performance merely by changing their agency status from employee to franchisee. IRFs could be considered an additional variant of the plural form, with plurality being manifested not only by systems operating company-owned stores and franchise stores, but also with another layer of pluralism provided when stores are franchised to IRFs or ERFs.

## 6. Managerial implications

From a practical point of view, given that a dearth of qualified franchisees has long plagued franchisors and stymied their growth (Bailey, 2018; Bradach, 1997; Frazer et al., 2012, 2014), this research provides important insights for franchisors who may decide to use IRFs as a partial solution to their future franchisee recruitment needs. More extensive use of IRFs could present a viable and effective option to counteract the shrinking pool of available franchisees (Bailey, 2018) however, the decision to do so should be viewed as a strategic imperative and implemented on a considered basis. In this research the pursuit of IRFs seemed to be somewhat *ad hoc* with the middle and lower level participants characterising many IRF decisions as being tactically driven by short-term pressures to meet unit growth numbers or organisational succession planning needs. Although some chains in this research still attained around 50 per cent IRFs, this outcome appears to not be premeditated but more the consequence of an emergent strategy (Mintzberg & Waters, 1985) resulting from expediency. This suggests a more deliberate strategy to pursue IRFs as part of an expansion plan should involve initially ensuring there is a sufficient employee pool to recruit from. Accordingly, franchise organisations that currently do not operate company owned units would need to alter their franchise structure to utilize a plural form (simultaneous use of company owned and franchised units) since this structure results in a larger workforce pool, providing a greater opportunity to recruit IRFs.

However simply having sufficient employees to recruit IRFs from is not the complete solution. The current research also indicates a requirement for the development of appropriate mechanisms for internal employees to make an effective transition to become franchisees. IRFs often lack the requisite financial capital demanded of a standard external franchisee applicant. Consequently in order to facilitate more IRFs, franchise organisations may need to develop another tier to their franchise agreements requiring less capital upfront from the IRF. As a result the standard structure would still exist primarily for ERFs, however an additional agreement structure primarily designed for IRFs would be offered requiring less capital but demanding a higher royalty. Such a structure emulates the approach the largest chain covered by this research undertook to overcome its IRF shortfall. The main caveat in the financial design of this new structure is that, to be compelling to IRFs it would need to retain the likelihood that the IRfs' prior employment salaries would be exceeded by their profits as franchisees.

## 7. Theoretical implications and future research directions

Numerous theoretical implications stem from this research. Currently the overall propensity of franchise chains to recruit internally is unknown. The variation in the perceived prevalence of IRFs between chains in this research (0 per cent to 50 per cent) suggests a priority exists to establish the prevalence of IRFs within not only the fast food industry, but the broader franchising community more generally.

The results of this research indicate that while IRFs confer advantages for unit growth and system uniformity, they are viewed as less adept than ERFs regarding local responsiveness and system-wide adaption. This suggests that chains that rely too heavily on either ERFs or IRFs may yield sub-optimal results in achieving the four strategic franchising imperatives. Consequently, just as prior research on plural form chains has attempted to formulate the optimal mix between company-owned units and franchise units (Madanoglu, Castrogiovanni, & Kizildag, 2018; Vázquez, 2007), so too the optimal mix of IRFs and ERFs within franchise systems needs investigation. Further, ERFs perceived superiority in the strategic imperative of system-wide adaption may indicate that IRFs and ERFs differ with respect to entrepreneurial orientation (EO). That ERFs may be superior in EO given they are perceived as more advanced in system-wide adaption. Dada and Watson (2013) analysed the effect of franchisor EO on franchise system performance outcomes finding a reasonably strong correlation while, Chien (2014) found among other things, that franchisee EO directly and positively affected franchisee performance. Thus any potential difference in EO between ERFs and IRFs and the implications this may have for franchise performance warrants further investigation. IRFs perceived deficiency in local responsiveness needs to be empirically tested by future research. If verified franchise systems may need to address this deficiency by implementing local engagement training programs for IRFs to mitigate this apparent shortcoming.

Finally, the establishment of a further category of franchisees in IRFs, presents implications in terms of how to reconcile IRFs with the main theories in the domain of franchising research of resource scarcity, agency theory and plural form symbiosis. While these implications are beyond the scope of this exploratory study, they present a fertile field for future research.

## 8. Limitations

As an exploratory study with a small purposively selected sample, this work has limitations in terms of representativeness, reliability and generalisability (Saunders et al., 2009). Consequently, a subsequent quantitative study incorporating a larger representative sample should seek to validate this study's results and preliminary model.

## 9. Conclusion

This study aims to commence a dialogue on the internal recruiting of franchisees, which although prevalent in some chains in today's marketplace, remains an under researched area of franchising. It is intended that future studies will build from the initial learnings of this study to enhance the body of literature around this emerging franchisee recruitment option. This exploratory research represents an important initial step in gaining insights into the circumstances that influence franchisors to choose internal franchisee recruiting arrangements and what differential outcomes they perceive this may provide in the areas of unit growth, system uniformity, local responsiveness and system-wide adaption.

## Disclosure statement

No potential conflict of interest was reported by the authors.

## Funding

No funding was provided for this research.

## ORCID

Peter Balsarini http://orcid.org/0000-0002-7825-4495
Claire Lambert http://orcid.org/0000-0002-0020-2599
Marie M. Ryan http://orcid.org/0000-0002-1270-0480

## References

Aaker, D., Kumar, V., & Day, G. (1997). *Marketing research* (6th ed.). New York, USA: Wiley.
Alchian, A., & Demsetz, H. (1972). Production, information costs, and economic organization. *The American Economic Review, 62*(5), 777–795.
Alon, I. (2001). The use of franchising by U.S.-based retailers. *Journal of Small Business Management, 39*(2), 111–122.
Attride-Stirling, J. (2001). Thematic networks: An analytic tool for qualitative research. *Qualitative Research, 1*(3), 385–405.
Bailey, M. (2018). Foodco grows profit despite 'misguided' franchising inquiry. *Australian Financial Review*. Retrieved from https://www.afr.com/business/retail/foodco-grows-profit-despite-misguided-franchising-inquiry-20181105-h17izh
Barney, J. (1991). Firm resources and sustained competitive advantage. *Journal of Management, 17*(1), 99–120.
Bender, J. (2015). Barking up the wrong tree: The NRLB's joint-employer standard and the case for preserving the formalities of business format franchising. *Franchise Law Journal, 35*(2), 209–235.
Bisio, R. (2015). Four reasons why former employees make the best franchisees. *Entrepreneur Magazine*. Retrieved from https://www.entrepreneur.com/article/250917
Bodey, K., Weaven, S., & Grace, D. (2011). Contrasting the four franchising imperatives across hybridized governance models: A preliminary investigation. *Journal of Asia-Pacific Business, 12*(3), 244–279.
Bodey, K., Weaven, S., & Grace, D. (2013). Multiple-unit franchising and performance outcomes. *Journal of Business Economics and Management, 14*(1), 279–312.

Bordonaba-Juste, M., & Polo-Redondo, Y. (2008). Differences between short and long-term relationships: An empirical analysis in franchise systems. *Journal of Strategic Marketing, 16*(4), 327–354.

Boulay, J., Caemmerer, B., Evanschitzky, H., & Duniach, K. (2016). Growth, uniformity, local responsiveness, and system-Wide adaptation in multiunit franchising. *Journal of Small Business Management, 54*(4), 1193–1205.

Bradach, J. (1995). Chains within chains: The role of multi-unit franchisees. *Journal of Marketing Channels, 4*(2), 65–81.

Bradach, J. (1997). Using the plural form in the management of restaurant chains. *Administrative Science Quarterly, 42*(2), 276–303.

Bradach, J., & Eccles, R. (1989). Price, authority, and trust: From ideal types to plural forms. *Annual Review of Sociology, 15*(1), 97–118.

Braun, V., & Clarke, V. (2006). Using thematic analysis in psychology. *Qualitative Research in Psychology, 3*(2), 77–101.

Camplin, A. (2013). From head office employee to franchisee. *Inside Franchise Business Magazine.* Retrieved from http://www.franchisebusiness.com.au/news/from-head-office-employee-to-franchisee-alex-campl

Caves, R., & Murphy, W. (1976). Franchising: Firms, markets, and intangible assets. *Southern Economic Journal, 42*(1–4), 572–587.

Chien, S. (2014). Franchisor resources, spousal resources, entrepreneurial orientation, and performance in a couple-owned franchise outlet. *Management Decision, 52*(5), 916–933.

Cliquet, G., & Penard, T. (2012). Plural form franchise networks: A test of bradach's model. *Journal of Retailing and Consumer Services, 19*(1), 159–167.

Combs, J., Ketchen Jr, D. J., & Short, J. (2011). Franchising research: Major milestones, new directions, and its future within entrepreneurship. *Entrepreneurship Theory and Practice, 35*(3), 413–425.

Combs, J., Michael, S., & Castrogiovanni, G. (2009). Institutional influences on the choice of organizational form: The case of franchising. *Journal of Management, 35*(5), 1268–1290.

Corbin, J. (2017). Grounded theory. *Journal of Positive Psychology, 12*(3), 301–302.

Creswell, J. (2014). *Research design: Qualitative, quantitative, and mixed methods approaches* (4th ed, International student ed.). Los Angeles: SAGE.

Croonen, E., Brand, M., & Huizingh, E. (2016). To be entrepreneurial, or not to be entrepreneurial? Explaining differences in franchisee entrepreneurial behavior within a franchise system. *International Entrepreneurship and Management Journal, 12*(3), 531–553.

Dada, O., & Watson, A. (2013). Entrepreneurial orientation and the franchise system. *European Journal of Marketing, 47*(5–6), 790–812.

Dada, O., Watson, A., & Kirby, D. (2015). Entrepreneurial tendencies in franchising: Evidence from the UK. *Journal of Small Business and Enterprise Development, 22*(1), 82–98.

Dant, R., Grunhagen, M., & Windsperger, J. (2011). Franchising research frontiers for the twenty-first century. *Journal of Retailing, 87*(3), 253–268.

Darr, E., Argote, L., & Epple, D. (1995). The acquisition, transfer, and depreciation of knowledge in service organizations: Productivity in franchises. *Management Science, 41*(11), 1750–1762.

Denzin, N., & Lincoln, Y. (2005). *The sage handbook of qualitative research* (3rd ed.). Thousand Oaks: Sage Publications.

Dick, B. (2016). *Convergent interviewing essentials.* Chapel Hill, Qld: Interchange. Retrieved from http://www.aral.com.au/resources/coin.pdf

Eisenhardt, K. (1989). Agency theory: An assessment and review. *Academy of Management Review, 14* (1), 57–74.

Fair Work Commission. (2019). Unfair dismissals benchbook. Retrieved from https://www.fwc.gov.au/unfair-dismissals-benchbook/overview-unfair-dismissal

Frazer, H. (2004). Doing narrative research: Analysing personal stories line by line. *Qualitative Social Work, 3*(2), 179–201.

Frazer, L., & Roussety, M. (2017). Both franchisees and franchisors benefit from company-owned stores. *The Conversation.* Retrieved from https://theconversation.com/both-franchisees-and-franchisors-benefit-from-company-owned-stores-81261

Frazer, L., Weaven, S., & Bodey, K. (2012). *Franchising Australia 2012*. Brisbane: Asia Pacific Centre for Franchising Excellence, Griffith University.

Frazer, L., Weaven, S., & Grace, A. (2014). *Franchising Australia 2014*. Brisbane: Asia Pacific Centre for Franchising Excellence, Griffith University.

Frazer, L., Weaven, S., Grace, A., & Selvanathan, S. (2016). *Franchising Australia 2016*. Brisbane: Asia Pacific Centre for Franchising Excellence, Griffith University.

Garg, V., Priem, R., & Rasheed, A. (2013). A theoretical explanation of the cost advantages of multi-unit franchising. *Journal of Marketing Channels, 20*(1–2), 52–72.

Garg, V., Rasheed, A., & Priem, R. (2005). Explaining franchisors' choices of organization forms within franchise systems. *Strategic Organization, 3*(2), 185–217.

Gillis, W., & Castrogiovanni, G. (2012). The franchising business model: An entrepreneurial growth alternative. *International Entrepreneurship and Management Journal, 8*(1), 75–98.

Grace, A., Frazer, L., Weaven, S., & Dant, R. (2016). Building franchisee trust in their franchisor: Insights from the franchise sector. *Qualitative Market Research, 19*(1), 65–83.

Grünhagen, M., & Mittelstaedt, R. (2005). Entrepreneurs or investors: Do multi-unit franchisees have different philosophical orientations? *Journal of Small Business Management, 43*(3), 207–225.

Guest, G., Bunce, A., & Johnson, L. (2006). How many interviews are enough?: An experiment with data saturation and variability. *Field Methods, 18*(1), 59–82.

Hizam-Hanafiah, M., & Li, J. (2014). Franchisee satisfaction of goal attainment: A discovery of a hierarchy of entrepreneur goals. *Journal of Entrepreneurship in Emerging Economies, 6*(3), 243–267.

Hussain, D., Sreckovic, M., & Windsperger, J. (2018). An organizational capability perspective on multi-unit franchising : Evidence from germany and switzerland. *Small Business Economics : An Entrepreneurship Journal, 50*(4), 717–727.

Inside Franchise Business. (2018), Parliamentary Inquiry into franchising sees Foodco and RFG in the firing line. Retrieved from http://www.franchisebusiness.com.au/news/parliamentary-inquiry-into-franchising-sees-foodco

Kaufmann, P. (1999). Franchising and the choice of self-employment. *Journal of Business Venturing, 14*(4), 345–362.

Kaufmann, P., & Dant, R. (1996). Multi-unit franchising: Growth and management issues. *Journal of Business Venturing, 11*(5), 343–358.

Kaufmann, P., & Eroglu, S. (1999). Standardization and adaptation in business format franchising. *Journal of Business Venturing, 14*(1), 69–85.

Ketchen, D., Ireland, R., & Snow, C. (2007). Strategic entrepreneurship, collaborative innovation, and wealth creation. *Strategic Entrepreneurship Journal, 1*(3/4), 371–385.

King, N., & Brooks, J. (2018). Thematic analysis in organisational research. In C. Cassell, A. L. Cunliffe, & G. Grandy (Eds.), *The sage handbook of qualitative business and management research methods* (pp. 219–236). London: SAGE Publications Ltd. doi:10.4135/9781526430236

Kroc, R., & Anderson, R. (1977). *Grinding it out: The making of McDonald's*. Chicago, IL: Contemporary Books, Inc.

Labuschagne, A. (2003). Qualitative research–airy fairy or fundamental? *The Qualitative Report, 8*(1), 100–103.

Lafontaine, F. (1992). Agency theory and franchising: Some empirical results. *Rand Journal of Economics, 23*(2), 263–283.

Lashley, C., & Morrison, A. (2000). *Franchising hospitality services*. Oxford: Butterworth/Heinmann.

MacPhail, C., Khoza, N., Abler, L., & Ranganathan, M. (2016). Process guidelines for establishing intercoder reliability in qualitative studies. *Qualitative Research, 16*(2), 198–212.

Madanoglu, M., Castrogiovanni, G., & Kizildag, M. (2018). Franchising and firm risk among restaurants. *International Journal of Hospitality Management*. doi:10.1016/j.ijhm.2018.10.021

Meiseberg, B. (2013). The prevalence and performance impact of synergies in the plural form. *Managerial and Decision Economics, 34*(3–5), 140–160.

Minkler, A. (1992). Why firms franchise: A search cost theory. *Journal of Institutional and Theoretical Economics, 148*(2), 240–259.

Mintzberg, H., & Waters, J. (1985). Of strategies, deliberate and emergent. *Strategic Management Journal, 6*(3), 257–272.

Nelson, N., Loken, B., & Bennett, C. (2009). Brand dilution effects on franchises. *Advances in Consumer Research, 36,* 951–952.

Norton, S. (1988a). An empirical look at franchising as an organizational form. *The Journal of Business, 61*(2), 197–218.

Norton, S. (1988b). Franchising, brand name capital, and the entrepreneurial capacity problem. *Strategic Management Journal, 9,* 105–114.

Oxenfeldt, A., & Kelly, A. (1969). Will successful franchise systems ultimately become wholly-owned chains? *Journal of Retailing, 44,* 69–83.

Perrigot, R., & Herrbach, O. (2012). The plural form from the inside. *International Journal of Retail & Distribution Management, 40*(7), 544–563.

Perryman, A., & Combs, J. (2012). Who should own it? An agency-based explanation for multi-outlet ownership and co-location in plural form franchising. *Strategic Management Journal, 33*(4), 368–386.

Ramaseshan, B., Rabbanee, F., & Burford, O. (2018). Combined effects of franchise management strategies and employee service performance on customer loyalty: A multilevel perspective. *Journal of Strategic Marketing, 26*(6), 479–497.

Rubin, P. (1978). The theory of the firm and the structure of the franchise contract. *The Journal of Law and Economics, 21*(1), 223–233.

Russell, J. (2014). *Elite Franchise Magazine.* Retrieved from http://elitefranchisemagazine.co.uk/peo ple/item/crossing-over-why-employees

Saunders, M., Lewis, P., & Thornhill, A. (2009). *Research methods for business students* (5th ed.). Harlow, Essex: Pearson.

Schaper, M., & Buchan, J. (2014). Franchising in Australia: A history. *International Journal of Franchising Law, 12*(4), 3–23.

Sirmon, D., Hitt, M., Ireland, R., & Gilbert, B. (2011). Resource orchestration to create competitive advantage: Breadth, depth, and life cycle effects. *Journal of Management, 37*(5), 1390–1412.

Storholm, G., & Scheuing, E. (1994). Ethical implications of business format franchising. *Journal of Business Ethics, 13*(3), 181–188.

Syed, R., & Syed, S. (2019). On the hunt for a franchisee? Take a look at your own employees. Smart Company. Retrieved from https://www.smartcompany.com.au/business-advice/franchising/find ing-franchisee-look-own-employees/

Teddlie, C., & Yu, F. (2007). Mixed methods sampling: A typology with examples. *Journal of Mixed Methods Research, 1*(1), 77–100.

Thaichon, P., Weaven, S., Quach, S., Baker, B., & Frazer, L. (2019). What to expect after the honey-moon: Evolutionary psychology of part-time franchising. *Journal of Strategic Marketing,* 1–25. doi:10.1080/0965254X.2019.1570315

Thaichon, P., Weaven, S., Quach, S., Bodey, K., Merrilees, B., & Frazer, L. (2018). Female franchisees; a lost opportunity for franchising sector growth? *Journal of Strategic Marketing,* 1–16. doi:10.1080/0965254X.2018.1482946

Vázquez, L. (2007). Proportion of franchised outlets and franchise system performance. *The Service Industries Journal, 27*(7), 907–921.

Vuong, B. (2017). IBISWorld industry report H4512 fast food and takeaway food services in Australia. *IBISWorld.* Retrieved from http://clients1.ibisworld.com.au.ezproxy.ecu.edu.au/reports/au/indus try/default.aspx?entid=2005

Watson, A., Dada, O., Grünhagen, M., & Wollan, M. (2016). When do franchisors select entrepreneurial franchisees? An organizational identity perspective. *Journal of Business Research, 69*(12), 5934–5945.

Weaven, S., & Frazer, L. (2007). Expansion through multiple unit franchising. *International Small Business Journal, 25*(2), 173–205.

Weaven, S., Isaac, J., & Herington, C. (2007). Franchising as a path to self-employment for Australian female entrepreneurs. *Journal of Management and Organization, 13*(4), 345–365.

Whalen, P., Uslay, C., Pascal, V., Omura, G., McAuley, A., Kasouf, C., … Deacon, J. (2016). Anatomy of competitive advantage: Towards a contingency theory of entrepreneurial marketing. *Journal of Strategic Marketing, 24*(1), 5–19.

Wilk, V., Soutar, G., & Harrigan, P. (2019). Tackling social media data analysis. *Qualitative Market Research: An International Journal, 22*(2), 94–113.

Zikmund, W., Ward, S., Lowe, B., Winzar, H., & Babin, J. (2011). *Marketing Research.* (2nd Asia Pacific ed). South Melbourne, Victoria: Cengage Learning Australia.

# Franchisee advisory councils and justice: franchisees finding their voice

Anthony Grace ⓘ, Lorelle Frazer, Scott Weaven ⓘ, Helen Perkins, Wei Shao
and Munyaradzi Nyadzayo ⓘ

**ABSTRACT**

Drawing on the four dimensions of justice: distributive, procedural, interactional, and informational justice, this research examines justice as an antecedent of franchisee performance. Empirical research tested a theoretical model using structural equation modelling techniques. Our results show significant support for two of the four dimensions: distributive and interpersonal justice. Furthermore, our model tested, and found support for the moderation of franchisee membership in the Franchisee Advisory Council (FAC). Perceptions of distributive justice is considered the most important contributor to franchisees' perceived performance in franchise systems that endorse and actively participate with the FAC through membership. Thus, one major implication of this research is the moderation effect of membership of the FAC on the influence of justice on franchisees' perceptions of positive performance outcomes. This speaks to the FAC's particular importance for facilitating best practice, strong, and financially viable franchise systems.

## 1. Introduction

Franchising is a widely used entrepreneurial growth strategy (Gillis et al., 2020). Globally, franchising is a popular strategy for arranging marketing channels (Dant et al., 2013; Thaichon et al., 2018), existing as both an economic entity and a complex social system. This study focuses on the latter, framing the franchising relationship as a complex social system (Strutton et al., 1995) whereby distributive, procedural, interactional, and informational decisions are made on a daily basis by both franchisee and franchisor which have consequences for both parties (Cochet et al., 2008). This study contributes to a theoretical examination of a franchise as a microcosm of society in which decisions have both economic and socioemotional consequences (Cropanzano & Schminke, 2001). According to Harmon and Griffiths (2008), franchisor success is predicated on franchisee performance, therefore this study makes an important contribution to the franchising literature, as well as real world practice, through an empirical investigation of a conceptual model that focuses on justice as an antecedent to franchisee performance.

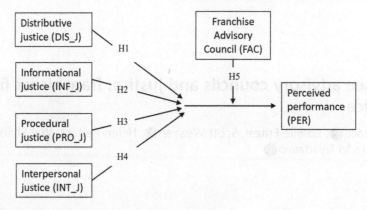

**Figure 1.** Conceptual model on the basis of justice theory.

This paper is organised as follows. The following section outlines the relevant market-ing channels literature laying the requisite theoretical foundation of this research by examining trust and justice as an essential component of relational exchange. Next, the five hypothesized relationships are discussed and a conceptual model is presented (Figure 1). The research method is then described, followed by a description of how the structural model was analysed. Then, our results are presented. Finally, the managerial implications, limitations, and areas for future research are discussed.

## 2. Marketing channels literature

A plethora of research has examined the intricacies of group cohesion in business-to-business settings, focusing on *conflict* (Anderson & Narus, 1990; Frazer et al., 2012), *power* (El-Ansary & Stern, 1972; Meehan & Wright, 2012) *trust* (Davies et al., 2011; Morgan & Hunt, 1994) and *justice* (Colquitt et al., 2001b; Griffith et al., 2006). Prior research suggests that the topic of justice forms a significant part of social interaction within marketing channels: behaviour that is right or good in society when members may have competing desires or opposing interests (Kolm, 2002). In a similar vein, justice within franchising is an important topic because individuals often have competing desires or opposing interests (Felstead, 1993). Indeed, from a social exchange theoretic perspective, franchisors and franchisees engage in a number of routine and irregular interactions focused on mutually beneficial outcomes, although the quality of such interactions are predicated on perceptions of interorganisational justice (Croonen & Hamming, 2019; Shaikh et al., 2017).

Despite this, one under-researched factor in the marketing channels literature is perceived unfairness (for notable exceptions see: Croonen, 2010; Kaufmann & Stern, 1988; Samaha et al., 2011). Perceived unfairness is a 'relationship-destroying factor' (Samaha et al., 2011, p. 99) as unfair acts are viewed as a direct threat to a person's self-identity and thus escalates the emotional imperative to punish unfair partners (Turillo et al., 2002). This is often further aggravated in the franchising context because of the unilateral contract between the two parties (Buchan, 2009). The franchisee and franchisor are considered to be in a business 'marriage' (Doherty & Alexander, 2004), one fraught with obstacles, macro-economic chal-lenges, incomplete information and as well as a business relationship subject to a myriad of ethical considerations (Hendrikse & Windsperger, 2011). Hence, the franchising relationship has been chosen as the context in which to investigate the implications of justice, and how this impacts on franchisee performance.

Trust is a multi-faceted construct (Yamagishi & Yamagishi, 1994) and an essential component of relational exchange within marketing channels (Fukuyama, 1995; Fulmer & Gelfand, 2012; Mayer et al., 1995; Rotter, 1967). According to Ring and Van de Ven (1994), trust in business relationships involve two key elements. The first considers trust from a business risk perspective whereby one party can confidently trust another because of the protection of formal mechanisms (Yakimova et al., 2019). These mechanisms include the law, insurance policies, organizational hierarchy, and industry codes such as the Franchising Code of Conduct (1998) found in Australia. The second emphasizes the moral integrity of individuals as reason enough to trust (Colquitt et al., 2007). Two crucial aspects of any relationship are the level of trust shared between the parties (Morgan & Hunt, 1994) and the duration of the relationship (Dwyer et al., 1987). Typically, the franchisee will interact with the franchisor over an extended period of time, thus it is not a discrete and simple transaction, instead, it is an enduring relational exchange (Croonen & Broekhuizen, 2019) with the capacity for both just and unjust behavior.

## 3. Hypothesized relationships

Colquitt (2001) discusses a measure for organizational justice along four dimensions: distributive justice, informational justice, procedural justice, and interpersonal justice. *Distributive justice* exists where the fairness of outcomes is perceived as reasonable for everyone according to the goals of a particular situation (Deutsch, 1975; Leventhal, 1976). This type of justice exists when the reward is reflective of the effort (Leventhal, 1976) and implies a positive incentive to co-operate (Narasimhan et al., 2013). Within the franchising context, under the umbrella of relational exchange, both the franchisee and the franchisor reasonably expect generalized reciprocity (Kaufmann & Dant, 1992; Shockley & Turner, 2016). Thus, we propose higher perceptions of distributive justice will have a positive influence on the financial goals of running the business (perceived performance). As justice is a social construct (Colquitt et al., 2001b), we propose to empirically examine the franchisee's subjective perception of both justice and their own business performance in comparison to other similar franchisees within the same franchise system (see Lado et al., 2008). Table 1 showcases the measure items for the constructs described in the following five hypotheses. For hypothesis one, we suggest:

*H1: Perceived distributive justice has a positive influence on perceived performance.*

*Informational justice* falls under the umbrella of the interactional justice construct first introduced by Bies and Moag (1986) whereby characteristics such as respect and truthfulness where assessed during the interaction of channel members. Informational justice has been discussed in the literature as contributing toward collective esteem (Colquitt, 2001), organisational citizenship behaviours (B. T. Lim & Loosemore, 2017), feelings of inclusion (Tyler & Bies, 1990), and salience of in-group membership (Luhtanen & Crocker, 1992). We consider information justice in terms of a franchisees willingness to feel comfortable disclosing sensitive and personal information to their franchisor; in other words, their willingness to trust their franchisor. We utilise Gillespie's (2003) Behavioral Trust Inventory

(BTI) scale in this research given its accuracy in assessing trust, rather than perceptions of trustworthiness. The BTI scale has been used or cited in many publications (for example, Heyns & Rothmann, 2016; Lam et al., 2013) and captures a person's willingness to be vulnerable (reliance-based trust) as well as a person's willingness to share work-related or personal information of a sensitive nature within a team setting (disclosure-based trust). This willingness to disclose sensitive information assesses the complexity of highly *inter-dependent* work relationships and requires the presence of informational justice. Accordingly, we hypothesize:

*H2: Perceived informational justice has a positive influence on perceived performance.*

*Procedural justice* exists when fairness is attributed to the type of processes and policies used to manage the exchange relationship (Tyler, 1994). In the context of franchising, franchisee confidence in the franchise system procedures and policies is important as the franchisee is dependent upon the franchisor to maintain brand equity and value (Shaikh et al., 2018). Furthermore, Walker et al. (1979) equated process controls with procedural justice. Within the franchising relationship, process controls belong with the franchisor (Doherty & Alexander, 2006). The perceived procedural justice of the franchisor contains two dimensions: the integrity of the individual and how they solve problems. Integrity is defined as the extent to which one acts in accordance with strong moral and ethical principles (Colquitt et al., 2007). Within franchising, the integrity of the franchisor will be deemed appropriate if they are seen to be honest, have a strong sense of procedural justice, and are consistent (Jackson & Jung, 2017). According to Davies et al. (2011) a franchisee is more likely to be compliant with system procedures and policies if they deem their franchisor to have high levels of integrity. The second dimension of franchisor fairness is their problem-solving orientation (PSO) defined as the franchisee's evaluation of their franchisor's capability to anticipate and satisfactorily resolve problems that may arise during the relationship. Problem solving is characterized by behaviors that are cooperative and integrative, and thus consistent with procedural justice components (Calantone et al., 1998). We propose a franchisee's perception of procedural justice will have a positive influence on perceived performance.

*H3: Perceived procedural justice has a positive influence on perceived performance.*

*Interpersonal Justice* refers to the degree to which people are treated with respect (Colquitt, 2001). The frequency of interpersonal interactions make it psychologically meaningful when people are recognized (Bies, 2005) and franchisees feel appreciated when their franchisor recognizes their successes and efforts; providing an enhanced sense of belonging (Strutton et al., 1993). This sense of belonging and recognition would impact on franchisee morale and willingness to share information with their franchisor (Shaikh, 2016). El Akremi et al. (2011) categorise this as entrepreneurial teamwork whereby interpersonal interaction among franchisees and franchisors leads to greater levels of shared experiences, sharing of vital information, socializing, and cohesion. The authors found support for their hypothesis testing perceptions of cohesion as negatively related to franchisee deviation from standards. Therefore, interpersonal justice is expected to have a positive influence on perceived performance because high levels of interpersonal justice promote a psychologically meaningful environment were entrepreneurial teamwork improves performance. While this construct is similar to informational justice – in that it falls under the same umbrella of interactional justice – there is evidence that these constructs have independent effects (Colquitt, 2001; Shapiro et al., 1994). Thus, we propose:

*H4: Perceived interpersonal justice has a positive influence on perceived performance.*

*Moderating role of Franchise Advisory Council.* In franchising, interfirm conflict among members inevitably arises because franchisors and franchisees have a different lens when it comes to solving problems (Cumberland, 2015). Mainly, this is because the power balance favors the franchisors (J. Lim & Frazer, 2002), as they retain the rights to the brand and it is also the franchisors that determine the contractual terms (Dant et al., 2011). However, franchisees are self-employed business owners who also play a critical role in the success of this marketing channel despite power imbalances. Thus, there is need for effective governance mechanisms that can foster collaborative interfirm relationships to build trust and enhance information exchange between firms (Sheng et al., 2005). As a result, Franchise Advisory Councils (FACs) were formed around the 1970 s to help counterbalance power and alleviate increasing tensions between franchisees and franchisors by offering a formal mechanism for franchisees' voice to be heard (Boroian & Boroian, 1987). Unlike other independent franchise associations, FACs (also referred to as franchisee councils/associations) were initiated and supported by franchisors with the goal of helping the franchise system to gain a competitive edge by drawing on the knowledge of franchisees and promoting a healthy franchisor–franchisee relationship (Bellin, 2016; Lawrence & Kaufmann, 2010). In other words, a franchisee council is 'an elected or selected group of franchisees who meet with representatives of the franchise headquarters to discuss and provide advice on issues of importance to all franchisees' (Dandridge & Falbe, 1994, p. 43). According to the International Franchise Association (IFA), FACs have a common goal of providing 'constructive two-way communications between a franchisor and the franchisees of the system' (Wulff, 2005, p. 4).

However, most studies in franchising have focused on the franchisor–franchisee relationship (see Harmon & Griffiths, 2008; Weaven et al., 2010). Yet, despite the unequivocal role played by FACs, there is very little empirical evidence on the impact they have on the relationship between the franchisees and franchisors (Cumberland, 2015). Croonen (2010, p. 194) adds that very few researchers have examined 'the role of FACs in franchise systems, their mechanisms, and their influence on franchisees' perceptions of trust and fairness'. Evidence shows that franchise systems that are governed by FACs have a competitive edge since franchisors rely on FACs to keep abreast of franchisees' concerns, collect market know-how, and offer a platform for effective horizontal communication rather than vertical top-down approach (Wulff, 2005). In other studies, the results have been inconsistent and research showed that the use of FACs proved to be ineffective in driving a firm's growth (McCosker et al., 1995). Moreover, Cochet and Ehrmann (2007) confirmed that institutional arrangements such as FACs tend to protect franchisees against moral hazards emanating from the franchisor. Given that the primary role of an FAC is to ensure homogeneity in interfirm practices (Miller-Millesen, 2003; Nicholson & Newton, 2010), we expect FACs to provide essential boundary mechanisms on the link between perceived justice and perceived performance in a franchisor–franchisee relationship. Croonen (2010) contends that franchisees' perceptions of distributive, procedural, and interactional fairness (also referred to as justice) are critical elements of franchisees' trust perceptions that drive firm performance especially during times of strategic change. We therefore expect the presence (absence) of FACs in a franchise system to strengthen (weaken) the effects of the dimensions of perceived justice on perceived performance. Hence:

*H5: Franchise Advisory Council membership moderates the relationship between perceived justice and perceived performance.*

## 4. Method

### 4.1. *Sample and data collection procedure*

Some 1,626 survey invitations were sent to the small business panel and the sample returned 209 usable responses for analysis purposes, or a response rate of approximately 13%. Data were collected using a global and reputable market research company (ISO 20252 accredited). The company utilised their localised business owner panel to provide the necessary sample. Table 2 shows the demographic characteristics of the sample. Respondents were asked a set of questions and asked to rate their agreement/disagreement based on a 7 point Likert scale ranging from 'strongly disagree' to 'strongly agree'. During the pre-test phase the data was analysed to check the psychometric properties such as reliability and effect size. Each scale had between items, some of which included reverse-coded questions. After reliability statistics were undertaken, the questionnaire was shortened by 27 items so that each construct was robust and reliable.

## 5. Analysis and Results

### 5.1. *Exploratory factor analysis*

We conducted EFA using principle component method with oblimin rotation. The pattern matrix is shown in Table 3. Oblique rotation was chosen because correlations between the justice factors were reasonably high (Corner, 2009). Kaiser-Meyer-Olkin (KMO) =.963 and the Barlett's Test of Sphericity test was significant at .000, indicating the suitability of conducting exploratory analysis on the sample (n = 209) (Kaiser, 1974). As shown in Table 3, a very clean five-factor structure emerged with high factor loadings. Factor loadings of .50 or higher will be considered significant (Henson & Roberts, 2006). Communalities vary between .725 and .874. Finally, the five-factor structure had a total variance explained of 80.48%, with all five extracted factors having eigenvalues above 1.0.

## 6. Confirmatory factor analysis

### 6.1. *Model fit*

We conducted CFA to test for the factorial validity of the independent variable, which is perceived justice, consisting distributive justice (DIS_J), informational justice (INF_J), procedural justice (PRO_J), and interpersonal justice (INT_J), and the dependent variable, which is perceived performance (PER). Table 4 shows that all the constructs have items

**Table 1.** Measure items.

| Construct | Measures | Source | Code |
|---|---|---|---|
| Distributive justice | Even if costs and benefits are not evenly shared between the franchisor and myself, in a given time period, they balance out over time. | Kaufmann and Dant (1992) | DIS_J1 |
| (DIS_J) | We each benefit and earn in proportion to the efforts my franchisor and I put in. (reverse coded) | Kaufmann and Dant (1992) | DIS_J2 |
| | My business usually gets a fair share of the rewards and cost-savings in doing business with the franchisor. | Kaufmann and Dant (1992) | DIS_J3 |
| | In our relationship, none of us benefits more than one deserves. | Kaufmann and Dant (1992) | DIS_J4 |
| Informational justice | Depend on your franchisor to handle an important issue on your behalf. | Gillespie (2003) | INF_J1 |
| (INF_J) | Depend on him or her to back you up in difficult situations. | Gillespie (2003) | INF_J2 |
| | Share your personal feelings with him or her. | Gillespie (2003) | INF_J3 |
| | Discuss work-related problems or difficulties with your franchisor that could potentially be used to disadvantage you. | Gillespie (2003) | INF_J4 |
| | Discuss how you honestly feel about your work, even negative feelings and frustration. | Gillespie (2003) | INF_J5 |
| | Share your personal beliefs with him or her. | Gillespie (2003) | INF_J6 |
| Procedural justice | The franchisor (CEO, founder, leader) has a strong sense of justice | Mayer et al. (1995) | PRO_J1 |
| (PRO_J) | The franchisor tries hard to be fair in dealing with others | Mayer et al. (1995) | PRO_J2 |
| | The franchisor (CEO, founder, leader) doesn't hesitate to take care of any problems I might have | Sirdeshmukh et al (2002) | PRO_J3 |
| | The franchisor goes out of their way to solve my problems | Sirdeshmukh et al (2002) | PRO_J4 |
| | Problems are dealt with in a timely manner | Sirdeshmukh et al (2002) | PRO_J5 |
| Interpersonal justice | I can count on a pat on the back from my franchisor when my store performs well. | Strutton et al. (1995) | INT_J1 |
| (INT_J) | My franchisor knows what my strengths are and lets me know it. | Strutton et al. (1995) | INT_J2 |
| | My franchisor is quick to recognise good performance. | Strutton et al. (1995) | INT_J3 |
| Performance(PER) | Compared to other similar franchisees in this franchise system, our performance is very high in terms of: Sales growth | Lado et al. (2008) | PER_1 |
| | Profit growth | Lado et al. (2008) | PER_2 |
| | Labor Productivity | Lado et al. (2008) | PER_3 |
| | Cash Flow | Lado et al. (2008) | PER_4 |

* Notes: All items use a 7-point scale with anchors of 1 = strongly disagree and 7 = strongly agree

with significant loadings (standardized regression weights equal and greater than .80). Table 5 shows that the goodness of fit for our measurement model is sufficient. We can conclude that the measurement model fits the data well.

## 6.2. Validity and reliability

In order to assess reliability, we computed composite reliability (CR) for each construct (see Table 6). In all cases, the CR was above the minimum threshold of .70 (Hair et al., 2010), indicating we have reliability in our constructs. The maximal reliability (MaxR) was also above .90 in all cases, indicating that MaxR and CR scores were consistent (Raykov et al., 2015). Convergent validity was estimated using average variance extracted (AVE). As shown in Table 6, all values of the AVE were above the recommended cutoff level of .50 (Fornell & Larcker, 1981). Thus, convergent validity of the constructs was established.

**Table 2.** Demographic characteristics of sample.

| Franchisee demographic characteristic | Total | Percentage |
|---|---|---|
| GENDER | | |
| Male | 125 | 59.8% |
| Female | 84 | 40.2% |
| AGE | | |
| 21–30 years | 46 | 23.4% |
| 31–40 years | 74 | 35.4% |
| 41–50 years | 46 | 23.4% |
| 51–60 years | 28 | 13.4% |
| Over 60 years | 15 | 7.2% |
| LENGTH OF OWNERSHIP OF FRANCHISE UNIT | | |
| Less than 6 months | 24 | 11.5% |
| 6 months to a year | 42 | 20.1% |
| 1 to 3 years | 65 | 31.1% |
| 4 to 7 years | 55 | 26.3% |
| 8 to 10 years | 14 | 6.7% |
| More that 10 years* | 8 | 3.8% |
| INITIAL INVESTMENT** | | |
| Below $100,000 | 75 | 35.9% |
| $100,001 to $200,00 | 40 | 19.2% |
| $200,001 to $300,000 | 53 | 25.3% |
| $300,001 to $400,00 | 29 | 13.9% |
| Over $400,000 | 12 | 5.7% |

\* The maximum length of ownership was 30 years.
\*\* Currency shown in AUD.

**Table 3.** Pattern matrix and reliability test.

| Items | Factor loadings | | | | |
|---|---|---|---|---|---|
| | 1Distributive jus-tice (DIS_J) | 2Informational justice(INF_J) | 3Procedural jus-tice(PRO_J) | 4Interpersonal justice (INT_J) | 5Perceived performance(PER) |
| DIS_J1 | .468 | | | | |
| DIS_J2 | .458 | | | | |
| DIS_J3 | .535 | | | | |
| DIS_J4 | .558 | | | | |
| Cronbach's alpha | .920 | | | | |
| INF_J1 | | .646 | | | |
| INF_J2 | | .725 | | | |
| INF_J3 | | .851 | | | |
| INF_J4 | | .679 | | | |
| INF_J5 | | .882 | | | |
| INF_J6 | | .992 | | | |
| Cronbach's alpha | | .939 | | | |
| PRO_J1 | | | −.604 | | |
| PRO_J2 | | | −.810 | | |
| PRO_J3 | | | −.745 | | |
| PRO_J4 | | | −.879 | | |
| PRO_J5 | | | −.833 | | |
| Cronbach's alpha | | | .937 | | |
| INT_J1 | | | | .548 | |
| INT_J2 | | | | .690 | |
| INT_J3 | | | | .675 | |
| Cronbach's alpha | | | | .900 | |
| PER1 | | | | | .824 |
| PER2 | | | | | .866 |
| PER3 | | | | | .632 |
| PER4 | | | | | .801 |
| Cronbach's alpha | | | | | .918 |

Extraction method: Principal Component Analysis.
Rotation Method: Oblimin with Kaiser Normalization.
Rotation converged in 16 iterations.

**Table 4.** Factor loadings in CFA.

| Construct | Items | Estimate (Standardized regression weights) |
|---|---|---|
| DISTRIBUTIVE JUSTICE | DIS_J→DIS1 | .888 |
| | DIS_J→DIS2 | .873 |
| | DIS_J→DIS3 | .861 |
| | DIS_J→DIS4 | .824 |
| INFORMATIONAL JUSTICE | INF_J→INF_J1 | .827 |
| | INF_J→INF_J2 | .855 |
| | INF_J→INF_J3 | .852 |
| | INF_J→INF_J4 | .813 |
| PROCEDURAL JUSTICE | PRO_J→PRO_J1 | .849 |
| | PRO_J→PRO_J2 | .849 |
| | PRO_J→PRO_J3 | .878 |
| | PRO_J→PRO_J4 | .867 |
| | PRO_J→PRO_J5 | .881 |
| | PRO_J→PRO_J6 | .850 |
| INTERPERSONAL JUSTICE | INT_J→INT_J1 | .883 |
| | INT_J→INT_J2 | .842 |
| | INT_J→INT_J3 | .871 |
| PERCEIVED PERFORMANCE | PER→PER1 | .888 |
| | PER→PER2 | .886 |
| | PER→PER3 | .793 |

**Table 5.** Goodness of fit statistics in CFA.

| Goodness of fit indices | Observed values | Recommended cutoff | References |
|---|---|---|---|
| Chi-square | 357.556 (df = 199) | p >.05 | Byrne (2010) |
| CMIN/DF ($\chi^2$/df) | 1.797 | 1< $\chi^2$/df <3 | Hu and Bentler (1998) |
| RMSEA | .062 | <.05 good fit | Hair et al. (2010) |
| | | <.06 mediocre fit | MacCallum and Austin (2000) |
| PCLOSE | .031 | >.05 | Jöreskog and Sörbom (1993) |
| GFI | .866 | >.90 | |
| AGFI | .830 | >.80 | |
| NFI | .924 | >.90 | |
| CFI | .965 | >.95 | |
| TLI | .959 | 0< TLI<1 | |

**Table 6.** Reliability and validity in CFA.

| | CR | AVE | MSV | MaxR(H) | PRO_J | DIS_J | INF_J | INT_J | PER |
|---|---|---|---|---|---|---|---|---|---|
| PRO_J | 0.937 | 0.748 | 0.728 | 0.938 | 0.865[a] | | | | |
| DIS_J | 0.920 | 0.742 | 0.837 | 0.923 | 0.853[b] | 0.861[a] | | | |
| INF_J | 0.935 | 0.706 | 0.726 | 0.936 | 0.852[b] | 0.796[b] | 0.840[a] | | |
| INT_J | 0.900 | 0.749 | 0.837 | 0.901 | 0.848[b] | 0.915[b] | 0.783[b] | 0.865[a] | |
| PER | 0.919 | 0.740 | 0.687 | 0.924 | 0.773[b] | 0.825[b] | 0.673[b] | 0.829[b] | 0.860[a] |

Square root of AVE.
Correlation between factors.

One of the advantages of confirmatory factor analysis using SEM is that this type of analysis is very flexible when examining a pattern of relationships between variables on the basis of theory or previous research. This flexibility includes the ability in SEM modelling to include and specify factors that are significantly correlated with each other (non-discriminant) as well as those that are independent of one another (discriminant) (de Vellis, 2003). To test for discriminant validity, we compared the mean shared variance (MSVs) to the AVEs. As shown in Table 6, the results have demonstrated evidence of discriminant validity for the construct of procedural justice (PRO_J) and perceived performance (PER) (MSVs < AVEs). For the other

**Table 7.** Hypotheses summary table.

| Hypotheses | | Model parameters | Supported |
|---|---|---|---|
| H1 | DIS_J→PER | .358* | Yes |
| H2 | INF_J→PER | −.125 | No |
| H3 | PRO_J→PER | .236 | No |
| H4 | INT_J→PER | .400* | Yes |
| Moderation | | | |
| H5 | DIS_J→PER (FAC = Yes) | .996*** | Yes |
| | DIS_J→PER (FAC = No) | −.487 | |
| | | $\Delta z$ score = −.3114*** | |
| | INT→PER (FAC = Yes) | .056 | |
| | INT→PER (FAC = No) | 1.138** | |
| | | $\Delta z$ score = 2.221** | |

*$p$ <.05.
**$p$ <.01.
***$p$ <.001.

three constructs, that is, distributional justice (DIS_J), informational justice (INF_J), and inter-personal justice (INT_J), MSVs > AVEs, indicating a lack of discriminant validity. However, examination of modification indices indicate that there was no cross-loading item in the model (Farrell & Rudd, 2009). Therefore, the measurement model was appropriately described and reliability and validity of the constructs were confirmed.

### 6.3. Invariance tests

As shown in the theoretical framework (Figure 1), the moderating variable was categorical (Yes or No) where respondents indicated whether or not their franchise system has a Franchise Advisory Council (FAC). We conducted the invariance tests to assess the equivalence of the two groups of respondents in relation to the four-factor structure of perceived justice.

The unconstrained measurement models (with two groups loaded separately) showed an adequate fit ($\chi^2$ = 741.052, df = 398, CMIN/DF = 1.862, CFI = .925, RMSEA = .065), indicating the measurement model was configurally invariant between two groups of respondents. After constraining the models to be equal, the model fit obtained was sufficient ($\chi^2$ = 759.747, df = 420, CMIN/DF = 1.809, CFI = .926, RMSEA = .063). Furthermore, the chi-square difference test was insignificant (chi-square difference = 18.7, df = 22, $p$ = .664). Thus, the model meets the metric invariance test between the two groups of respondents.

### 6.4. Structural model and hypotheses testing

The overall structural model (moderator not included) displays a good model fit (chi-square = 357.6, df = 199, CMIN/DF ($\chi^2$/df) = 1.797), the same as the full measurement model in CFA (see Table 5). Figure 2 shows the standardized parameters of the structural model (n = 209). The two significant predictors of perceived performance were distributive justice (β = .358, $p$ = .031) and interpersonal justice (β = .400, $p$ = .016). Thus, H1 and H4 were supported. However, informational justice (β = −1.25, $p$ = .216) and procedural

**Structural model (n=209)**

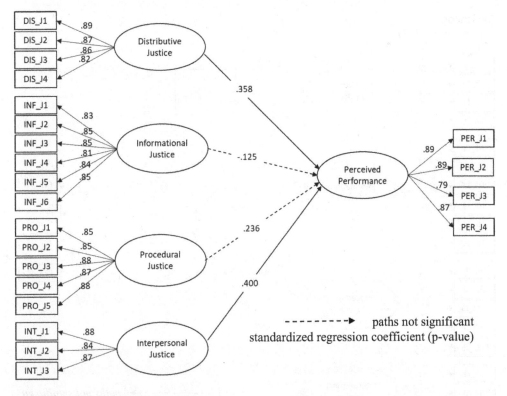

**Figure 2.** Structural model (n = 209).

justice (β = .236, *p* = .016) were not significant. Thus, H2 and H 3 were not supported. The results are summarized in the hypotheses summary (Table 7).

### 6.5. Multi-group differences

We also tested the moderating effect of FAC membership. The results indicated that when respondents indicated their franchise system belongs to a Franchise Advisory Council (FAC), the significant predictor was distributive justice (β = .966, p = .000). When respondents indicated that their franchise system does not belong to a FAC, the significant predictor was interpersonal justice (β = 1.138, p = .008), whereas distributive justice was not significant (β = −.487, p = .187). Figure 3 shows the standardized parameters of the structural model as influenced by the moderator FAC. Further analyses shows that the two groups (FAC = YES/NO) were significantly different in relation to distributive justice as a predictor variable of perceived performance (z-score difference = −3.114, p < .001), and the two groups were significantly different in relation to interpersonal justice as a predictor variable of perceived performance (z-score difference = 2.221, p < .01). Thus, H5 was supported.

**Testing moderating effect of FAC**

Moderator:
FAC = Yes (n=112)

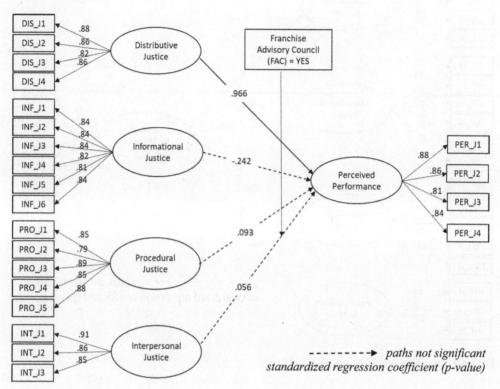

**Figure 3.** Testing moderating effect of FAC.

## 6. Discussion

In accordance with prior recommendations (Paterson et al., 2002) we developed a bank of justice measures that were customized for application in the context of asymmetric exchange relationships. Couched in an equity theoretical lens, our findings reveal significant support for distributive and interpersonal justice as predictors of franchisee perceived performance outcomes. This suggests that franchisee perceptions of unit performance are predicated on their perceptions of fairness on how rewards are allocated to exchange partners proportionate to their efforts, and how they perceive their treatment within the franchise system to be characterized by politeness, respect and with dignity. Given that franchising is a relational business model that permits franchisees to be in business 'for themselves, not by themselves' (Weaven et al., 2009), perceived business performance is contingent upon the assessment of the quality of interpersonal exchanges (for example, provision of guidance with local marketing initiatives and advice pertaining to day-to-day operations). Moreover, as partners in the franchise system, how franchisee contributions (for example, royalty fees, advertising levies) are distributed in

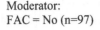

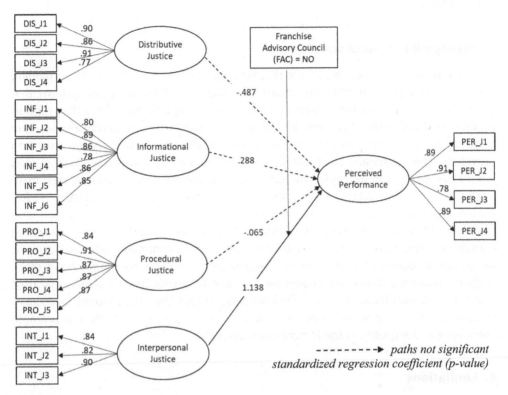

**Figure 3.** (Continued).

the system will impact business performance perceptions. The insignificant effects for both procedural and informational justice may be due to the unique characteristics of franchising compared to other organizational arrangements. Franchisees may perceive the legal franchising agreement as representative of a fair, truthful and transparent mechanism which clearly explicates the roles, rights and responsibilities of both parties throughout the term of the relationship.

Perhaps, the most salient findings arising from our research lie in revealing support for the moderating effects of FAC membership. Franchisees in systems with FACs do not rely upon perceived interpersonal justice to the extent exhibited by franchisees within non-FAC systems. Instead, franchisees in FAC systems rely predominantly on perceptions of *distributive justice* (e.g. fair distribution of rewards as compared with effort put in) as the most important contributor to their perceived performance. This may be because the FACs provide franchisees with a 'voice' ensuring respectful two-way communications with recourse to procedures aimed at rectifying any interpersonal difficulties that may affect performance outcomes. In contrast, franchisees within systems that do not have an operational FAC consider *interpersonal justice* in the form of depth of interpersonal understanding, appropriate recognition, and respectful treatment of franchisees by their franchisors, as more important than distributive justice. In this way, the absence of a franchisee collective relegates fairness in interpersonal exchanges (and concomitant perceptions of unit performance) to the level of the individual.

## 7. Managerial implications

Our findings reveal the significant role that Franchisee Advisory Councils play in shaping the justice and performance perceptions of franchisees. Franchisors in systems that encourage FAC membership should emphasise processes and operations that support positive distributive justice perceptions. For instance, franchisors could provide clear and ongoing details on how royalty fees are being utilised (and what services are being provided), how advertising funds are being distributed across franchisee localities, and ensure transparency in franchisor earnings. Non-FAC franchisee members are best managed via high-quality interpersonal interactions. For these franchisees, positive performance expectations are best encouraged through ensuring polite, dignified and respectful interactions. Franchisors should adhere to these standards when providing operational support, marketing assistance, recommending continuing education, and so on, across all points of contact in the organization (e.g. area managers, head office support). However, should franchisors be less able to demonstrate interpersonal trust when dealing with franchisees, our findings suggest that the establishment and maintenance of FACs may serve to boost franchisee perceptions of fairness and promote confidence in the quality of the franchising relationship.

## 8. Limitations

Although the contributions of this study to the relational sentiments literature in franchising is manifest, it is not without some limitations. Although the data were collected online via a market research company, the low sample size (n = 209) may not be fully representative of the Australian franchisee population. Second, our study did not capture objective franchisee performance data. However, we argue that explanatory power of such data may be impacted by macro-level conditions. For example, measures of distributive justice may be inflated in thriving economic conditions, however, through no fault of the franchisor or franchises system, performance may be influenced by macroeconomic uncertainty and difficult business conditions. Accordingly, we follow Lado et al.'s (2008) approach in capturing franchisee ratings of their own performance. While this may be subject to some bias and inflation, prior research has argued that it is a valid measure in that it seeks franchisee performance assessments against other (similar) franchisees in the system (of which they would possess detailed knowledge). However, future research utilising objective financial performance measures may be of value in future investigations.

## 9. Future research

This empirical examination sheds light on relational exchange within the franchise channel relationship: examined within the context of organizational justice, both distributive and interpersonal justice were found to play an important role in the franchising relationship and support was found for a link to high levels of performance.

If trust is generally considered to be an essential component of exchange (Mayer et al., 1995; Fulmer et al., 2012), research-linking justice and trust is of significant value. However, this continues to be a challenging endeavour because as Colquitt and Rodell (2011) elucidate, conventional wisdom assumes that justice leads to trust. Consistent with their insight, this research suggests that it is distributive and inter-personal justice that leads to firm performance. As an entrepreneurial enterprise, the franchisee is engaged in an effort to secure a 'good life' (Storholm & Scheuing, 1994) and perhaps it is not so much trust that provides this (i.e. their willingness to be vulnerable) instead it is the mutually satisfying influence of fairness of outcome (distributive justice) and recognition from the franchisor (interpersonal justice) linked to strong financial performance. However, as procedural justice in organizations develop over time (Pignata et al., 2016) further investigation on how the quality of franchisor–franchisee interactions impacts procedural justice perceptions (and trust in the relationship) is warranted. Moreover, the lack of support for informational justice may require further investigation as a lack of transparency in franchisor communica-tions has been linked to lower levels of perceived trust in franchising relationships (S. K. Weaven et al., 2014).

We found clear support for the moderating effect of FAC membership. However, prior research provides evidence of the downside of FACs in which franchisees have cited 'favoritism', 'unfairness', and 'fake franchisee involvement' caused by a lack of clear procedures on how franchisee representatives are selected as well as their rights and obligations (Brand et al., 2016). Therefore, future research should investigate the dark side of FACs and how they can negatively impact franchise performance, or perhaps how the dark side of FACs impacts the four dimensions of justice.

## Acknowledgments

In memory of Professor Rajiv P. Dant, with thanks and with admiration

## Informed Consent

Informed consent was obtained from all individual participants included in the study.

## Research involving human participants

All procedures performed in studies involving human participants were in accordance with the ethical standards of the institutional and/or national research committee and with the 1964 Helsinki declaration and its later amendments or comparable ethical standards. GU Ethics approved ethical clearance number: MKT/11/13/HREC.

## ORCID

Anthony Grace http://orcid.org/0000-0001-7899-7646
Scott Weaven http://orcid.org/0000-0001-9150-7111
Munyaradzi Nyadzayo http://orcid.org/0000-0003-0802-2119

# References

Anderson, J. C., & Narus, J. A. (1990). A model of distributor firm and manufacturer firm working partnerships. *Journal of Marketing, 54*(1), 42–58. https://doi.org/10.1177/002224299005400103

Bellin, H. (2016). Good Franchising. *Journal of Marketing Channels, 23*(1–2), 77–80. https://doi.org/10.1080/1046669X.2016.1147893

Bies, R. J. (2005). Are procedural justice and interactional justice conceptually distinct? In J. Greenberg & J. A. Colquitt (Eds.), *Handbook of organizational justice* (pp. 85–112). Lawrence Erlbaum.

Bies, R. J., & Moag, J. F. (1986). Interactional justice: Communication criteria of fairness. In R. J. Lewicki, B, H, Sheppard, & M. H. Bazerman. (Eds). *Research on Negotiation in Organizations, 1*, 43–55.

Boroian, D. D., & Boroian, P. J. (1987). *The franchise advantage: Make it work for you.* National Bestseller Publication.

Brand, M. J., Croonen, E. P., & Welsh, D. H. (2016). Successfully managing chain-wide transformational change. *Organizational Dynamics, 45*(2), 94–103. https://doi.org/10.1016/j.orgdyn.2016.02.003

Buchan, J. (2009). Consumer protection for franchisees of failed franchisors: Is there a need for statutory intervention. *Queensland University of Technology Law & Just for Fun, 9*(2) 232–250. https://doi.org/10.5204/qutlr.v9i2.30

Byrne, B. (2010). *Structural equation modeling with AMOS: Basic concepts, applications, and programming* (2nd ed.). Routledge: New York.

Calantone, R. J., Graham, J. L., & Mintu-Wimsatt, A. (1998). Problem-solving approach in an international context: Antecedents and outcome. *International Journal of Research in Marketing, 15*(1), 19–35. https://doi.org/10.1016/S0167-8116(97)00028-1

Cochet, O., Dormann, J., & Ehrmann, T. (2008). Capitalizing on franchisee autonomy: Relational forms of governance as controls in idiosyncratic franchise dyads. *Journal of Small Business Management, 46*(1), 50–72. https://doi.org/10.1111/jsbm.2008.46.issue-1

Cochet, O., & Ehrmann, T. (2007). Preliminary evidence on the appointment of institutional solutions to franchisor moral hazard—the case of franchisee councils. *Managerial and Decision Economics, 28*(1), 41–55. https://doi.org/10.1002/()1099-1468

Colquitt, J. A. (2001). On the dimensionality of organizational justice: A construct validation of a measure. *Journal of Applied Psychology, 86*(3), 386. https://doi.org/10.1037/0021-9010.86.3.386

Colquitt, J. A., Conlon, D. E., Wesson, M. J., Porter, C. O., & Ng, K. Y. (2001b). Justice at the millennium: A meta-analytic review of 25 years of organizational justice research. *Journal of Applied Psychology, 86*(3), 425. https://doi.org/10.1037/0021-9010.86.3.425

Colquitt, J. A., & Rodell, J. B. (2011). Justice, trust, and trustworthiness: A longitudinal analysis integrating three theoretical perspectives. *Academy of Management Journal, 54*(6), 1183–1206. https://doi.org/10.5465/amj.2007.0572

Colquitt, J. A., Scott, B. A., & LePine, J. A. (2007). Trust, trustworthiness, and trust propensity: A meta-analytic test of their unique relationships with risk taking and job performance. *Journal of Applied Psychology, 92*(4), 909. https://doi.org/10.1037/0021-9010.92.4.909

Corner, S. (2009). Choosing the right type of rotation in PCA and EFA. *JALT Testing & Evaluation SIG Newsletter, 13*(3), 20–25. http://hosted.jalt.org/test/PDF/Brown31.pdf

Croonen, E. P. (2010). Trust and fairness during strategic change processes in franchise systems. *Journal of Business Ethics, 95*(2), 191–209. https://doi.org/10.1007/s10551-009-0354-z

Croonen, E. P., & Broekhuizen, T. L. (2019). How do franchisees assess franchisor trustworthiness? *Journal of Small Business Management, 57*(3), 845–871. https://doi.org/10.1111/jsbm.v57.3

Croonen, E. P., & Hamming, R. (2019). They are jolly good fellows! A framework for antecedents and consequences of peer trust in franchise networks. In J. Windsperger, G. Cliquet, G. Hendrikse, M. Srećković (Eds.), *Design and Management of Interfirm Networks.* Contributions to Management Science. Springer, Cham. https://doi.org/10.1007/978-3-030-29245-4_3

Cropanzano, R., & Schminke, M. (2001). Using social justice to build effective work groups. In M. Turner (Ed.), *Groups at work: Theory and research* (pp. 143–171). Erlbaum.

Cumberland, D. M. (2015). Advisory councils in franchising: Advancing a theory-based typology. *Journal of Marketing Channels, 22*(3), 175–191. https://doi.org/10.1080/1046669X.2015.1071587

Dandridge, T. C., & Falbe, C. M. (1994). The influence of franchisees beyond their local domain. *International Small Business Journal, 12*(2), 39–50. https://doi.org/10.1177/0266242694122004

Dant, R. P., Grünhagen, M., & Windsperger, J. (2011). Franchising research frontiers for the twenty-first century. *Journal of Retailing, 87*(3), 253–268. https://doi.org/10.1016/j.jretai.2011.08.002

Dant, R. P., Weaven, S. K., & Baker, B. L. (2013). Influence of personality traits on perceived relationship quality within a franchisee-franchisor context. *European Journal of Marketing, 47*(1/2), 279–302. https://doi.org/10.1108/03090561311285556

Davies, M. A., Lassar, W., Manolis, C., Prince, M., & Winsor, R. D. (2011). A model of trust and compliance in franchise relationships. *Journal of Business Venturing, 26*(3), 321–340. https://doi.org/10.1016/j.jbusvent.2009.09.005

Deutsch, M. (1975). Equity, equality, and need: What determines which value will be used as the basis of distributive justice? *Journal of Social Issues, 31*(3), 137–149. https://doi.org/10.1111/josi.1975.31.issue-3

Doherty, A. M., & Alexander, N. (2004). Relationship development in international retail franchising: Case study evidence from the UK fashion sector. *European Journal of Marketing, 38*(9/10), 1215–1235. https://doi.org/10.1108/03090560410548942

Doherty, A. M., & Alexander, N. (2006). Power and control in international retail franchising. *European Journal of Marketing, 40*(11/12), 1292–1316. https://doi.org/10.1108/03090560610702821

Dwyer, F. R., Schurr, P. H., & Oh, S. (1987). Developing buyer-seller relationships. *Journal of Marketing, 51*(2), 11–27. https://doi.org/10.1177/002224298705100202

El Akremi, A., Mignonac, K., & Perrigot, R. (2011). Opportunistic behaviors in franchise chains: The role of cohesion among franchisees. *Strategic Management Journal, 32*(9), 930–948. https://doi.org/10.1002/smj.v32.9

El-Ansary, A. I., & Stern, L. W. (1972). Power measurement in the distribution channel. *Journal of Marketing Research, 9*(1), 47–52. https://doi.org/10.1177/002224377200900110

Farrell, A. M., & Rudd, J. M. (2009). *Factor analysis and discriminant validity: A brief review of some practical issues.* Anzmac.

Felstead, A. (1993). *The corporate paradox: Power and control in the business franchise.* Routledge.

Fornell, C., & Larcker, D. F. (1981). Structural equation models with unobservable variables and measurement error. *Algebra and Statistics, 18*(3), 382–388. https://doi.org/10.1177%2F002224378101800313

Frazer, L., Weaven, S., Giddings, J., & Grace, D. (2012). What went wrong? Franchisors and franchisees disclose the causes of conflict in franchising. *Qualitative Market Research: An International Journal, 15*(1), 87–103. https://doi.org/10.1108/13522751211192017

Fukuyama, F. (1995). *Trust: Social virtues and the creation of prosperity.* Free Press.

Fulmer, C. A., & Gelfand, M. J. (2012). At what level (and in Whom) we trust trust across multiple organizational levels. *Journal of Management, 38*(4), 1167–1230. https://doi.org/10.1177%2F0149206312439327

Fulmer, C. A., & Gelfand, M. J. (2012). At what level (and in Whom) we trust trust across multiple organizational levels. *Journal of Management, 38*(4), 1167–1230. https://doi.org/10.1177/0149206312439327

Gillespie, N. (2003). Measuring trust in working relationships: The behavioral trust inventory. In *Academy of management conference, Seattle, WA.*

Gillis, W. E., Combs, J. G., & Yin, X. (2020). Franchise management capabilities and franchisor performance under alternative franchise ownership strategies. *Journal of Business Venturing, 35*(1), 1. https://doi.org/10.1016/j.jbusvent.2018.09.004

Griffith, D. A., Harvey, M. G., & Lusch, R. F. (2006). Social exchange in supply chain relationships: The resulting benefits of procedural and distributive justice. *Journal of Operations Management, 24*(2), 85–98. https://doi.org/10.1016/j.jom.2005.03.003

Hair, J. F., Black, W. C., Babin, B. J., & Anderson, R. E., (2010). *Multivariate data analysis* (7th ed.). Englewood Cliffs: Prentice Hall.

Harmon, T. R., & Griffiths, M. A. (2008). Franchisee perceived relationship value. *Journal of Business & Industrial Marketing, 23*(4), 256–263. https://doi.org/10.1108/08858620810865834

Hendrikse, G., & Windsperger, J. (2011). Determinants of contractual completeness in franchising. In M. Tuunanen, J. Windsperger, G. Cliquet, G. Hendrikse (Eds.), *New developments in the theory of networks* Contributions to Management Science.. Heidelberg: Physica.https://doi.org/10.1007/978-3-7908-2615-9_2

Henson, R. K., & Roberts, J. K. (2006). Use of exploratory factor analysis in published research: Common errors and some comment on improved practice. *Educational and Psychological Measurement, 66*(3), 393–416. https://doi.org/10.1177/0013164405282485

Heyns, M., & Rothmann, S. (2016). Comparing trust levels of male and female managers: Measurement invariance of the Behavioural Trust Inventory. *South African Journal of Psychology, 46*(1), 74–87. https://doi.org/10.1177/0081246315596732

Hu, L. T., & Bentler, P. M. (1998). Fit indices in covariance structure modeling: Sensitivity to under-parameterized model misspecification. *Psychological Methods, 3*(4), 424. https://doi.org/10.1037/1082-989X.3.4.424

Jackson, L. A., & Jung, H. (2017). The lodging franchise relational model: A model of trust, commitment, and resource exchanges. *The Journal of Hospitality Financial Management, 25*(1), 56–73. https://doi.org/10.1080/10913211.2017.1314125

Jöreskog, K. G., & Sörbom, D. (1993). *LISREL 8: Structural equation modeling with the SIMPLIS command language*. Scientific software international. Hillsdale, NJ: Lawrence Erlbaum Associates.

Kaiser, H. F. (1974). An index of factorial simplicity. *Psychometrika, 39*(1), 31–36. https://doi.org/10.1007/BF02291575

Kaufmann, P. J., & Dant, R. P. (1992). The dimensions of commercial exchange. *Marketing Letters, 3*(2), 171–185. https://doi.org/10.1007/BF00993996

Kaufmann, P. J., & Stern, L. W. (1988). Relational exchange norms, perceptions of unfairness, and retained hostility in commercial litigation. *Journal of Conflict Resolution, 32*(3), 534–552. https://doi.org/10.1177/0022002788032003007

Kolm, S. C. (2002). *Modern theories of justice*. MIT Press: Cambridge, Massachusetts.

Lado, A. A., Dant, R. R., & Tekleab, A. G. (2008). Trust-opportunism paradox, relationalism, and performance in interfirm relationships: Evidence from the retail industry. *Strategic Management Journal, 29*(4), 401–423. https://doi.org/10.1002/()1097-0266

Lam, L. W., Loi, R., & Leong, C. (2013). Reliance and disclosure: How supervisory justice affects trust in supervisor and extra-role performance. *Asia Pacific Journal of Management, 30*(1), 231–249. https://doi.org/10.1007/s10490-011-9249-5

Lawrence, B., & Kaufmann, P. J. (2010). Franchise associations: Strategic focus or response to franchisor opportunism. *Journal of Marketing Channels, 17*(2), 137–155. https://doi.org/10.1080/10466691003635119

Leventhal, G. S. (1976). The distribution of rewards and resources in groups and organizations. In L. Berkowitz, and E. Walster, (Eds.), *Advances in experimental social psychology* (Vol. 9, pp. 91–131). New York: Academic Press.

Lim, B. T., & Loosemore, M. (2017). The effect of inter-organizational justice perceptions on organizational citizenship behaviors in construction projects. *International Journal of Project Management, 35*(2), 95–106. https://doi.org/10.1016/j.ijproman.2016.10.016

Lim, J., & Frazer, L. (2002). Introducing franchising regulation: An analysis of the Australian franchising code of conduct. *Journal of Marketing Channels, 10*(2), 39–56. https://doi.org/10.1300/J049v10n02_04

Luhtanen, R., & Crocker, J. (1992). A collective self-esteem scale: Self-evaluation of one's social identity. *Personality and Social Psychology Bulletin, 18*(3), 302–318. https://doi.org/10.1177%2F0146167292183006

MacCallum, R. C., & Austin, J. T. (2000). Applications of structural equation modeling in psychological research. *Annual Review of Psychology, 51*(1), 201–226. https://doi.org/10.1146/annurev.psych.51.1.201

Mayer, R., Davis, J., & Schoorman, F. (1995). An integrative model of organizational trust. *The Academy of Management Review, 20*(3), 709–734. https://doi.org/10.5465/amr.1995.9508080335

McCosker, C., Frazer, L., & Pensiero, D. (1995). An exploration of franchise advisory councils: Expectations and relationships. In *Proceedings of the society for franchising*, A. Dugan (ed.). Society of Franchising: Minneapolis.

Meehan, J., & Wright, G. H. (2012). The origins of power in buyer–seller relationships. *Industrial Marketing Management, 41*(4), 669–679. https://doi.org/10.1016/j.indmarman.2011.09.015

Miller-Millesen, J. L. (2003). Understanding the behavior of non-profit boards of directors: A theory-based approach. *Nonprofit and Voluntary Sector Quarterly, 32*(4), 521–547. https://doi.org/10.1177%2F0899764003257463

Morgan, R. M., & Hunt, S. D. (1994). The commitment-trust theory of relationship marketing. *Journal of Marketing, 58*(3), 20–38. https://doi.org/10.1177%2F002224299405800302

Narasimhan, R., Narayanan, S., & Srinivasan, R. (2013). An investigation of justice in supply chain relationships and their performance impact. *Journal of Operations Management, 31*(5), 236–247. https://doi.org/10.1016/j.jom.2013.05.001

Nicholson, G., & Newton, C. (2010). The role of the board of directors: Perceptions of managerial elites. *Journal of Management & Organization, 16*(2), 204–218. https://doi.org/10.1017/S1833367200002133

Paterson, J. M., Green, A., & Cary, J. (2002). The measurement of organizational justice in organizational change programmes: A reliability, validity and context-sensitivity assessment. *Journal of Occupational and Organizational Psychology, 75*(4), 393–408. https://doi.org/10.1348/096317902321119565

Pignata, S., Winefield, A. H., Provis, C., & Boyd, C. M. (2016). A longitudinal study of the predictors of perceived procedural justice in Australian University staff. *Frontiers in Psychology, 7*(August), 1271. https://doi.org/10.3389/fpsyg.2016.01271

Raykov, T., Gabler, S., & Dimitrov, D. M. (2015). Maximal reliability and composite reliability: A latent variable modeling approach to their difference evaluation. *Structural Equation Modeling A Multidisciplinary Journal, 23*(3), 1–8. https://doi.org/10.1080/10705511.2016.1155414

Ring, P. S., & Van de Ven, A. H. (1994). Developmental processes of cooperative interorganizational relationships. *Academy of Management Review, 19*(1), 90–118. https://doi.org/10.5465/amr.1994.9410122009

Rotter, J. (1967). A new scale for the measurement of interpersonal trust. *Journal of Personality, 35*(4), 651–665. https://doi.org/10.1111/j.1467-6494.1967.tb01454.x

Samaha, S. A., Palmatier, R. W., & Dant, R. P. (2011). Poisoning relationships: Perceived unfairness in channels of distribution. *Journal of Marketing, 75*(3), 99–117. https://doi.org/10.1509%2Fjmkg.75.3.99

Shaikh, A. (2016). Conceptualizing fairness in franchisor–franchisee relationship: Dimensions, definitions and preliminary construction of scale. *Journal of Retailing and Consumer Services, 28*(1), 28–35. https://doi.org/10.1016/j.jretconser.2015.08.010

Shaikh, A., Biswas, S. N., Yadav, V., & Mishra, D. (2017). Measuring fairness in franchisor-franchisee relationship: A confirmatory approach. *International Journal of Retail & Distribution Management, 40*(2), 156–176. https://doi.org/10.1108/IJRDM-11-2015-0174

Shaikh, A., Sharma, D., Vijayalakshmi, A., & Yadav, R. S. (2018). Fairness in franchisor–franchisee relationship: An integrative perspective. *Journal of Business & Industrial Marketing, 35*(4), 550–562. https://doi.org/10.1108/JBIM-04-2017-0093

Shapiro, D. L., Buttner, E. H., & Barry, B. (1994). Explanations: What factors enhance their perceived adequacy? *Organizational Behavior and Human Decision Processes, 58*(3), 346–368. https://doi.org/10.1006/obhd.1994.1041

Sheng, S., Brown, J. R., & Nicholson, C. Y. (2005). The mediating role of communication in interorganizational channels. *Journal of Marketing Channels, 13*(2), 51–80. https://doi.org/10.1300/J049v13n02_04

Shockley, J., & Turner, T. (2016). A relational performance model for developing innovation and long-term orientation in retail franchise organizations. *Journal of Retailing and Consumer Services, 32*(September), 175–188. https://doi.org/10.1016/j.jretconser.2016.06.013

Sirdeshmukh, D., Singh, J., & Sabol, B. (2002). Consumer trust, value, and loyalty in relational exchanges. *Journal of Marketing, 66*(1), 15–37. https://doi.org/10.1509%2Fjmkg.66.1.15.18449

Storholm, G., & Scheuing, E. E. (1994). Ethical implications of business format franchising. *Journal of Business Ethics, 13*(3), 181–188. https://doi.org/10.1007/BF02074817

Strutton, D., Pelton, L. E., & Lumpkin, J. R. (1993). The influence of psychological climate on conflict resolution strategies in franchise relationships. *Journal of the Academy of Marketing Science, 21*(3), 207–215. https://doi.org/10.1177%2F0092070393213004

Strutton, D., Pelton, L. E., & Lumpkin, J. R. (1995). Psychological climate in franchising system channels and franchisor-franchisee solidarity. *Journal of Business Research, 34*(2), 81–91. https://doi.org/10.1016/0148-2963(94)00053-H

Thaichon, P., Weaven, S., Quach, S., Bodey, K., Merrilees, B., & Frazer, L. (2018). Female franchisees; a lost opportunity for franchising sector growth? *Journal of Strategic Marketing, 28*(2), 1–16. https://doi.org/10.1080/0965254X.2018.1482946

Turillo, C. J., Folger, R., Lavelle, J. J., Umphress, E. E., & Gee, J. O. (2002). Is virtue its own reward? Self-sacrificial decisions for the sake of fairness. *Organizational Behavior and Human Decision Processes, 89*(1), 839–865. https://doi.org/10.1016/S0749-5978(02)00032-8

Tyler, T. R., & Bies, R. J. (1990). Beyond formal procedures: The interpersonal context of procedural justice. In J. Carroll (Ed.), *Applied social psychology and organizational settings* (Vol. 77, pp. 98). Psychology Press.

Tyler, T. R. (1994). Psychological models of the justice motive: Antecedents of distributive and procedural justice. *Journal of Personality and Social Psychology, 67*(5), 850. https://psycnet.apa.org/doi/10.1037/0022-3514.67.5.850

Walker, L., Lind, E. A., & Thibaut, J. (1979). Relation between procedural and distributive justice. *The Virginia Law Review, 65*(8), 1401. https://www.jstor.org/stable/1072580

Weaven, S., Frazer, L., & Giddings, J. (2010). New perspectives on the causes of franchising conflict in Australia. *Asia Pacific Journal of Marketing and Logistics, 22*(2), 135–155. https://doi.org/10.1108/13555851011026917

Weaven, S., Grace, D., & Manning, M. (2009). Franchisee personality. *European Journal of Marketing, 43*(1/2), 90–109. https://psycnet.apa.org/doi/10.1108/03090560910923256

Weaven, S. K., Grace, D. A., Frazer, L., & Giddings, J. (2014). Processual antecedents of perceived channel conflict in franchising. *Journal of Business Economics and Management, 15*(2), 316–334. https://doi.org/10.3846/16111699.2012.711362

Wulff, E. (2005). *Advisory councils: Effective two-way communications for franchise systems.* International Franchise Association. accessed 03 April 2019. Retrieved from https://www.franchise.org/sites/default/files/uploaded_documents/Advisory%2520Councils.pdf

Yakimova, R., Owens, M., & Sydow, J. (2019). Formal control influence on franchisee trust and brand-supportive behavior within franchise networks. *Industrial Marketing Management, 76*(1), 123–135. https://doi.org/10.1016/j.indmarman.2018.07.010

Yamagishi, T., & Yamagishi, M. (1994). Trust and commitment in the United States and Japan. *Motivation and Emotion, 18*(2), 129–166. https://doi.org/10.1007/BF02249397

# Determinants of overall franchisee satisfaction: application of the performance feedback theory

Michal Jirásek, Susanne Maria Gaffke and Josef Windsperger

**ABSTRACT**

Franchisee satisfaction in a franchise network has various consequences, from stimulating the implementation of new practices up
to the decision to stay in or leave the network. This paper aims to
examine the performance antecedents of overall franchisee satisfaction. We posit that satisfaction is influenced by three performance
dimensions: financial, service, and relationship performance. We
argue that increasing performance on any of these three dimensions
leads to higher franchisee satisfaction. Based on a sample of franchisees from Germany and Austria, the findings show that relationship
performance (quality) consistently predicts changes in satisfaction and
mediates the effect on satisfaction of the other important performance
factor – financial performance relative to competitors. Overall, this
study contributes to the franchising and retail literature by applying
Cyert and March's performance feedback theory to explain overall
franchisee satisfaction.

## Introduction

Franchising generates numerous economic (e.g., Kalargyrou et al., 2018) and non-
economic (e.g., Cumberland, 2015) benefits for the franchisor and franchisees as partners
in a franchise network. Franchising has been addressed through several theory lenses
(e.g., Combs et al., 2011) that tend to apply a rather franchisor-centric perspective (e.g.,
Grünhagen & Mittelstaedt, 2005; Wu, 2015); consequently, they cannot fully explain the
complex relational structures within a franchise network that determine the behavior of
the franchisor and franchisees (e.g., Jang & Park, 2019). Yet franchisees' actions contribute
to brand positioning, customer retention, and, most importantly, to the overall success of
the franchise network (e.g., Yakimova et al., 2019).

Previous research has mainly focused on the consequences, rather than the antecedents, of overall franchisee satisfaction (e.g., Kalargyrou et al., 2018). We aim to fill this
gap and enrich the existing franchising and retail literature with new insights from
a behavioral theory perspective (Cyert & March, 1963), on which basis we posit that
franchisees aim at satisficing rather than maximizing their goals. If a franchisee is
dissatisfied with its performance compared to earlier periods or its peers, it will adjust
its goals with the franchisor or exit the franchise network (Croonen et al., 2016).

Therefore, this paper aims to examine the performance antecedents of overall franchisee satisfaction – specifically the roles of financial, service, and relationship performance – by applying the performance feedback theory (Cyert & March, 1963; Greve & Gaba, 2015). We hypothesize that feedbacks on financial, service, and relationship performance are positively related to overall franchisee satisfaction within the franchise network.

This study's contribution to the franchising and retail literature is to explore franchise relationships from a behavioral standpoint by applying the performance feedback theory (Cyert & March, 1963; Greve, 2003; Greve & Gaba, 2015). Focusing on the franchisee's perspective gives voice to them as a major stakeholder in the franchise network, recognizing that the network's success is based on a value co-creation process between the franchisor and franchisees (Facca, 2013; Kalargyrou et al., 2018). Specifically, we highlight the role of three performance dimensions – financial, service, and relational (Achrol & Etzel, 2003) – that capture the antecedents of overall franchisee satisfaction. Moreover, two of them – service performance and relationship quality – establish the importance of relationship marketing in the franchise context, which is underexplored in the franchising literature (e.g., Beitelspacher et al., 2018). Overall, our study reveals that all three of these performance dimensions have complex linkages that should be acknowledged by both researchers and practitioners to determine the failure and success of franchise networks.

The paper is structured as follows: The second section overviews the literature on franchisee satisfaction and develops hypotheses using the performance feedback theory. In the third section, we describe the study's methodology. The fourth section presents the results of analyses using regression models. Finally, the last section discusses the findings and their implications for both theory and management practice.

## Theory and hypotheses

Satisfaction is generally understood as a positive affective state (Anderson & Narus, 1984) that is perceived by an individual when certain expectations seem to be met. On the consequences of franchisee satisfaction, the literature offers a wealth of findings. High levels of franchisee satisfaction predict 'higher morale, greater cooperation, fewer terminations of relationships, fewer lawsuits, and a lower likelihood of seeking protective legislation' (Hunt & Nevin, 1974, p. 191). Indeed, other studies have indicated that franchisee satisfaction constitutes a key factor in the franchise network's success (e.g., Bordonaba-Juste & Polo-Redondo, 2008; Kalargyrou et al., 2018) as it promotes persistence (Gauzente, 2003; Morrison, 1997), performance (Abdullah et al., 2008), and coordination (Tuunanen, 2002). Moreover, franchisor–franchisee collaboration can be encouraged through satisfaction (Kalargyrou et al., 2018), which leads to fewer conflicts (Davis, 2012), a lower franchisee turnover rate (Frazer et al., 2012), and greater overall productivity (Tuunanen, 2002). In addition, scholars have revealed that satisfied franchisees tend to support the development of the franchise network by building an affirmative position toward the network (Grace & Weaven, 2011), engaging continuously in it (Chiou et al., 2004; Gauzente, 2003), and actively promoting the franchise firm through word-of-mouth (Kalargyrou et al., 2018).

### Antecedents of franchisee satisfaction

While franchisee satisfaction constitutes an essential aspect of franchise system success (e.g., Jang & Park, 2019; Kalargyrou et al., 2018), the current literature only partially explains the antecedents of franchisee satisfaction. Scholars contend that franchisee satisfaction results from support provided by the franchisor (e.g., Hing, 1995) and increases with the degree of closeness of the franchisor–franchisee relationship (e.g., Bordonaba-Juste & Polo-Redondo, 2008; Kalargyrou et al., 2018). Furthermore, Chiou and Droge (2015) found that trust and financial performance positively influence overall franchisee satisfaction. Similarly, Tuunanen and Hyrsky (2001) indicated that key roles are played by financial performance, support by the franchisor, work as a franchisee, and market performance. Morrison (1997) showed that personal and situational factors influence franchisee job satisfaction. Relatedly, Roh and Yoon (2009) found that selecting franchisees with suitable attitudes and similar expectations to the franchisor's leads to greater franchisee satisfaction in general. Based on these results, franchisee satisfaction is arguably a multidimensional construct (Abdullah et al., 2008; Kalargyrou et al., 2018; Tuunanen & Hyrsky, 2001).

According to Lim and Frazer (2004), the franchisee plays the following roles: a customer purchasing a franchise shop (e.g., Abdullah et al., 2008), a business partner similar to that in channel partnerships (e.g., Grünhagen & Dorsch, 2003), and an employee (e.g., Morrison, 1997). Therefore, based on the assumption that the franchisee–franchisor relationship is hybrid in nature (Dant et al., 2013), it is essential to combine the different satisfaction constructs to holistically assess the determinants of overall franchisee satisfaction. For this reason, we attempt to enrich the literature by approaching the topic from a behavioral perspective, drawing particularly on the performance feedback theory (Cyert & March, 1963).

### Performance feedback theory and organizational goals

Performance feedback theory (Cyert & March, 1963; Greve, 2003; Greve & Gaba, 2015) argues that satisfaction is driven by the attainment of goal-based aspiration levels. Aspiration levels are performance outcomes that are satisfactory for the decision-maker – a concept derived from bounded rationality (Simon, 1955). Thus, decision-makers – franchisees in our case – do not attempt to maximize their performance but rather aim to attain their performance goals.

As the behavioral theory predicts (Cyert & March, 1963), strategies leading to goal attainment are less likely to be replaced by alternatives. By contrast, when strategies lead to unsatisfactory results (goals are not attained), the decision-maker initiates a search for alternative courses of action that will likely achieve better performance. The performance feedback deriving from the comparison between performance and goals explains why organizations change during times when they underperform (Greve, 2003; Greve & Gaba, 2015).

Besides particular levels of performance, differences of satisfaction are caused by each franchisee aiming to achieve different economic, social, or psychological goals (Grace & Weaven, 2011; Tuunanen, 2002). The entrepreneurial perspective on franchisees has formulated their performance goal dimensions based on their motivation to start a franchise outlet, concentrating on the interdependency impetus or on the financial interest in owning a franchise outlet (e.g., Hatten, 2009). Compared to the traditional entrepreneur, franchisees follow similar performance dimensions but also focus on relational components that determine the franchisor–franchisee relationship (e.g., Grace et al., 2013).

Nevertheless, little systematic attention has been paid to goal formulation in the long run, i.e., when the franchisee already owns a franchise outlet (as in Chiou & Droge, 2015). Achrol and Etzel (2003) elaborated and determined three strategic performance dimensions from this perspective: productivity, market-adaptation, and channel-integration goals. First, productivity goals refer to the firm's efficiency and financial performance. Second, market-adaptation goals empower a firm to differentiate against competitors and emphasize a customer-centric focus. Third, channel-integration goals relate to structural and relational ties within the channel (franchise network).

Two major benchmarks determining the level of performance considered satisfactory are own historical performance and the performance of comparable peers (Greve, 2003). This gives the organization two types of performance feedback. Historical performance feedback provides information about performance compared to previous periods, while social performance feedback provides information about the organization's relative standing compared to peers. For this reason, when considering aspirations, it is important to distinguish not only different performance dimensions but also different performance levels (Washburn & Bromiley, 2012).

### Hypotheses

In general, performance is a multidimensional construct and comprises both financial and non-financial elements (e.g., Combs et al., 2005; Patiar et al., 2012). Two of Achrol and Etzel (2003) strategic goals – productivity and market-adaptation – largely correspond to financial and service performance as outlined by Chiou and Droge (2015) in relation to franchisee satisfaction. While the financial aspects illustrate the skill-set of management in allocating limited resources and achieving profitability (e.g., Sainaghi, 2010), service aspects reflect the management of staff and customers (e.g., Patiar et al., 2012). Although some scholars have investigated performance as a one-dimensional construct, performance encompasses economic and non-economic elements that should be examined separately (Chiou & Droge, 2015; Kalargyrou et al., 2018; Patiar et al., 2012).

The job satisfaction literature about employee bonuses, which are closely related to franchisee remuneration, highlights the importance of financial performance (Chiou & Droge, 2015). Following the marketing literature on satisfaction, higher levels of franchisee satisfaction can be achieved by, for instance, extrinsic motivation such as profits (Abdullah et al., 2008) or sales (Chiou & Droge, 2015).

Since the franchisor creates value through franchisees providing the service to customers (Facca, 2013), service performance should be explored in that context. Service performance has a relational character since it reflects the relationship between the franchisee and its customers. In essence, the franchisee's service performance can be achieved by addressing customer needs (Liao & Chuang, 2004). The better the adaptation of the service offering to the customer base, the greater the satisfaction of both exchange partners (franchisee and customer), potentially resulting in better overall business performance (Ramaseshan et al., 2018). Prior research suggests that the franchisee's perception of service performance also promotes franchisee satisfaction (e.g., Chiou & Droge, 2015). Accordingly, we propose the following hypotheses:

*H1a: The higher the financial performance (compared to the social benchmark), the higher is the franchisee satisfaction.*

*H1b: The higher the financial performance (compared to the historical benchmark), the higher is the franchisee satisfaction.*

*H2a: The higher the service performance (compared to the social benchmark), the higher is the franchisee satisfaction.*

*H2b: The higher the service performance (compared to the historical benchmark), the higher is the franchisee satisfaction.*

The three preeminent theories used to explain franchisor–franchisee interdependence are the resource-based view, principal-agent theory, and transaction-cost theory (Combs et al., 2011; Dant et al., 2011; Rosado-Serrano et al., 2018). Despite the importance of these theories in franchising research, they mostly overlook the specifics of relational exchanges between franchisor and franchisee, along with the emerging behavioral concerns (e.g., Jang & Park, 2019). Since franchisees' actions can substantially influence the franchise network's perfor- mance, some scholars argue that relational exchange is pivotal in the franchisor–franchisee relationship as it determines franchisee satisfaction (Chiou & Droge, 2015; Chiou et al., 2004). Relatedly, there is a value co-creation process between franchisor and franchisee that deter- mines the franchise network's performance (Facca, 2013; Lusch & Vargo, 2014).

We consider the third performance dimension posited by Achrol and Etzel (2003) – channel integration – different from the previous two. This goal focuses on relationship quality, thus deviating from pure financial and non-financial performance. Scholars have found that, in channel partnerships, relationship quality is crucial for long-term success (e.g., Ulaga & Eggert, 2006). Franchisees perceive higher levels of relationship quality when they experience fair, equal, and respectful treatment by their franchisor (Bordonaba-Juste & Polo-Redondo, 2008). According to Lee (2017), the franchisee is satisfied when their relationship quality with the franchisor exceeds their own economic, psychological, and social expectations. Furthermore, Kalargyrou et al. (2018) and Squire (2009) emphasize that better relationships increase franchisee satisfaction. Since relation- ship quality (performance) is easily observed by the franchisee only in its own relationship with the franchisor, we do not consider the social benchmark to be salient here. Therefore, the following hypothesis is suggested:

*H3: The higher the perceived relationship performance (quality), the higher is the franchisee satisfaction.*

To summarize our research model (see Figure 1), we posit that overall franchisee satisfaction is positively related to financial and service performance (both separately compared to social and historical benchmarks) and to relationship performance.

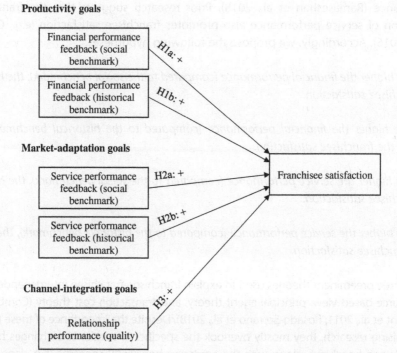

**Figure 1.** Research model.

## Methodology

### *Data collection and sample*

The data were collected online and through paper-and-pen questionnaires sent to franchisees in Germany and Austria between April 2018 and March 2019. The final sample comprised only respondents that own and manage one or more outlets, excluding managers of company-owned outlets. Based on Grace et al. (2013), we expected franchisees to be reluctant to complete the questionnaire because they fear confidential information expressly connected to them or the company being disclosed to the public. Attempting to overcome this obstacle, the cover letter promised that information would be aggregated and treated anonymously. The models are calculated using 113 responses, representing a response rate of 8%.

The respondents had managed their franchise outlets for an average of eight years. A slight majority of the sample were German franchisees (51.3%). Respondents varied by industry (30% in fitness, 23% in education services) and age (13.3% are 30 years old or younger, 20.4% between 31 and 40 years old, 31.9% between 41 and 50 years old, and 34.4% older than 50).

### *Measurement*

### *Dependent variable*

The dependent variable is overall (franchisee) satisfaction, which describes the level of satisfaction of franchisees with their respective franchise network. The six items for this latent variable (calculated as a mean score) were adopted from Chiou et al. (2004), Chiou and Droge (2015), and Wu (2015). Cronbach's alpha for overall satisfaction is 0.946. Details on the measurements of this and other variables are given in Appendix A. We also conducted factor analyses of the variables, which is reported in Appendix B. All the scales yielded single factors for all items.

### Performance measures

All independent variables are latent variable constructs and measured as mean scores. With respect to the hypotheses, performance feedback on both the service and financial benchmarks was based on separate comparisons of the franchisee's outlet with (a) others in the area and (b) its own performance a year ago. Accordingly, four performance feedback variables were used.

We used a four-item scale to measure financial performance (based on Chiou & Droge, 2015; Delgado-García et al., 2012) and a three-item scale to measure service performance (based on Chiou & Droge, 2015). Factor analyses of both social and historical benchmarks distinguished financial performance and service performance. Cronbach's alphas for historical performance feedback are 0.907 for financial performance and 0.930 for service performance. Cronbach's alphas for social performance feedback are 0.875 for financial performance and 0.844 for service performance.

Using a seven-item scale adapted from Grace and Weaven (2011), Grace et al. (2013), and Weaven et al. (2017), franchisees were asked to assess the relationship performance (quality) between them and their respective franchisor. Factor analysis yielded one factor based on the seven-item scale. Cronbach's alpha for relationship performance is 0.965.

### Control variables

We controlled for industry segments (fitness, education, other) to rule out different satisfaction levels caused by industry differences. Since the ownership of multiple outlets may reflect higher (historical) satisfaction with the franchise network, we also included a dummy for this. Then, we controlled for respondent's age (up to 30 years, 31–40 years, 41–50 years, older), which reflects general work experience. Finally, we controlled for potential survivor-bias by including the natural logarithm of years of business age, since those dissatisfied with the franchise network are more likely to exit over time.

## Results

### Descriptive statistics

The descriptive statistics of the variables and their correlations are reported in Table 1. A test of variance inflation factors showed no important indications of multicollinearity, with scores well below 5. All the models reported below were calculated using HC3 robust standard errors to avoid potential problems with heteroskedasticity.

Since common method bias is a serious concern in behavioral research, especially in single informant surveys (Podsakoff et al., 2012), we employed a marker variable technique (Lindell & Whitney, 2001). First, we selected a marker variable theoretically unrelated to the variables of interest (in this case, the importance respondents place on risk reduction,

**Table 1.** Descriptive statistics and correlations.

| | Mean | SD | Min | Max | 1 | 2 | 3 | 4 | 5 | 6 | 7 | 8 | 9 | 10 | 11 | 12 | 13 |
|---|---|---|---|---|---|---|---|---|---|---|---|---|---|---|---|---|---|
| 1 Overall Satisfaction | 3.960 | 1.111 | 1.000 | 5.000 | 1.00 | | | | | | | | | | | | |
| 2 Financial Performance (soc.) | 3.440 | 0.847 | 1.000 | 5.000 | 0.64 | 1.00 | | | | | | | | | | | |
| 3 Service Performance (soc.) | 4.081 | 0.807 | 1.667 | 5.000 | 0.53 | 0.56 | 1.00 | | | | | | | | | | |
| 4 Financial Performance (his.) | 3.449 | 0.905 | 1.000 | 5.000 | 0.56 | 0.74 | 0.48 | 1.00 | | | | | | | | | |
| 5 Service Performance (his.) | 3.811 | 0.857 | 1.667 | 5.000 | 0.46 | 0.49 | 0.58 | 0.61 | 1.00 | | | | | | | | |
| 6 Relationship Performance | 3.791 | 1.102 | 1.000 | 5.000 | 0.86 | 0.59 | 0.61 | 0.50 | 0.51 | 1.00 | | | | | | | |
| 7 Dummy Industry 1 (Fitness) | 0.301 | 0.461 | 0.000 | 1.000 | 0.00 | -0.06 | -0.05 | -0.01 | -0.01 | -0.04 | 1.00 | | | | | | |
| 8 Dummy Industry 2 (Educ.) | 0.230 | 0.423 | 0.000 | 1.000 | -0.09 | -0.02 | -0.06 | 0.02 | -0.01 | -0.16 | -0.36 | 1.00 | | | | | |
| 9 Dummy Age 1 (≤ 30) | 0.133 | 0.341 | 0.000 | 1.000 | 0.06 | -0.03 | 0.11 | 0.09 | 0.02 | 0.07 | 0.26 | -0.15 | 1.00 | | | | |
| 10 Dummy Age 2 (31–40) | 0.204 | 0.404 | 0.000 | 1.000 | -0.04 | -0.07 | -0.01 | -0.05 | 0.09 | -0.05 | 0.24 | -0.22 | -0.20 | 1.00 | | | |
| 11 Dummy Age 3 (41–50) | 0.319 | 0.468 | 0.000 | 1.000 | 0.06 | 0.05 | 0.05 | 0.04 | 0.03 | 0.11 | 0.05 | -0.01 | -0.27 | -0.35 | 1.00 | | |
| 12 Dummy Multiple Outlets | 0.478 | 0.502 | 0.000 | 1.000 | 0.07 | -0.02 | 0.09 | -0.01 | -0.06 | 0.10 | -0.13 | 0.15 | 0.20 | -0.26 | 0.03 | 1.00 | |
| 13 Business Age (ln) | 1.958 | 0.745 | 0.000 | 3.989 | -0.10 | 0.14 | -0.08 | 0.02 | 0.06 | -0.14 | -0.21 | -0.25 | -0.25 | 0.02 | -0.12 | -0.12 | 1.00 |

n = 113

measured on a scale from 1 'Not important at all' to 5 'Very important'). Second, we took the smallest positive correlation between a marker variable and a variable of interest (r = 0.008) and used it to adjust correlations across variable pairs. Third, we checked whether correlations that were significant before adjustment remained significant. As they did, the correlations cannot be attributed to common method bias. Although we cannot completely rule out the effect, the test indicated that its impact is likely to be minimal. We also used paired t-tests to assess whether responses from the earlier part of the data collection differ from responses from the later part; we found no significant differences (at the 5% level).

### Hypotheses testing

To test our research model, we calculated four ordinary least squares (OLS) regression models with franchisee satisfaction as the dependent variable (see Table 2). OLS models were preferred as we did not hypothesize a complex structure among variables. For this reason, we chose a parsimonious approach that did not impose any unnecessary assumptions on our dataset.

Model 1 includes only the control variables. In Model 2 we added the financial and service performance (social benchmark) measures, and financial and service performance (historical benchmark) measures. Financial performance feedback based on the social benchmark was found to be strongly significant (p = 0.003), thus supporting H1a. However, none of the other sources of performance feedback yielded significant results, so H1b, H2a, and H2b were not supported. It is also important to note that with an estimated coefficient of 0.605, the effect size of financial performance feedback based on the social benchmark is very large. In Model 2, the adjusted R-squared is 0.441, considerably more than in Model 1.

In Model 3, only relationship performance (quality) supplemented the control variables. It was found to be strongly significant, with a considerably high effect size (coefficient of 0.887), thus supporting H3. In this model, the adjusted R-squared is 0.723, again, considerably more than in the previous model. Model 4 included all aspiration measures, and its

**Table 2.** Regression of overall satisfaction.

| | Model 1 | Model 2 | Model 3 | Model 4 |
|---|---|---|---|---|
| Financial Performance (soc.) | | 0.605 (0.003)*** | | 0.224 (0.039)** |
| Service Performance (soc.) | | 0.225 (0.174) | | −0.084 (0.480) |
| Financial Performance (his.) | | 0.136 (0.463) | | 0.133 (0.163) |
| Service Performance (his.) | | 0.083 (0.594) | | −0.063 (0.479) |
| Relationship Performance | | | 0.887 (0.000)*** | 0.782 (0.000)*** |
| Business Age (ln) | −0.137 (0.300) | −0.226 (0.066)* | 0.056 (0.521) | −0.018 (0.838) |
| Dummy Multiple Outlets | −0.122 (0.595) | 0.069 (0.694) | −0.123 (0.279) | −0.038 (0.742) |
| Dummy Age 1 (≤ 30) | 0.226 (0.567) | −0.070 (0.858) | 0.025 (0.932) | 0.030 (0.920) |
| Dummy Age 2 (31–40) | −0.031 (0.927) | −0.010 (0.961) | 0.028 (0.873) | 0.031 (0.841) |
| Dummy Age 3 (41–50) | 0.184 (0.535) | 0.008 (0.974) | −0.058 (0.676) | −0.069 (0.606) |
| Dummy Industry 1 (Fitness) | −0.213 (0.424) | −0.034 (0.855) | 0.140 (0.375) | 0.106 (0.492) |
| Dummy Industry 2 (Education) | −0.294 (0.357) | −0.192 (0.479) | 0.195 (0.193) | 0.140 (0.313) |
| Adj. R-Square | −0.036 | 0.441 | 0.723 | 0.748 |
| AIC | 358.094 | 292.029 | 210.017 | 203.014 |
| BIC | 382.640 | 327.485 | 237.291 | 241.197 |
| N | 113 | 113 | 113 | 113 |

Notes. Dependent variable: Overall Satisfaction. Constant not reported.
$^\S p < 0.1$; $^*p < 0.05$; $^{**}p < 0.01$; $^{***}p < 0.001$; p-values in parentheses, HC3 standard errors.

**Table 3.** Mediation model.

|  | Model M |
| --- | --- |
| Financial Performance (soc.) | 0.487* (0.013) |
| Service Performance (soc.) | 0.396** (0.004) |
| Financial Performance (his.) | 0.003 (0.985) |
| Service Performance (his.) | 0.186 (0.177) |
| Business Age (ln) | −0.266* (0.010) |
| Dummy Multiple Outlets | 0.136 (0.396) |
| Dummy Age 1 (≤ 30) | −0.128 (0.712) |
| Dummy Age 2 (31–40) | −0.053 (0.810) |
| Dummy Age 3 (41–50) | 0.097 (0.634) |
| Dummy Industry 1 (Fitness) | −0.178 (0.315) |
| Dummy Industry 2 (Education) | −0.424 (0.108) |
| Adj. R-Square | 0.487 |
| N | 113 |

*Dependent variable: Relationship performance. Constant not reported.*
$^{s}p < 0.1$; $^{*}p < 0.05$; $^{**}p < 0.01$; $^{***}p < 0.001$; *p-values in parentheses, HC3 standard errors.*

adjusted R-squared is 0.748, slightly more than in Model 3. Financial performance feedback based on the social benchmark remained significant ($p = 0.039$), although its effect size decreased to around one-third of its value in Model 2. Relationship performance (quality) was strongly significant ($p < 0.001$), which further supports H3, although the effect size was slightly smaller than in Model 3. This indicates that relationship performance may mediate the relationships between performance feedback and overall franchisee satisfaction. To provide further support for this claim, we regressed performance feedback variables and controls on relationship performance (see Table 3). We found significant coefficients for both service and financial performance feedbacks with the social benchmark ($p = 0.013$ and $p = 0.004$, respectively). Therefore, both of these performance feedbacks are mediated by relationship performance in their effect on overall franchisee satisfaction.

### Robustness check

To support our findings, we also tested our research model with structural equation modeling (SEM). In this SEM analysis, we used a mediation structure implied by the reported results. The outputs fully support that relationship quality mediates both service and financial performance feedbacks with the social benchmark. We do not report the SEM results in detail as the small sample size may undermine their reliability.[1]

## Discussion and conclusions

### Findings

In this paper, we developed and tested a new perspective on the antecedents of franchisee satisfaction by applying performance feedback theory (Cyert & March, 1963; Greve, 2003).

First, our results show a paramount positive impact of relationship quality on overall franchisee satisfaction (Nijmeijer et al., 2014; Weaven et al., 2010). Relationship quality is vital for sustainable relationships inside the franchise network (Jang & Park, 2019), and the mediation role of relationship quality between performance feedback and overall franchisee satisfaction supports that notion. Fundamentally, it indicates that ongoing investment in franchisor–franchisee relationships can support higher perceived relationship quality between both exchange partners and, in turn, improve cooperation and performance (Blut et al., 2011).

Second, consistent with the findings of Grace et al. (2013) and Chiou and Droge (2015), we found no direct effect of service performance feedback on overall franchisee satisfaction. One possible explanation is that the level of service performance may be considered relatively irrelevant in competitive markets since it cannot be transformed directly into higher profits (Chiou & Droge, 2015). We offer an alternative explanation with our post-hoc mediation test. It shows that performance feedback (based on social benchmarks) is at least partially mediated by relationship quality. Thus, instead of directly influencing satisfaction, it influences the relationship between franchisee and franchisor. Negative service performance feedback may create tensions between the franchisee and franchisor, thereby straining the relationship (Kirtland, 2015).

Third, regarding performance feedbacks on historical (own performance) benchmarks, we posit that the franchisee attributes this performance to itself, rather than the franchisor. Since the framing of the franchisee's business by the franchise network remains the same over time (unless the network makes major changes affecting performance), the historical benchmark does not influence overall franchisee satisfaction in the franchise network.

### Theoretical implications

Focusing on organizational goals enabled us to consider the franchisee from the behavioral theory perspective (Delgado-García et al., 2012) – a novel theoretical view scarcely used in prior research. We argue that the determinants of franchisee satisfaction cannot be fully explained by the classical theories in franchising (the resource-based view, principal-agent theory, and transaction-cost theory), because they mainly adopt a one-sided perspective and do not recognize that the value-creation process relies on the quality of the relationship between franchisor and franchisee (Facca, 2013; Lusch & Vargo, 2014). Hence, in future studies, applying a behavioral theory perspective in combination with the service-dominant logic of Lusch and Vargo (2014) may offer new research opportunities.

Furthermore, this study enriches the performance feedback theory. Most related studies focus on corporate-level decision-making, so our research model on franchisee satisfaction contributes to the scarce literature on lower levels of decision-making (e.g., Blettner et al., 2015; Washburn & Bromiley, 2012). As the literature often treats such decision-making processes as black boxes (Posen et al., 2018), we also provide empirical evidence of how various goal dimensions interact. Whereas most empirical studies use only one performance dimension, usually financial (one exception is Audia & Brion, 2007), the performance feedback theory assumes that there are multiple dimensions (Cyert & March, 1963). Our findings reveal that the three goal dimensions proposed by Achrol and Etzel (2003) are hierarchical, with financial and service performance being determinants of the higher-order goal of relationship quality. Finally, as empirical research on the performance feedback theory uses mostly secondary financial data, we offer an alternative by collecting primary data through questionnaires (e.g., Kaleka & Morgan, 2019; Villagrasa et al., 2018).

### Managerial implications

Low satisfaction can lead to franchisees leaving the franchise system, with potentially severe implications for the franchisor and its business. Hence, we recommend that franchisors should implement timely measures to guarantee high satisfaction levels among franchisees (Croonen et al., 2016). Notably, satisfaction support is necessary when the franchisee is in 'routine' and 'crossroads' stages of the life cycle, characterized by relatively low relationship quality between the parties (Blut et al., 2011). Accordingly, franchisors need to regularly inspect relationship quality, and should invest in developing relationships that franchisees perceive as fair, respectful, and high quality (Bordonaba-Juste & Polo-Redondo, 2008).

Nevertheless, franchisors should not neglect the existence of other factors that may affect the relationship. Our research indicates that social performance feedback may strongly influence the perceived relationship quality. As franchisee-centered research already shows, poor levels or even the absence of economic satisfaction will weaken the durability of the franchisor–franchisee relationship (Jang & Park, 2019). Furthermore, the mediating role of relationship quality between performance feedback and overall franchisee satisfaction is an important consideration for the franchisor. Since negative performance feedback does not directly translate into dissatisfaction (and subsequent intention to leave the franchise network), the franchisor can proactively use relationship quality to keep the franchisee in the network despite poor performance.

### Limitations and further research

This study has one major limitation: while our findings show that franchise partners' goals have a hierarchical structure (consistent with Achrol & Etzel, 2003), the relatively small number of observations prevented us from testing a more complex structure among franchisee goals. As service performance feedback seems to be fully mediated, while the mediation of financial performance feedback is only partial, we expect there is much more to discover besides the mediation we identified. Therefore, future research should address the hierarchical relationship between different performance goals and overall satisfaction. One possible empirical approach to this topic is to study performance attribution between the franchisee and the franchisor. We believe that qualitative (case study) research can provide an initial insight into this topic.

### Conclusions

This study aimed to develop an alternative perspective on the antecedents of overall franchisee satisfaction based on the performance feedback theory. One of its main findings supports the view that relationship performance (quality) has a considerable impact on overall franchisee satisfaction. The results also highlight that relationship quality is a mediator between social-benchmark-based financial and service performance feedbacks and overall franchisee satisfaction. The franchisor can profit from the study's insights by attempting to discover particular strategic goals that shape franchisees' expectations and applying this knowledge to enhance the level of overall franchisee satisfaction. In doing so, the franchisor would acknowledge the value co-creation process with the franchisee, which is conducive to better meeting customer needs, leading ultimately to better overall performance outcomes. Implementing this behavioral strategy allows franchise managers to act proactively and create a substantial competitive advantage for the franchise network.

## Note

1. The results can be obtained from the authors.

## Disclosure statement

No potential conflict of interest was reported by the author(s).

## References

Abdullah, F., Rashidee Alwi, M., Lee, N., & Boo, H. V. (2008). Measuring and managing franchisee satisfaction: A study of academic franchising. *Journal of Modelling in Management, 3*(2), 182–199. https://doi.org/10.1108/17465660810890144

Achrol, R. S., & Etzel, M. J. (2003). The structure of reseller goals and performance in marketing channels. *Journal of the Academy of Marketing Science, 31*(2), 146–163. https://doi.org/10.1177/0092070302250899

Anderson, J. C., & Narus, J. A. (1984). A model of the distributor's perspective of distributor-manufacturer working relationships. *Journal of Marketing, 48*(4), 62–74. https://doi.org/10.1177/002224298404800407

Audia, P. G., & Brion, S. (2007). Reluctant to change: Self-enhancing responses to diverging performance measures. *Organizational Behavior and Human Decision Processes, 102*(2), 255–269. https://doi.org/10.1016/j.obhdp.2006.01.007

Beitelspacher, L. S., Baker, T. L., Rapp, A., & Grewal, D. (2018). Understanding the long-term implications of retailer returns in business-to-business relationships. *Journal of the Academy of Marketing Science, 46*(2), 252–272. https://doi.org/10.1007/s11747-017-0553-6

Blettner, D. P., He, Z.-L., Hu, S., & Bettis, R. A. (2015). Adaptive aspirations and performance heterogeneity: Attention allocation among multiple reference points. *Strategic Management Journal, 36*(7), 987–1005. https://doi.org/10.1002/smj.2260

Blut, M., Backhaus, C., Heussler, T., Woisetschläger, D. M., Evanschitzky, H., & Ahlert, D. (2011). What to expect after the honeymoon: Testing a lifecycle theory of franchise relationships. *Journal of Retailing, 87*(3), 306–319. https://doi.org/10.1016/j.jretai.2010.06.003

Bordonaba-Juste, V., & Polo-Redondo, Y. (2008). The effect of relationship marketing strategy on franchise channels: Evidence from Spanish franchisees. *Journal of Marketing Channels, 15*(1), 71–91. https://doi.org/10.1080/10466690802081392

Chiou, J.-S., & Droge, C. (2015). The effects of standardization and trust on franchisee's performance and satisfaction: A study on franchise networks in the growth stage. *Journal of Small Business Management, 53*(1), 129–144. https://doi.org/10.1111/jsbm.12057

Chiou, J.-S., Hsieh, C.-H., & Yang, C.-H. (2004). The effect of franchisors' communication, service assistance, and competitive advantage on franchisees' intentions to remain in the franchise network. *Journal of Small Business Management, 42*(1), 19–36. https://doi.org/10.1111/j.1540-627X.2004.00095.x

Combs, J. G., Crook, T. R., & Shook, C. (2005). The dimensionality of organizational performance and its implications for strategic management research. In D. Ketchen & D. Bergh (Eds.), *Research methodology in strategy and management* (Vol. 2, pp. 259–286). Emerald Group Publishing Limited.

Combs, J. G., Ketchen, D. J., Jr, & Short, J. C. (2011). Franchising research: Major milestones, new directions, and its future within entrepreneurship. *Entrepreneurship Theory & Practice, 35*(3), 413–425. https://doi.org/10.1111/etap.2011.35.issue-3

Croonen, E., Brand, M., & Broekhuizen, T. (2016). Time to say goodbye: Explaining franchisees' exit intentions and behaviors. In G. Atinc (Ed.), *Academy of management proceedings* (Vols. 2016, No. 1, p. 16636). Academy of Management.

Cumberland, D. M. (2015). Advisory councils in franchising: Advancing a theory-based typology. *Journal of Marketing Channels, 22*(3), 175–191. https://doi.org/10.1080/1046669X.2015.1071587

Cyert, R. M., & March, J. G. (1963). *A behavioral theory of the firm*. Prentice-Hall.

Dant, R. P., Grünhagen, M., & Windsperger, J. (2011). Franchising research frontiers for the twenty-first century. *Journal of Retailing, 87*(3), 253–268. https://doi.org/10.1016/j.jretai.2011.08.002

Dant, R. P., Weaven, S. K., Baker, B. L., & Jeon, H. J. (2013). An introspective examination of single-unit versus multi-unit franchisees. *Journal of the Academy of Marketing Science, 41*(4), 473–496. https://doi.org/10.1007/s11747-011-0265-2

Davis, P. J. (2012). A model for strategy implementation and conflict resolution in the franchise business. *Strategy & Leadership, 40*(5), 32–38. https://doi.org/10.1108/10878571211257168

Delgado-García, J. B., Rodríguez-Escudero, A. I., & Martín-Cruz, N. (2012). Influence of affective traits on entrepreneur's goals and satisfaction. *Journal of Small Business Management, 50*(3), 408–428. https://doi.org/10.1111/j.1540-627X.2012.00359.x

Facca, T. M. (2013). Using discriminant analysis to classify satisfaction data to facilitate planning in a franchise context. *Journal of Strategic Marketing, 21*(2), 125–139. https://doi.org/10.1080/0965254X.2012.752400

Frazer, L., Weaven, S., Giddings, J., & Grace, D. (2012). What went wrong? Franchisors and franchisees disclose the causes of conflict in franchising. *Qualitative Market Research: An International Journal, 15*(1), 87–103. https://doi.org/10.1108/13522751211192017

Gauzente, C. (2003). Measuring franchisee satisfaction: Theoretical considerations and empirical testing. *International Journal of Retail & Distribution Management, 31*(10), 508–517. https://doi.org/10.1108/09590550310497030

Grace, D., & Weaven, S. (2011). An empirical analysis of franchisee value-in-use, investment risk and relational satisfaction. *Journal of Retailing, 87*(3), 366–380. https://doi.org/10.1016/j.jretai.2010.06.001

Grace, D., Weaven, S., Frazer, L., & Giddings, J. (2013). Examining the role of franchisee normative expectations in relationship evaluation. *Journal of Retailing, 89*(2), 219–230. https://doi.org/10.1016/j.jretai.2012.12.002

Greve, H. R. (2003). *Organizational learning from performance feedback: A behavioral theory perspective on innovation and change*. Cambridge University Press.

Greve, H. R., & Gaba, V. (2015). Performance feedback in organizations and groups: Common themes. In L. Argote & J. M. Levine (Eds.), *Oxford Handbook of group and organizational learning* (pp. 3–52). Oxford University Press.

Grünhagen, M., & Dorsch, M. J. (2003). Does the franchisor provide value to franchisees? Past, current, and future value assessments of two franchisee types. *Journal of Small Business Management, 41*(4), 366–384. https://doi.org/10.1111/1540-627X.00088

Grünhagen, M., & Mittelstaedt, R. A. (2005). Entrepreneurs or investors: Do multi-unit franchisees have different philosophical orientations? *Journal of Small Business Management, 43*(3), 207–225. https://doi.org/10.1111/j.1540-627X.2005.00134.x

Hatten, T. S. (2009). *Small business management: Entrepreneurship and beyond* (4th ed.). Nelson Education.

Hing, N. (1995). Franchisee satisfaction: Contributors and consequences. *Journal of Small Business Management, 33*(2), 12–25. https://search.proquest.com/docview/220957601

Hunt, S. D., & Nevin, J. R. (1974). Power in a channel of distribution: Sources and consequences. *Journal of Marketing Research, 11*(2), 186–193. https://doi.org/10.1177/002224377401100210

Jang, S. S., & Park, K. (2019). A sustainable franchisor-franchisee relationship model: Toward the franchise win-win theory. *International Journal of Hospitality Management, 76*, 13–24. https://doi.org/10.1016/j.ijhm.2018.06.004

Kalargyrou, V., Aliouche, E. H., & Schlentrich, U. (2018). Antecedents and consequences of franchisee satisfaction in the U.S. restaurant industry. *Journal of Human Resources in Hospitality & Tourism, 17*(1), 60–79. https://doi.org/10.1080/15332845.2017.1328261

Kaleka, A., & Morgan, N. A. (2019). How marketing capabilities and current performance drive strategic intentions in international markets. *Industrial Marketing Management, 78*, 108–121. https://doi.org/10.1016/j.indmarman.2017.02.001

Kirtland, A. (2015). *Towards an understanding of the nature of the breakdown in relationship between a Franchisee and a Franchisor: An approach using psychological contract theory.* University of Pretoria.

Lee, K. J. (2017). Knowledge sharing in franchise system: Franchisee self-leadership, satisfaction, and compliance. *International Journal of Contemporary Hospitality Management, 29*(12), 3101–3118. https://doi.org/10.1108/IJCHM-03-2016-0178

Liao, H., & Chuang, A. (2004). A multilevel investigation of factors influencing employee service performance and customer outcomes. *Academy of Management Journal, 47*(1), 41–58. https://doi.org/10.5465/20159559

Lim, J., & Frazer, L. (2004). Exploring the link between goal congruence and satisfaction in the franchising channel. *Academy of World Business Conference*, 1–9.

Lindell, M. K., & Whitney, D. J. (2001). Accounting for common method variance in cross-sectional research designs. *Journal of Applied Psychology, 86*(1), 114–121. https://doi.org/10.1037/0021-9010.86.1.114

Lusch, R. F., & Vargo, S. L. (2014). *Service-Dominant Logic: Premises, Perspective, Possibilities.* Cambridge University Press.

Morrison, K. A. (1997). How franchise job satisfaction and personality affects performance, organizational commitment, franchisor relations, and intention to remain. *Journal of Small Business Management, 35*(3), 39–67. https://search.proquest.com/docview/220956728

Nijmeijer, K. J., Fabbricotti, I. N., & Huijsman, R. (2014). Making franchising work: A framework based on a systematic review. *International Journal of Management Reviews, 16*(1), 62–83. https://doi.org/10.1111/ijmr.12009

Patiar, A., Davidson, M. C. G., & Wang, Y. (2012). Competition, total quality management practices, and performance: Evidence from upscale hotels. *Tourism Analysis, 17*(2), 195–211. https://doi.org/10.3727/108354212X13388995267904

Podsakoff, P. M., MacKenzie, S. B., & Podsakoff, N. P. (2012). Sources of method bias in social science research and recommendations on how to control it. *Annual Review of Psychology, 63*(1), 539–569. https://doi.org/10.1146/annurev-psych-120710-100452

Posen, H., Keil, T., Kim, S., & Meer, F. (2018). Renewing research on problemistic search: A review and research agenda. *Academy of Management Annals, 12*(1), 208–251. https://doi.org/10.5465/annals.2016.0018

Ramaseshan, B., Rabbanee, F. K., & Burford, O. (2018). Combined effects of franchise management strategies and employee service performance on customer loyalty: A multilevel perspective. *Journal of Strategic Marketing, 26*(6), 479–497. https://doi.org/10.1080/0965254X.2017.1293137

Roh, E. Y., & Yoon, J. (2009). Franchisor's ongoing support and franchisee's satisfaction: A case of ice cream franchising in Korea. *International Journal of Contemporary Hospitality Management, 21*(1), 85–99. https://doi.org/10.1108/09596110910930205

Rosado-Serrano, A., Paul, J., & Dikova, D. (2018). International franchising: A literature review and research agenda. *Journal of Business Research, 85*, 238–257. https://doi.org/10.1016/j.jbusres.2017.12.049

Sainaghi, R. (2010). Hotel performance: State of the art. *International Journal of Contemporary Hospitality Management, 22*(7), 920–952. https://doi.org/10.1108/09596111011066617

Simon, H. A. (1955). A behavioral model of rational choice. *Quarterly Journal of Economics*, *69*(1), 99–118. https://doi.org/10.2307/1884852

Squire, J. (2009). Experienced franchisors weigh in on tactics: Is no news, good news? *Franchising World*, *41*(4), 82–84.

Tuunanen, M. (2002). An ounce of prevention is worth a pound of cure: Findings from national franchisee (dis-)satisfaction study. *Journal of Marketing Channels*, *10*(2), 57–89. https://doi.org/10.1300/J049v10n02_05

Tuunanen, M., & Hyrsky, K. (2001). Entrepreneurial paradoxes in business format franchising: An empirical survey of Finnish franchisees. *International Small Business Journal: Researching Entrepreneurship*, *19*(4), 47–62. https://doi.org/10.1177/0266242601194003

Ulaga, W., & Eggert, A. (2006). Relationship value and relationship quality: Broadening the nomological network of business-to-business relationships. *European Journal of Marketing*, *40*(3/4), 311–327. https://doi.org/10.1108/03090560610648075

Villagrasa, J., Buyl, T., & Escribá-Esteve, A. (2018). CEO satisfaction and intended strategic changes: The moderating role of performance cues. *Long Range Planning*, *51*(6), 894–910. https://doi.org/10.1016/j.lrp.2017.12.002

Washburn, M., & Bromiley, P. (2012). Comparing aspiration models: The role of selective attention. *Journal of Management Studies*, *49*(5), 896–917. https://doi.org/10.1111/j.1467-6486.2011.01033.x

Weaven, S., Baker, B. L., & Dant, R. P. (2017). The influence of gratitude on franchisor-franchisee relationships. *Journal of Small Business Management*, *55*(S1), 275–298. https://doi.org/10.1111/jsbm.12263

Weaven, S., Frazer, L., & Giddings, J. (2010). New perspectives on the causes of franchising conflict in Australia. *Asia Pacific Journal of Marketing and Logistics*, *22*(2), 135–155. https://doi.org/10.1108/13555851011026917

Wu, C.-W. (2015). Antecedents of franchise strategy and performance. *Journal of Business Research*, *68*(7), 1581–1588. https://doi.org/10.1016/j.jbusres.2015.01.055

Yakimova, R., Owens, M., & Sydow, J. (2019). Formal control influence on franchisee trust and brand-supportive behavior within franchise networks. *Industrial Marketing Management*, *76*, 123–135. https://doi.org/10.1016/j.indmarman.2018.07.010

# APPENDIX A

## *Measurement of Scale Variables*

**Overall satisfaction**. Mean of six items (Cronbach's alpha = 0.946) measured on a five-point Likert-type scale (1 = strongly disagree, 5 = strongly agree):

(1) It is my pleasure to introduce this franchise network to others.
(2) I am willing to collaborate with this franchisor in the future.
(3) I still consider the current franchisor as my first priority, although I can look for other franchisors.
(4) I am happy about my decision to choose this franchise network.
(5) I believe that I did the right thing when I chose this franchise network.
(6) Overall, I am satisfied with this franchise relationship.

**Social financial performance feedback**. Mean of four items (Cronbach's alpha = 0.875) measured on a five-point Likert-type scale (1 = much worse, 5 = much better):
Compare your outlet with others in the area on

(1) ... sales
(2) ... sales growth
(3) ... profitability
(4) ... efficiency

**Social service performance feedback.** Mean of three items (Cronbach's alpha = 0.844) measured on a five-point Likert-type scale (1 = much worse, 5 = much better):
Compare your outlet with others in the area on

(1) ... service level
(2) ... service quality
(3) ... service value

**Historical financial performance feedback.** Mean of four items (Cronbach's alpha = 0.907) measured on a five-point Likert-type scale (1 = much worse, 5 = much better):
Compare your outlet with a year ago on

(1) ... sales
(2) ... sales growth
(3) ... profitability
(4) ... efficiency

**Historical service performance feedback.** Mean of three items (Cronbach's alpha = 0.930) measured on a five-point Likert-type scale (1 = much worse, 5 = much better):
Compare your outlet with a year ago on

(1) ... service level
(2) ... service quality
(3) ... service value

**Relationship quality.** Mean of seven items (Cronbach's alpha = 0.965) measured on a five-point Likert-type scale (1 = strongly disagree, 5 = strongly agree):
Overall, do you consider your relationship with the franchisor to be:

(1) Satisfying
(2) Friendly
(3) Fair
(4) Supportive
(5) Considerate
(6) Healthy
(7) Cordial

# APPENDIX B

## *Factor Analysis*

| Factors | Items | Factor loadings |
|---|---|---|
| **Overall satisfaction:** KMO 0.876; Bartlett's test ~ 0.000; Variance explained 79.785% | It is my pleasure to introduce this franchise network to others. | 0.877 |
| | I am willing to collaborate with this franchisor in the future. | 0.779 |
| | I still consider the current franchisor as my first priority, although I can look for other franchisors. | 0.887 |
| | I am happy about my decision to choose this franchise network. | 0.655 |
| | I believe that I did the right thing when I chose this franchise network. | 0.747 |
| | Overall, I am satisfied with this franchise relationship. | 0.841 |
| **Social financial performance feedback:** KMO 0.822; Bartlett's test ~ 0.000; Variance explained 72.928% | Compare your outlet with others in the area on | |
| | ... sales | 0.814 |
| | ... sales growth | 0.860 |
| | ... profitability | 0.891 |
| | ... efficiency | 0.848 |
| **Social service performance feedback:** KMO 0.654; Bartlett's test ~ 0.000; Variance explained 77.277% | Compare your outlet with others in the area on | |
| | ... service level | 0.757 |
| | ... service quality | 0.874 |
| | ... service value | 0.687 |
| **Historical financial performance feedback:** KMO 0.736; Bartlett's test ~ 0.000; Variance explained 78.305% | Compare your outlet with a year ago on | |
| | ... sales | 0.811 |
| | ... sales growth | 0.800 |
| | ... profitability | 0.808 |
| | ... efficiency | 0.714 |
| **Historical service performance feedback:** KMO 0.751; Bartlett's test ~ 0.000; Variance explained 88.001% | Compare your outlet with a year ago on | |
| | ... service level | 0.893 |
| | ... service quality | 0.907 |
| | ... service value | 0.840 |
| **Relationship quality:** KMO 0.943; Bartlett's test ~ 0.000; Variance explained 82.751% | Overall, do you consider your relationship with the franchisor to be: | |
| | Satisfying | 0.834 |
| | Friendly | 0.761 |
| | Fair | 0.877 |
| | Supportive | 0.794 |
| | Considerate | 0.846 |
| | Healthy | 0.879 |
| | Cordial | 0.802 |

# Index

Note: Figures are indicated by *italics*. Tables are indicated by **bold**. Endnotes are indicated by the page number followed by 'n' and the endnote number e.g., 20n1 refers to endnote 1 on page 20.